What practising managers say about
You Lead, They'll Follow Volume 3:

'The book is not just easy to read, using everyday, easy-to-understand language, but is nicely broken up into background "lectures", examples to reinforce points, *Cosmopolitan*-style self checks, cartoons and quotations … "Tell 'em and then tell 'em what you've just told them" never fails and works well in Dan's book … All in all, it provides leaders with additional items for their leadership tool bag'.
Ian Jackson, Director, Africa Business Unit,
Woodside Energy Ltd

'When faced with the everyday issues of management, *You Lead, They'll Follow* provides a ready reference of ideas and suggestions to help managers solve real problems in a practical and professional manner. Over time I have found that the more I have adopted the ideas outlined in the *You Lead, They'll Follow* series of books, the less problems I have had to solve!'
Frank Humphreys, Operations Manager,
Cement Australia, Rockhampton

'This volume again covers a wide range of topics in a practical and easy-to-follow manner. The concepts can easily be adopted and adapted by any organisation, big or small. It provides practical templates which can be easily used by leaders and managers. There is a current trend in organisations to adopt a Learning Organisation philosophy, but sometimes it can be difficult to convert this strategic goal into action plans. Dan's latest book builds on the concepts in earlier volumes and continues to provide many examples of how the everyday actions and words of everyday managers and supervisors can contribute to the attainment of this goal.'
Helen Rogerson, Training & Development Manager,
Wesfarmers Federation Insurance

'An easy, engaging read. It calls for introspection which proved refreshing, it avoids esoteric definitional debate and stance which also proved refreshing, and generally provides a wide variety of useful "how to" pointers for the reader. A very good book— for seasoned managers and management aspirants alike.'
Stuart Bodey, Mine Superintendent, Jubilee Mines

'A further valuable, straightforward reference tool for all supervisors and managers, both new and experienced.'
Eric Baines, Manager Human Resources,
Racing & Wagering Western Australia

'Following on from volumes one and two, *You Lead, They'll Follow* Volume 3 provides more valuable tips for all managers, new and experienced alike. The self-contained chapters allow you to dip into the book as required and instantly "cut to the chase" with practical, action-oriented solutions to everyday management challenges. Avoiding the usual textbook focus on theories and models, this book uses real-life examples and humorous cartoons to get the message across. This series of books deserves a place on every manager's bookshelf.'
Vivien Whitehead, People Services Manager,
SKG Radiology, West Perth

'An excellent hands-on and practical guide to the often elusive skills required to lead and manage an organisation, group of people or an individual. Highly recommended.'
Chris Godden, CEO, Opticon Australia,
a business unit of UXC Limited

'As with volumes one and two, the third volume of *You Lead, They'll Follow* proves to be an excellent manager's handbook that is full of real truths with practical answers to many of the HR problems encountered in today's workplaces.'
Senior Sergeant Janet Makepeace,
APM Queensland Police Service

'You lead, they'll follow—but don't expect to plant seedlings today and fell timber tomorrow. Leadership is a journey and Dan Kehoe has, in this third in a series, captured the balance of leadership and the need for continuous self- and organisational improvement. The practical "how to" advice mixed with reflective and yet motivating articles on leadership practice will add to your knowledge base and improve your leadership and management skills.'
Wayne L Belcher, Chief Executive, Churches of Christ Homes and
Community Services Incorporated, Western Australia

I had dedicated this book to some special friends, Gina, Sherry, Senia, Aileen, Carolyn, Shelley and Deb, but just prior to publication, my father died on 7 April 2004. So I also dedicate this book to the loving memory of my father Kevin Redmond Kehoe. My dad was a veteran of the Second World War—he flew with Beaufort Bomber Squadrons Numbers 8, 25 and 35. Apart from losing two of his brothers in that war, Austin and Desmond, the war had a profound effect on him. As with most men who served in this war, he never talked about it unless you initiated a conversation. He is loved and remembered for his great kindness and compassion, for his honesty and his selfless devotion to his wife, Carmel, and his family and friends. His smile warmed the hearts of everyone he met and he never ever lost his ability to laugh and smile at himself even as his life began to ebb away. I love and miss him deeply.

You Lead, They'll Follow

*How to inspire, lead and manage people.
Really.*

DANIEL KEHOE

with Peter Baartz and Harry Bate

Contributing authors

**Glyn Ashley, Helen Crossing, David Deane-Spread,
Kevin Poynton and Warren Sare**

Cartoons by Dean Alston

The **McGraw·Hill** Companies

Sydney New York San Francisco Auckland
Bangkok Bogotá Caracas Hong Kong
Kuala Lumpur Lisbon London Madrid
Mexico City Milan New Delhi San Juan
Seoul Singapore Taipei Toronto

National Library of Australia Cataloguing-in-Publication data:

Kehoe, Daniel
You lead, they'll follow: how to inspire, lead and manage
people. Really. Volume 3.

Includes index.
ISBN 0 074 71376 0.

1. Personnel management. 2. Leadership.
II. Title.

658.3

Published in Australia by
McGraw-Hill Australia Pty Ltd
Level 2, 82 Waterloo Road, North Ryde NSW 2113
Acquisitions Editor: Eiko Bron
Production Editor: Rosemary McDonald
Editor: Rosemary McDonald
Proofreader: Tim Learner
Indexer: Diane Harriman
Designer (cover and interior): R.T.J Klinkhamer
Illustrator: Lorenzo Lucia, Tech View Studio
Cover image: gettyimages
Cartoonist: Dean Alston
Typeset in 12/13 Adobe Garamond by R.T.J Klinkhamer
Printed on 70 gsm bulky woodfree by Pantech Limited, Hong Kong.

The **McGraw·Hill** Companies

CONTENTS

CONTENTS

PART 5

Facilitating group performance

PART 6

Understanding behaviour

PART 7

Implementing change and improvement

CONTENTS

PART 8

Improving relationships

PART 9

Improving learning and development

PART 10

Improving sales and service

ABOUT THE AUTHORS

Daniel Kehoe (principal author) has worked as a management consultant since 1979. In that time he has worked with over 4500 managers, ranging from chief executives to frontline managers, in all states of Australia, in Indonesia, Malaysia, Singapore, Dubai (United Arab Emirates) and the United States of America. As a management consultant, he has spent thousands of hours listening to and discussing with practising managers how to solve the real-life issues and problems related to leading and managing people.

Dan is director of M•A•P•P™ Systems International based in Perth, Western Australia. He is the creator and designer of the M•A•P•P™ System—an innovative management process for improving any aspect of organisation performance (www.mappsystem.com). He is also the principal designer of the *SPACE* Continuum®—creating the space for sustainable improvement (www.space123.com). He holds tertiary and post-graduate qualifications in the field of applied behavioural science. He is a past member of the Institute of Management Consultants and has been awarded the grading of CMC—Certified Management Consultant. He is a certified Att-C® Attitudinal Competence facilitator and is an Open Space Technology facilitator.

Dean Alston (cartoonist) is internationally recognised as one of the world's best cartoonists, having won two awards at the 1999 International Cartoon Festival at Ayr, Scotland. His keen and intelligent insights into the human condition, combined with his outstanding artistic skills, have won him nineteen national awards for cartooning in his home country, Australia, including the prestigious Walkley Award. Apart from being the world's busiest man, he is also a seriously funny man. He is the editorial cartoonist and resident humorist for *The West Australian* and is being sued by Dan Kehoe for sleep loss.

Peter Baartz (contributing author) has had a career in sales, marketing and management spanning more than twenty-five years. Before joining the commercial world, Peter was a maths and science teacher in high schools. He has degrees in science, education and marketing, has lectured in Marketing Process Analysis at University of NSW, is an accomplished trainer and was previously contracted to one of the world's largest training companies. Through serving on boards and in senior management positions for large companies, Peter has gained a thorough understanding of business principles, processes and practices from both the supplier and retailer perspectives. He started Tethys Consulting (www.tethys.com.au) in 1999 to assist companies to develop and implement processes that bring about business improvements. Peter is also a certified M•A•P•P™ System facilitator.

Harry Bate (contributing author) has spent over twenty-five years in leadership positions in a diverse range of engineering-oriented businesses, including thirteen years as Chief Executive of overseas-owned companies in Australia. He has experience in manufacturing and marketing, including many years with responsibility for sales throughout Asia as well as Australia and New Zealand. His experience includes company start-up, achieving major sales growth, developing strong marketing campaigns, team building, and operation of a market leader and of a market challenger. Harry has also spent time in the food industry, including the meat and rice industries. He has worked as a consultant in a developing country leading a team financed by the World Bank. He has tertiary qualifications in engineering and business administration. Harry is also a certified M•A•P•P™ System facilitator. (hbate@optusnet.com.au)

David Deane-Spread (contributing author) is a senior executive coach and a specialist facilitator for attitudinal competency, leadership and group development. His private and corporate clients embrace government, commerce and industry. He has more than thirty years operational leadership and training expertise spanning the military, law enforcement and commerce, in Australia, Asia and Europe. He is a graduate of both military and law enforcement commissioned officer academies. He is an NLP master practitioner, an emotional therapist, a reiki master and trainer, and a qualified Open Space Technology facilitator. He is a member of the Open Space Institute of Australia and the National Speakers Association of Australia. His study and experience in human behaviour resulted in his development of Att-C®, a model for training for attitudinal competence. With Dan Kehoe, he codeveloped the *SPACE* Continuum® (www.space123.com).

Glyn Ashley (contributing author) has four decades of direct involvement in major manufacturing and process industries and this has provided him with an approach to management that is entirely pragmatic and experience based. He spent twenty years in senior management with one of the world's largest and most successful aluminium smelters, Dubai Aluminium Company Ltd. The structured change model that Glyn designed and introduced with that organisation formed the basis for a self-driven culture of continuous improvement that is coveted by competitors and emulated by many others (it also won international awards in Europe, USA and the Middle East). Glyn supported the Dubai Government as Chairman of the Technical Committee responsible for implementing a national quality award based on the USA Malcolm Baldridge model. He is the proud Founding Chairman of the Dubai Quality Group, which he formed to share knowledge of best practice with over four hundred participating organisations. (www.space123.com)

Kevin Poynton (contributing author) is currently the Chief Executive Officer of Mindarie Regional Council. He has been an accomplished 'journeyman of leadership'—from the corridors of the Royal Military College at Duntroon, through the jungles of Papua New Guinea in his position as Lieutenant Colonel in the Royal Australian Engineers within the Australian Regular Army, to the wilds of North-west Australia and the demanding environments of a major teaching hospital and key local government appointments. Kevin has consistently generated successful outcomes through the application of 'learned leadership' and the academic strategies obtained through his tertiary engineering and administration studies. (kpoynton@mrc. wa.gov.au)

Helen Crossing (contributing author) is an organisational psychologist with over twenty years of consulting experience. She has worked closely with management and employees in finance, manufacturing, service, retail, IT industry groups and government. The organisations vary in size from multinationals and large corporations to small companies in start-up. Her work is varied but with the central and recurring theme of working with people to create the relationships and culture that is best able to deliver business objectives while also ensuring the quality of work environment for management and employees. Helen draws on her experience from conducting assessments of managers, designing and delivering development programs for individuals and groups, as well as working to build productive teams. She also works closely with senior managers and CEOs to help them achieve their visions for their organisations. (www.hcaconsulting.com.au)

Warren Sare (contributing author) graduated from the University of South Australia with a degree in Business and Management Information Systems in 1993 and has since been involved in a variety of different roles within the information technology and communications arena. These include software support, client application implementations, technology roll-outs and a diversity of other roles. These have provided a solid understanding of the issues faced by organisations and their people when dealing with applications and the integration of information technology. From ensuring the end users have the tools and the ability to use them to work efficiently, through to information management and support of strategic direction, Warren has built up an extensive knowledge of information technology within the workplace. (www.bsnappy.com)

PREFACE

The all-new Volume 3 continues the success of Volumes 1 and 2 in the best-selling *You Lead, They'll Follow* series. In this volume, while I remain the major contributor, I have invited contributions from seven other suitably qualified and experienced people.

This adds to the value for the reader because these other writers broaden the depth of experience and perspective brought to bear on the subject of successfully leading and managing people.

There are literally hundreds of books on leadership and management released every year around the world. We wanted to find a niche—a series of books that would offer something very different (and in our view, better) to the reader.

We feel we found it. Firstly, we had to write books that managers would be motivated to buy. Secondly, they had to be books that managers would use in the workplace to create a better managed workforce. To achieve these aims, we set the following criteria. The books had to be:

- very user friendly
- quick and easy-to-read
- ageless
- full of realistic, action-based solutions that provide immediate answers and solutions
- illustrated with humorous and relevant cartoons
- supplemented with inspirational quotations from the best thinkers and doers in the world
- relevant to the real world of the workplace.

The *You Lead, They'll Follow* books are not textbooks, nor are they written in an academic style. They do not describe theories and models about leadership and management as many other books do. They are practical toolkits—'how to' books. They provide the reader with hundreds of actions that can be applied in a wide variety of situations.

Managing people issues is the most difficult part of a manager's job. The *You Lead, They'll Follow* series will help make it easier. It is full of practical, down-to-earth solutions to the many issues managers, team leaders and supervisors have to manage. It is a handy reference collection that is stimulating, humorous, enjoyable and easy-to-read. The series is based on discussions with over 5000 real, practising managers—from all industry and public sectors—what they do and say to deal with the complex issues and problems they face in their daily work life.

Using the books is simple. Select the area in which you want to improve from the 'Improving Leadership and Management' model. Check the subject headings and select the issue of interest. While some articles aim to stimulate your thinking, most will provide you with a range of actions to take in relation to the issue.

If you are involved in a Frontline Management Initiative (FMI), then refer to the FMI Reference Table. Suggested articles are shown for each of the 11 units of competence for frontline management. These may be useful to you as a learning resource or as a tool to enable you to provide evidence related to the performance criteria for that unit of competence.

These books are designed to be dipped into over and over again. They can be opened at any section because most articles are self-contained over two-pages. In some cases you will find a variety of articles on the same issue with each adding a different perspective. More complex subjects are linked by a number of self-contained articles.

A critical goal for managers is to win and maintain the respect of their people. With that respect, a manager can achieve much; without that respect, a manager is doomed. Fundamental to respect are dignity and selfworth. In dealings with their people, the successful manager tries to say and do things that enhance the sense of dignity and selfworth of those people.

Being a manager is not a popularity contest. You are required to make hard decisions that will not always meet the wants of all of your people. But the complex task of managing people becomes more productive, much easier and more rewarding when you have the respect of your people.

The *You Lead, They'll Follow* series of books shows you what real managers say and do in real situations with real people to be successful.

Daniel Kehoe
(www.space123.com)

ACKNOWLEDGMENTS

My thoughts about managing and being managed have been shaped by a number of people during my work life. First and foremost, the late Gwynn Gibbons, a brave, intelligent, wise and sensitive man who saw something others didn't, took a risk and gave me an opportunity. Brian McSweeney, who brought out the best in me. Mary Ballantine and Elizabeth Mulrennan, for their intelligence, practical wisdom, great humour and counsel (Liz). Tony Power, who dared to do things and also took a risk giving me a fantastic opportunity. Dr Peter Saul, for his great intelligence and humour who taught me much about managing and management consulting. Sally Jardine, for her wisdom, compassion, great fun and joie de vivre. Helen Crossing, for her intelligent observations about organisations and people and for her spirit. Steve Godden, for his patience, humour, dedication, high-quality thinking, counsel and the constant reminder that there's more than one way to skin a cat. Kevin Poynton, for demonstrating good leadership in action and providing living proof that when you enhance the dignity and selfworth of your people, they respond positively. Jim Runciman, for his good leadership example and for his toughness and softness all wrapped up in one and for the many learning experiences he has given me.

To Yasmin Naglazas for her never-ending love and support, and to my long-time friends Dennis Smith, Michael Kehoe and Sherry Abrahmsen, and my mother, Carmel, all of whom helped me out when the going got tough.

To all the 5000 or so managers, supervisors and team leaders over the years who have shared the highs and lows, the frustrations and successes, the insights and learnings about the greatest challenge facing the manager—leading and managing the world's potentially greatest asset—our workforce.

Daniel Kehoe

Quotations

Many of the quotations used in *You Lead, They'll Follow* are sourced from *The Manager's Book of Quotations* by Lewis D Eigen and Jonathan P Siegel, AMACOM, 1989 and *The International Thesaurus of Quotations* compiled by Rhoda Thomas Tripp, Penguin Reference Books, 1976. Both of these books are highly recommended as sources of quotations on inspiration, humour, wisdom, practical advice, writing and public speaking.

IMPROVING LEADERSHIP AND MANAGEMENT MODEL

1. Improving leadership— strategic and tactical

2. Improving communication

3. Improving your performance

4. Improving individual performance

5. Facilitating group performance

6. Understanding behaviour

7. Implementing change and improvement

8. Improving relationships

9. Improving learning and development

10. Improving sales and service

FRONTLINE MANAGEMENT INITIATIVE (FMI) REFERENCE TABLE

While the *You Lead, They'll Follow* series is applicable to all levels of management, many of the articles provide 'how to' guidelines to assist with the implementation or demonstration of frontline management competencies.

	Frontline Management Competencies	Relevant articles from You Lead, They'll Follow series, volume 3
1	Manage personal work priorities and professional development	30, 38, 46, 66, 72, 74, 76, 78, 100, 158
2	Provide leadership in the workplace	2, 4, 7, 19, 32, 34, 36, 84, 113, 116, 119, 122, 180, 196, 198, 305, 308
3	Establish and manage effective workplace relationships	14, 82, 86, 110, 124, 142, 144, 176, 190, 250, 252, 254, 258, 260, 262
4	Participate in, lead and facilitate work teams	55, 58, 126, 128, 130, 135, 140, 148, 150, 152, 154, 156, 160, 168, 170, 184
5	Manage operations to achieve planned outcomes	10, 12, 22, 24, 96, 162, 229, 231, 310
6	Manage workplace information	44, 49, 90, 92, 94, 102, 106
7	Manage quality customer service	200, 296, 299, 301, 303
8	Develop and maintain a safe workplace and environment	165
9	Implement and monitor continuous improvement systems and procedures	98, 208, 210, 212, 214, 216, 219, 221, 223, 225, 233, 235, 237, 239, 242
10	Facilitate and capitalise on change and innovation	40, 202, 205, 245
11	Contribute to the development of a workplace learning environment	27, 52, 137, 266, 268, 270, 273, 276, 279, 282, 284, 286, 288, 290, 292, 313

PART 1

Improving leadership— strategic and tactical

Women and children first, after me

THE TITLE OF OUR BOOK SERIES IS *You Lead, They'll Follow* but what does 'lead' really mean? 'Show the way by going with or ahead' is one of many definitions for the word 'lead' from the *Collins English Dictionary.*

Unbeknown to most of you who are out there quietly or loudly practising management and leadership in the real world, there is an ongoing debate about leadership amongst academics, management consultants and other purveyors of the leadership publishing and training industry. Are leaders born or can they be made?

Who knows? Who cares? The above-mentioned group may not know, but believe me they do care. After all, we are talking about a worldwide multi-billion dollar industry here.

If you ask this question of a management consultant or trainer who is in the business of providing leadership training programs, how do you think they would answer? Don't hold your breath waiting for them to tell you that leaders are born, not made.

Digressing for a moment, a lot of our notions about leadership are derived from the battlefield where acts of leadership are more readily obvious and easier to define. Transferring these notions into the context of the workplace presents several difficulties, not the least being that in a combat situation, there are many different factors at play that cause soldiers to behave in certain ways that can have nothing to do with the inspirational qualities, or lack of, of the leader. These include a desire to avoid being shot or court-martialled by their own officers for deemed cowardice, a desire to avoid the stigma of being branded a coward, a desire to not let down their mates, a burning desire to show their patriotism, a belief that the cause is just and worth the sacrifice of their life, anger and hatred bred by the death of a mate or the killing of innocent civilians, not wanting to live with the self-imposed guilt of not behaving admirably on the battlefield, or simply a desire to kill before they are killed—the powerful instinct for self-preservation. Combat veterans know that there are many examples of officers who were trained in the world's best military academies who proved incompetent in the battlefield, unfortunately to the extreme detriment of their troops.

On the other side of the coin, the 'leaders are born' brigade are pushing the idea of a leadership gene. If that were so, you might expect that there would be many instances where the sons and daughters, and grandsons and grand-daughters of great leaders also excelled at leadership. If you think about it you will be able to cite examples where this is so. However, you will also be able to cite examples where this is not so.

Back to the question. To my way of thinking anybody can be a leader provided they are capable of taking actions which guide, direct, support or inspire behaviour depending on the circumstances. Leadership is defined in the eyes of the followers by the actions the leader performs. Maybe some people instinctively or inherently know how to do these things while others have to be shown. Many managers are ineffective as leaders because they don't know how to act as leaders or they don't have the desire to.

In our *You Lead, They'll Follow* series we don't attempt to answer the question about leaders being born or made for two simple reasons: One, we don't know. Two, we think it is immaterial. We believe that if you apply the actions described in our books you will be demonstrating leadership behaviours in the eyes of your people. Both you and your people will experience leadership.

> Managers are people who do things right,
> and leaders are people who do the right thing.
> **Warren G Bennis and Burt Nanus, *Leaders*, Harper and Row, 1985**
>
> Leadership is practised not so much in words as in attitudes and in actions.
> Leadership cannot really be taught. It can only be learned.
> **Harold Geneen (1910–1977), CEO, IT&T, *Managing*, Doubleday, 1984**
>
> Management techniques are obviously essential,
> but what matters is leadership … Leading the whole organisation
> needs wisdom and flair and vision and they are another matter;
> they cannot be reduced to a system and incorporated
> into a training manual.
> **Anthony Jay et al., *Management and Machiavelli*,
> Holt, Rinehart and Winston, 1967**
>
> Contrary to the opinion of many people, leaders are not born.
> Leaders are made, and they are made by effort and hard work.
> **Vince Lombardi (1913–1970), professional football coach,
> quoted in John Wiebusch, *Lombardi*, Follett, 1971**

Are you being assertive?

ASSERTIVENESS...

FROM A VERY EARLY AGE, every individual begins to assert their personal needs on others. In the first instance, this expression of needs and requirements is most likely directed to parents who often comply with the wishes of the infant. Even at this early stage, the concept of reward (smiles) and punishment (tears) is well understood and utilised by almost all infants.

As needs become more complex, young children learn to state likes and dislikes more clearly in support of their demands. Having discovered the value of bargaining (reward or punishment) they also begin to realise that it is not always necessary to provide reasons for their needs. It is possible to establish and maintain their rights without constantly having to explain themselves.

Assertiveness, as a management style or tool, is arguably the most effective manner to achieve the positive outcomes desired by those with ultimate responsibility for the company's performance. It should not be confused with aggressiveness or autocracy. Indeed, an assertive management style invites others to join in an exchange to agree to meet the needs of all concerned. Such agreements deliver mutual satisfaction because of the climate that is created.

In people management, assertiveness involves three fundamental behavioural patterns:

1. Communicating personal needs, demands, expectations, requirements or standards.
2. Evaluating the behaviour of others based on your own personal standards
3. Offering incentives, rewards and pressures to motivate others.

To determine whether you have an assertive management style, simply read each of the following statements and circle Y to indicate 'Yes, I do that' or N to indicate 'No, I don't do that'.

1.	Explain to others exactly what they are expected to do.	Y	N
2.	Use the power of position or authority respectfully to get others to agree.	Y	N
3.	Let people know the standards by which they will be evaluated.	Y	N
4.	Obtain the support of others by offering something in return.	Y	N
5.	Inform people when they do not meet standards or requirements.	Y	N
6.	Identify for others the common goals and values of the group.	Y	N
7.	Negotiate to obtain personal objectives.	Y	N
8.	Correct others' mistakes immediately.	Y	N
9.	Make your personal needs clearly and unambiguously known to others.	Y	N
10.	Through reiteration, ensure that expectations are understood.	Y	N
11.	Make sure that other people know what is needed from them.	Y	N
12.	Compliment others (publicly and immediately) when they do something well.	Y	N
13.	Exert pressure on people to achieve an objective.	Y	N
14.	Use praise to reinforce required and desired actions.	Y	N
15.	Give corrective personal feedback constructively.	Y	N
16.	Tell others about the negative impact of their actions and behaviour.	Y	N
17.	Gain others' support by offering to personally help overcome obstacles.	Y	N

18. Hold to a position until others show a willingness to
move towards agreement.   Y   N
19. State personal objectives or expectations clearly
and firmly.   Y   N
20. Engage others in working towards achieving your
objectives.   Y   N

If you have circled 'Y' fifteen or more times then you have a
predominantly assertive management style. If you have circled 'Y' less
than fifteen times then you are perhaps not being assertive enough in
your position.

To develop a more assertive management style, take a note of the
actions that you circled 'N' and try to incorporate some of them in
your behaviour.

A winning combination

FEW PEOPLE CAN RESIST A CHALLENGE and everyone enjoys success. It makes excellent business sense, therefore, to continuously challenge people at all levels of the organisation and create a formal basis for celebrating success.

Some years ago I watched a father teaching his young daughter to swim. The child's inflatable armbands blurred into a foaming mass as she battled a couple of metres into daddy's arms. The proud father lifted the child above his head and loudly cheered her achievement. The joy on the face of the child was as memorable as it was delightful.

Every one of us achieves satisfaction and joy at overcoming a difficult challenge and our degree of pleasure is further enhanced if and when others recognise our success and join our celebrations.

It made me question why many organisations seem reticent about celebrating the successful contribution of their people. This is particularly true when time seems always available for reprimand and retribution when things go wrong.

In my experience whenever people are challenged with reasonable tasks and given the necessary support and information to produce the goods, they invariably succeed. Just like the child in the swimming pool they become motivated by an inherent need for personal satisfaction and a human desire to prove their capabilities. If, in addition, their success is celebrated and afforded formal recognition the experience is further enhanced to a point where a proud memory generates a desire to replicate the experience.

Strange that such a powerful motivational tool has not been seized upon by the world of business? In most organisations people operate within confined functional boundaries and job specifications without ever being challenged to push the boundaries and demonstrate their true potential.

Testing the theory

To test this challenge/response/celebration motivational theory I was fortunate to conduct a controlled experiment within a large industrial organisation. Ten projects were selected to test the theory. These projects emanated from an examination of problem issues within the organisation that had been dogging management for some considerable time. These included areas of high cost, low productivity, low material recoveries, severe breakdowns, unsafe situations, quality issues and various other issues.

Having identified a selection of projects we produced written outlines to define the scope and the criteria by which success or failure would be measured. In effect we defined a series of specific management challenges for presentation to the workforce.

To set things in motion we examined the knowledge base required to successfully beat the challenge. We subsequently identified suitable project teams with the appropriate collective ability to deliver success.

At first the reaction from the selected teams was one of confusion and uncertainty with prevailing questions like:

- Why is management doing this?
- Why have we been selected?
- What if we don't succeed?
- What if we don't want to do this?
- Will we receive any support?
- Where do we start?
- When will we meet?
- Who will lead the team?

Everyone was reassured that their selection was based on ability and attitude. Involvement was not compulsory. They were also advised that management had agreed to the experiment to test a theory and therefore had no predetermined expectations regarding the eventual outcome.

Initially a facilitator (industrial engineer) supported the team to promote synergy and teach the basics of systematic problem identification, examination and improvement. The role of the facilitator was to coax the team through the improvement processes without dominating or leading the investigation.

Without exception all of the teams delivered excellent results although only two teams completed within the agreed deadline. The next step, however, was more traumatic than anticipated because I requested each team leader to make a formal presentation of recommendations to senior management. As it turned out the thought of entering the boardroom and delivering a presentation was infinitely more demanding than the actual project. This was overcome by coaching and practice together with the reassurance that entire teams would also be in attendance.

I don't really know what gave me the most pleasure: observing the astounded, delighted reaction of management or seeing the look of pride and joy on the face of the team members. It was also a wonderful experience to witness the growth of confidence in the presenters as they realised personal capabilities that had previously never been tested.

To seal their success each team was allocated a budgeted sum to celebrate their achievement in any way that they wished. The only condition was that they must celebrate as a team.

It is difficult to measure the full benefits that have been achieved through the application of this concept. Certainly the financial benefits over the years have been measured in tens of millions of dollars but in reality the financial considerations represent only a part of the story.

The culture throughout the business was changed beyond recognition as management developed increasing trust and respect for the capabilities of its workforce and the workforce was allowed to realise potential that otherwise may never have been identified. Effectively, the process of problem solving and continuous improvement has been progressively devolved to levels that are both economical and highly effective.

In our own image

WHAT IS THE IMAGE of your organisation in the broader community? Many service organisations, especially in the public sector, rely heavily on community support to help them function effectively. The extent and usefulness of that support is directly related to the community's perception of the organisation.

Would you like to start working on improving the image of your organisation within the community? No? Then on your bike. Yes? Read on.

Gather together a group of people who are in a position to influence your image in the community. A group size around eight people is ideal. Use the following issues to stimulate discussion around actions to put into place to improve community image:

- [ ] Agree the reasons why you need to improve your image.
- [ ] Explain the connection between service effectiveness and public image.
- [ ] Explain the connection between reduced stress levels, increased job satisfaction and a good public image.
- [ ] Agree incidents and behaviours that give your organisation a bad image.
- [ ] Agree the causes of these incidents or behaviours.
- [ ] Agree the things you can do to improve community image.
- [ ] Identify ways to involve the community in your activities.
- [ ] Identify policies and procedures which need to be improved.
- [ ] Identify the support required from senior management to improve image.
- [ ] Seek opportunities to explain to the community what you are trying to do and how you are trying to help them.
- [ ] Ask members of the community how you can improve your image.
- [ ] Develop skills in non-confrontational conflict resolution techniques.
- [ ] Participate in community activities.
- [ ] Thank members of the community when they have helped you.
- [ ] Train staff in ways to improve your image.

- ☐ Coach offending staff in better ways to deal with the community.
- ☐ Practise responding not reacting to conflict situations.
- ☐ Discuss within the team the best ways to implement required changes to the way you do things that will improve your image.
- ☐ Acknowledge and support staff that actively promote your services in a positive way.
- ☐ Check that the new changes now become a standard practice for community relations.
- ☐ Seek the assistance of community groups to help you communicate to their members.
- ☐ Speak with people on the street and foster relationships.
- ☐ Explain your services to school students.
- ☐ Seek feedback from the community about your image.
- ☐ Seek the cooperation of local media to print examples of ways you have helped the community.
- ☐ Counsel/discipline staff who continue to create a bad image.
- ☐ Establish a communication liaison with the community.
- ☐ Discuss and implement new, different and better ways to help you improve your image.

> We try to anticipate some of your questions
> so that I can respond 'no comment' with
> some degree of knowledge.
> William Baker, spokesman, CIA, *Newsweek*, 2 May 1988
>
> A good name is like a precious ointment; it filleth all around
> about, and will not easily away; for the odors of
> ointments are more durable than those of flowers.
> Sir Francis Bacon (1561–1626), Lord Chancellor of England,
> 'Of Praise', *The Essays*, 1601

Some tips from the military

YOU HAVE SEEN THEM ALL—*A Bridge Too Far* about the Battle of Arnhem in World War II, *Gallipoli*, which depicts the abortive landing by Allied forces in World War I in Turkish territory, *Stalingrad*, which describes the German folly of advancing into Russia during winter.

You may have wondered what makes the military mind tick when it comes to planning and decision making. The answer? The appreciation process, meaning appreciate the factors and develop your plan.

So what are the steps?

1. **Establish your aim.** What is it that you want to achieve or do? Build a bridge, operate a business, run a hotel?
2. **Identify the key factors that are likely to impact on your plan.** For example, the competition, the environment, your resources, time frames.
3. **Compile information on these key factors.** What do you actually know about this project or situation?
4. **Analyse this information and develop deductions.** For example, if you only have $10,000 then extra people are probably out of the question. Deductions derive from the question 'so what' to a piece of fact.
5. **Marshall your deductions and then develop options or courses.** For example, option one: buy products overseas, option two: buy products locally.

6. **Establish your criteria for scrutineering these options.** John Viljoen in his book *Strategic Management* has some handy ones:
   * compatibility with the external environment
   * compatibility with the internal environment
   * measurability
   * consistency with the organisation's mission
   * resource availability
   * competitive advantage
   * support from the people within
   * risk
   * flexibility
   * motivation
   * social responsibility
   * clarity.

7. **Select your preferred option and then develop the detailed plan of attack.**

These steps are simple, methodical and versatile. Have a go when you next need to make a decision. And by the way, it works—ask any great military commander!

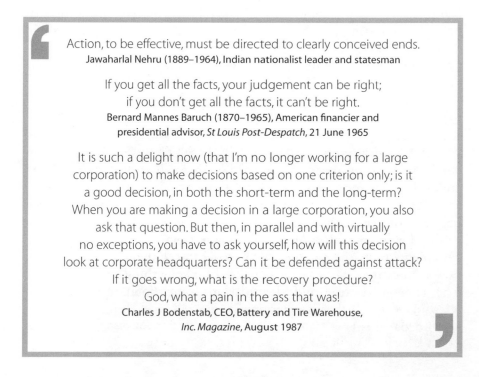

Action, to be effective, must be directed to clearly conceived ends.
Jawaharlal Nehru (1889–1964), Indian nationalist leader and statesman

If you get all the facts, your judgement can be right;
if you don't get all the facts, it can't be right.
Bernard Mannes Baruch (1870–1965), American financier and
presidential advisor, *St Louis Post-Despatch*, 21 June 1965

It is such a delight now (that I'm no longer working for a large
corporation) to make decisions based on one criterion only; is it
a good decision, in both the short-term and the long-term?
When you are making a decision in a large corporation, you also
ask that question. But then, in parallel and with virtually
no exceptions, you have to ask yourself, how will this decision
look at corporate headquarters? Can it be defended against attack?
If it goes wrong, what is the recovery procedure?
God, what a pain in the ass that was!
Charles J Bodenstab, CEO, Battery and Tire Warehouse,
Inc. Magazine, August 1987

How much could it cost you?

IMAGINE THIS. You are a senior level manager of a medium-sized organisation. You are on a six-figure salary package and enjoy a comfortable lifestyle in a prestigious suburb. You are at a conference put on by your organisation to celebrate the end of a successful financial year. Your team and other employees are attending. It is around 10.00 p.m., the formal dinner is over and a group of people has gathered around the bar. You notice a female member of staff in the midst of the group whose name is Meg. She is having fun, and in your eyes, flirting with her male colleagues. She appears animated and confident as she talks and you are attracted to her. Buoyed by the fact that you have been drinking for much of the evening, you join the group. The laughter and joking continues but eventually people start to drift back to their rooms. Meg excuses herself too. Some time later, you leave but you do not go back to your own room, instead, you head for Meg's room, having found this out by checking the registration list. Before you know it you are standing outside her room. You knock once, twice firmly. There is silence and then the door opens. You miss the surprised look on her face and push your way into the room. Meg is initially polite, put stands at a distance from you. You move towards her and try putting your arm around her but she pulls away. You are in Meg's room for close to half an hour. For you, it seems like minutes but for Meg it feels like hours. Eventually she manages to push you to the door. You leave and nothing more is said. However, traumatised by the event, Meg takes several days off after the conference to pull herself together.

Back at work, you go about your business and fortunately you do not have to deal with Meg on a daily basis. However, some months later, an important meeting is scheduled that will mean the two of you are in the same room. You take action to have Meg taken off the list of attendees so you do not have to face her and you invite someone else instead. You realise that this will sideline Meg but you still proceed.

On being informed of her omission from the meeting, Meg is extremely upset. She held her silence over the conference incident, but now realises that she is being penalised for something she did not do. The feelings of fear and degradation come flooding back. After wrestling with all that has happened, she calls the Human Resources (HR) department.

Later that day you receive a call from the director of HR. He sounds frosty over the phone and you wonder what can be the problem as you head to his office. After a brief conversation, you find yourself terminated summarily. You struggle to deal with what has just happened. You hear the HR director's voice requesting your keys and telling you to leave your car in the basement. It is only 4.00 p.m. Do you go home early? What will you say to your wife, to your children and to your friends?

This scenario is a compilation of many examples of harassment and discrimination that occur in organisations. The difference being that it is unusual for such decisive action to be taken.

Some questions you might reflect on:

1. What stopped Meg complaining to HR straight away?
2. Why did Meg complain once she was excluded from the meeting?
3. Did the manager deserve to be terminated?

Analysis

The impact of the conference incident on Meg

Meg was attacked in her room. She had to fend off unwanted sexual advances from a person she thought she could trust and who is in a position of greater power and status. In other circumstances, she may well have been more on guard. The abuser takes advantage of the power differential.

The result of abuse leaves the person feeling powerless and shakes their confidence in their judgment and actions. 'Victims' doubt themselves and go through a period of soul searching, trying to understand the experience and the reason for it happening to them. Sadly, this works in favour of their abuser as the victim often chooses not to take action against them. So the abuser is then free to reabuse.

Depending on what actually happened while the manager was in the room, an apology might be what is needed. However, the abuser is unlikely to apologise, as this would be an admission of guilt. They often do not comprehend the degree of trauma they have inflicted due to a lack of empathy or more severe psychological disturbance that prevents them connecting with their actions.

Meg chose not to raise the issue. However, this does not mean the problem goes away.

The impact of exclusion from the meeting on Meg

Meg would only have had to look at the list of attendees to guess the reason for her exclusion. Meg's exclusion from the project-briefing meeting sends a message to her colleagues and staff that she is less suited to undertaking the project challenges than her substitute. The colleague is likely to gain valuable experience that will give him/her an edge when it comes to promotion. Meg will be at a disadvantage when competing for promotion against them. To date, Meg had been a star performer and was the best person for the project.

The act of excluding Meg also impacts at an emotional level leaving her feeling hurt, rejected and angry. Meg was already carrying unresolved emotions as a result of the incident at the conference. Her fright and feelings of self-loathing as a result of the 'attack' in her room flood back. Fuelled by her anger and the injustice of the situation, Meg takes her problem to HR.

The senior manager's side

He had too much to drink. He assumed that Meg would be interested in his advances, as it appeared to him that she was flirting with other men. He could not remember too much about what happened the next day, but he did realise that he had overstepped the mark. He considered a few options for dealing with this problem. One was to avoid her and the other was to have her leave the organisation somehow.

When the meeting was scheduled he was suddenly consumed by fear and under no circumstances did he want to risk having to face her. He reflected on the possibility of her raising the issue with him and other people overhearing her. It was then that he knew that he had to cut her out of the meeting and as soon as possible raise concerns about her performance so she would have to leave.

Options available

The best option for Meg would have been for her to raise her complaint with HR as soon after the event as possible. This would have created an opportunity for the organisation and those involved to resolve the problem internally. However, the willingness of people to discuss their grievances will depend on the nature of the complaint and their personal resilience. Whatever the situation, no-one should be forced to do anything. The person who has been abused may refuse point blank to be in the same room as their abuser. If HR is unable to resolve the situation, then the person can contact an anti-discrimination agency.

Meg could also have taken her case directly to an anti-discrimination agency. She need not have discussed her complaint with anyone in the organisation. The head of the organisation would receive a letter outlining the complaint. This direct access to an anti-discrimination agency is important as, in some instances, raising a problem results in further acts of discrimination or harassment.

The responsible organisation

Interpersonal conflicts that arise from discrimination or harassment are extremely disruptive to productivity. It is each manager's responsibility to ensure that the workplace is safe—not just physically safe but that it is emotionally safe for all people in the organisation.

It is important to:

- Measure and reward managers on the morale of their department or teams.
- Have a clear code of conduct for your workplace. Outline how you expect people to act towards each other. Put your effort into emphasising 'right' conduct rather than telling people what you do not want. Provide people with the reasons for requiring certain behaviours in the workplace.
- Outline the consequences that will be applied should inappropriate behaviour continue. State the consequences in a matter of fact way rather than as a threat. Be prepared to act on the consequences.
- Educate people about their rights and what to do if they are on the receiving end of discrimination or harassment.
- Inform everyone of the risks associated with acting in a discriminatory manner or harassing others in the workplace. People need to understand that they can be personally taken to court in a civil action and will not be able to hide behind the organisation.
- Establish a complaint process in consultation with managers and employees. Identify resources external to the organisation such as mediators or facilitators who can be called in to provide an impartial perspective.
- Ensure that each complaint is followed up to check that the issue has been resolved to the satisfaction of the complainant.

Final thoughts

Citing performance as a reason for discriminatory behaviour has been tried and is usually unsuccessful in escaping the implications of harassment and discrimination.

If there are performance problems with a particular person, harassment and discrimination are not methods that will serve to enhance performance. On the contrary, such approaches only serve to further reduce the person's effectiveness and result in the person taking stress leave as well as following through with a formal complaint.

If there are performance problems, be sure to document them. Note the date and time and outline the situation, including those present and what was said or not said as well as what was done or not done. If you are unsure how to deal with the issue, consult HR, a senior manager or a colleague.

Create an open communication system so that people can find the assistance they need to resolve such problems. People need to be able to raise issues or concerns openly. Silencing people will only serve to send problems underground.

The more open the communication, the healthier the culture and the healthier the culture, the less likely the organisation will experience the problems you have been reading about.

Importantly, remember the following:

- Client- or customer-focused cultures are dependent upon people within the organisation treating each other with respect.
- Use this article as a case study to run a session with managers to raise the issue of discrimination and harassment.

Discussion questions could include:

- What are the underlying causes that created this situation?
- What parallels exist between the case study and our organisation?
- What learnings or awareness do we need to apply?
- What are the covert and overt ways that discrimination and harassment take place?
- How effective are our mechanisms and policy to prevent and deal with discrimination and harassment?
- What actions do we need to initiate to make improvements in this area?

Will? Skill? Nil? Dill?

OST PERFORMANCE PROBLEMS usually relate more to a lack of will than to a lack of skill. Consider these questions: How are you going to influence your people to increase their level of commitment? How do you incorporate the following four aspects of leadership:
• direction/context
• space
• boundaries
• support
into your own leadership behaviour?

Procedure

Here are some guidelines to follow. In practice, always consider your prevailing circumstances:

1. Identify a person whose performance could be improved (low commitment and possibly moderate competence), or a person who is capable of being 'stretched' (high commitment and high competence).
2. Identify a key performance indicator (KPI), a key part of their role, a major task or major project, or a new initiative related to the person where their performance is down or where they are ready to be 'stretched'.
3. Using the scale from 1 to 10, rate them against each criterion based on your perception with 1 = definitely no and 10 = definitely yes.
4. Obtain a total score—the perfect score would be 320 points.
5. Circle the item numbers where you have assessed them as 7 or less.
6. Prepare yourself for a discussion with the person by planning what you would say in regards to each issue related to the identified KPI/task/project/initiative. What are the specific things you would like to discuss with this person?
7. Involve them in this leadership action by getting them to do a self-assessment. Use your assessment and their assessment as a basis for creating learning and understanding.
8. Agree two or three things that you will both focus on over the next month or so. Review the application of these and pick two or three new things and so on.

Direction and context

1. Understands the context. 1 2 3 4 5 6 7 8 9 10
2. Understands the purpose. 1 2 3 4 5 6 7 8 9 10
3. Understands the direction. 1 2 3 4 5 6 7 8 9 10
4. Understands the what and the why. 1 2 3 4 5 6 7 8 9 10
5. Explores options. 1 2 3 4 5 6 7 8 9 10
6. Applies creativity and innovation. 1 2 3 4 5 6 7 8 9 10
7. Is motivated to perform. 1 2 3 4 5 6 7 8 9 10
8. Understands the key drivers. 1 2 3 4 5 6 7 8 9 10

Space

1. Acts independently. 1 2 3 4 5 6 7 8 9 10
2. Shows there is sufficient trust in our
   relationship. 1 2 3 4 5 6 7 8 9 10
3. Tries new ways of doing things. 1 2 3 4 5 6 7 8 9 10
4. Explores best practice options. 1 2 3 4 5 6 7 8 9 10
5. Uses initiative to solve problems. 1 2 3 4 5 6 7 8 9 10
6. Uses initiative to make decisions. 1 2 3 4 5 6 7 8 9 10

Boundaries

1. Knows and accepts the boundaries. 1 2 3 4 5 6 7 8 9 10
2. Constructively challenges the boundaries. 1 2 3 4 5 6 7 8 9 10
3. Demonstrates their accountabilities. 1 2 3 4 5 6 7 8 9 10
4. Acts within acceptable levels of risk-taking. 1 2 3 4 5 6 7 8 9 10
5. Acts to our ethics. 1 2 3 4 5 6 7 8 9 10
6. Acts to our standards. 1 2 3 4 5 6 7 8 9 10
7. Acts to our principles. 1 2 3 4 5 6 7 8 9 10

Support

1. Feels that contribution is acknowledged and
   rewarded. 1 2 3 4 5 6 7 8 9 10
2. Learns from experience. 1 2 3 4 5 6 7 8 9 10
3. Overcomes setbacks. 1 2 3 4 5 6 7 8 9 10
4. Is self-motivated. 1 2 3 4 5 6 7 8 9 10
5. Receives adequate coaching and mentoring. 1 2 3 4 5 6 7 8 9 10
6. Initiates and develops ideas. 1 2 3 4 5 6 7 8 9 10
7. Feels that ideas are heard and considered. 1 2 3 4 5 6 7 8 9 10
8. Feels failure is supported by me. 1 2 3 4 5 6 7 8 9 10
9. Feels creativity, innovation and risk-taking
   are supported by me. 1 2 3 4 5 6 7 8 9 10

10. Feels a needed part of the team.   1 2 3 4 5 6 7 8 9 10

11. Receives adequate emotional and
intellectual support from me.   1 2 3 4 5 6 7 8 9 10

Score

256–320   Congratulations. Take a bow. You are providing outstanding
leadership and a very positive influence.

192–255   You are doing many good things and you both have plenty of room
for improvement.

128–191   Some good signs but a heck of a lot of work to do here.

64–127   If you are inexperienced, at least you now know the size of your
learning curve. If not, leadership is not really your bag, is it?

Less than 63   Leadership? What's that? Who? Me?

First impressions

I F YOU ARE READING THIS AT WORK and you need to clear the brain, here's a little exercise to do now. In a moment, walk beyond the front gate of your facility and pretend that you are a visitor who is coming onto the site for the first time. What do they see? Take in everything. Pan slowly across the site from side to side and top to bottom. Inspect the whole site. What is the general image conveyed by a visual inspection of the site? What does your yard or site say about the efficiency and management of your organisation?

Make a note of things that suggest slack standards, poor planning, untidiness, visual pollution, poor or dangerous access, neglect, inefficiency, wasted space, etc. Okay. Off you go.

How does it look to the customer? Neat, tidy, clean, well-organised, efficient, well-managed? Yes? Then you can skip the rest of this article. No? Then carry on.

Here is a checklist to use to get started:

☐ Create a group of six to eight people made up of equal numbers of people responsible for yard management and people whose jobs are most affected by the state of the yard. Set up this group to meet once a fortnight and give them the simple brief: to improve yard management.

☐ Explain the context, define the space, boundaries and level of support.

☐ Appoint a facilitator, if not yourself, making sure that this person has the authority to make decisions.

☐ Review the list below and agree the first five things that this group will start working on.

☐ Allocate specific tasks from these five actions to members of this group making sure that the load is spread evenly. Document agreements on individual action plans.

☐ Agree to meet in two weeks to report on progress or to discuss results. At this meeting, also agree on the next five actions for the group to implement.

☐ Continue this process until the group believes that they have achieved optimum yard management.

Use the following list to add, delete or modify actions to suit your circumstances:

☐ Agree the need for improving yard management.

☐ Agree and produce a ground plan for product storage areas; scrap; rubbish; scale; empty drums; raw materials; quality assurance hold areas; damaged materials for rework; containers; lifting equipment; maintenance materials; scrap drums; access for trucks and fork lifts; oil, fuel and chemical storage; flammable goods storage; miscellaneous, etc.

☐ Agree a logical sequence for the siting of all above areas.

☐ Discuss and agree the usage of the ground plan with key personnel.

☐ Develop storage and stacking procedures.

☐ Train operating crews in storage and stacking procedures.

☐ Develop a routine system for informing crews where product and other materials are to be stored.

☐ Train key personnel in the usage of the ground plan.

☐ Check that stacking and storage procedures are being followed correctly.

☐ Advise other managers/forepersons of the requirements for storage and stacking.

☐ Minimise distance travelled when loading containers.

☐ Identify inefficiencies in storage and stacking, and take action to improve.

☐ Agree with key personnel what cooperation is required from them.

☐ Agree with the management what direction/support you require from them.

☐ Eradicate loose, raw materials at the end of the production run.

☐ Develop and implement procedures for receiving goods and raw materials.

☐ Train all key personnel in procedures for receiving.

☐ Check that all materials are stacked and stored in optimum locations with optimum accessibility.

☐ Check that suppliers of raw materials follow correct delivery procedures.

☐ Check that raw materials are delivered efficiently to internal areas.

☐ Agree the actions required of other areas to assist in yard management.

☐ Consult with users of the yard on ways you could improve yard management.

☐ Implement new, different and better ways to improve yard management.

Ignore now, pay later

A S WE ESTABLISHED IN *You Lead, They'll Follow* Volume 2, time spent on 'on condition' observation and preventative maintenance is preferable to time spent repairing plant and equipment after breakdown.

Operators and maintenance people need to work hand in hand to ensure optimum maintenance. That's obvious, but it doesn't always happen that way due to the foibles of human nature. Here is a way to get greater cooperation happening between the operators and the maintenance personnel. Create a group of six to eight people made up of equal numbers of operators and maintenance people. Set up this group to meet fortnightly and give them the simple brief: to improve maintenance.

Here is a checklist to use to get started:

☐ Explain the context, define the space, boundaries and level of support.

☐ Appoint a facilitator, if not yourself, making sure that this person has the authority to make decisions.

☐ Review the list below and agree the first five things that this group will start working on.

☐ Allocate specific tasks from these five actions to members of this group making sure that the load is spread evenly. Document agreements on individual action plans.

☐ Agree to meet in two weeks to report on progress or to discuss results. At this meeting, also agree the next five actions for the group to implement.

☐ Continue this process until the group believes that they have achieved the optimum maintenance level.

Use the list below or add, delete or modify actions to suit your circumstances:

☐ Discuss the reasons for, and benefits of, improving maintenance.

☐ Identify all plant and equipment requiring maintenance.

☐ Develop a maintenance plan for each area.

☐ Agree an annual maintenance budget.

☐ Clarify individual management roles in relation to maintenance requirements.

☐ Identify and plan maintenance periods around best times to halt production.

☐ Inform the maintenance area of likely/possible unscheduled shutdowns.

☐ Inform the maintenance area of impending scheduled shutdowns.

☐ Develop maintenance procedures for key plant and equipment.

☐ Check that all stakeholders understand the organisation's policy and procedures in relation to maintenance activities.

☐ Train people in procedures related to maintenance activities.

☐ Develop a maintenance cycle to meet production requirements.

☐ Investigate maintenance contracts with new plant and equipment.

☐ Conduct regular meetings between maintenance and production to ensure all interests are met.

☐ Discuss the consequences of poor maintenance of plant and equipment.

☐ Agree the time for plant/equipment to be out of action during maintenance.

☐ Inform all areas within the organisation about impending maintenance activities and likely shutdowns.

☐ Check that all areas within the organisation are aware of impending maintenance shutdowns and have actioned their work appropriately.

☐ Inform customers of the impact a maintenance shutdown may have on our ability to supply product.

☐ Check that crews are able to complete maintenance within agreed time frames.

☐ Check that adequate skills exist within the maintenance crew to enable them to complete the job to the required standard.

☐ Identify where warranty conditions may impact on maintenance activities.

☐ Discuss and implement ways to improve maintenance activities.

☐ Identify where, how and why maintenance is not meeting the required standards.

☐ Develop and implement a simple, easy-to-use process to enable operators to provide regular feedback on the condition of plant and equipment.

☐ Remove obstacles/mental blockages and provide incentives (non-monetary) for operators to provide feedback on the condition of plant and equipment.

Idle minds are the devil's playground

WE HAVE WRITTEN AT LENGTH (see *You Lead, They'll Follow* Volume 1 pp. 246, 250 and 254) about the necessity of thoroughly briefing and debriefing people who are taken off the job to participate in formal management training. What about those who aren't involved—the rest of the people who make up the work group? In the absence of accurate information, the mischief makers will spread their destructive comments and do their best to foster suspicion. The 'grapevine' will be flourishing and spreading its counterproductive 'grapes' everywhere. (In fact, one of the reasons why there is a problem with the transfer of learning from the training room into application in the workplace is because the participants fear the reactions from their staff.)

I was working with a group of nine people with the aim of improving leadership. During one session, a few of the team leaders expressed their annoyance at the attitude of the people in their work group who were not part of this learning process. They said that they had to put up with derisive remarks and ridicule from some of the people in their work group. They found this off-putting, counterproductive and unnecessary. This made it harder for them to put into practice the desired or required leadership actions agreed to as part of the process.

Even though the actions they were taking with their work group were in the best interests of the group, they still experienced low cooperation and ridicule from some of their people.

Context/information for those left behind

It will produce more positives than negatives to hold a session with the uninvolved people and discuss these sorts of issues:

- Why are we doing this?
- What is the purpose?
- What is the training connected to?
- What is the rationale?
- What is the background that has led to this process being undertaken?
- What are the areas of focus for this process—the content of the program?
- When and where and how often we will be doing this?
- How will we be attempting to apply the learnings from this process?
- How will you be involved?
- How could you benefit?
- The support we would like from you to help us improve the quality of work life for all of us.
- Any concerns or issues that the people who are not taking part in the training may want to raise.
- Ask them for their reactions to this initiative. Ask them for their thoughts and feelings about the exercise. Ask what they could do to help use this initiative to produce a positive impact in the workplace.
- For any negative thoughts expressed, ask them to consider this question in relation to each negative comment: What are other ways to think about this initiative which could apply and be true and serve us all better?

They won't fully understand the process you are going through, but the fact you took the time to include them will make it worthwhile. You will still probably get a couple of mischief makers trying their best to sabotage the training, but their mischief making will fall on less fertile ground.

'
With the rapidity of a burning powder train, information
flows like magic out of the woodwork, past the
water fountain, past the manager's door, past the
janitor's mop closet. As elusive as a summer zephyr, it filters
through steel walls, bulkheads, or construction glass partitions,
from the sub-basement to the rafters, from office boy
to executive … It carries good news and bad, fact as well
as fancy, without discrimination. It cares nothing for
reputation, nothing about civil rights; it will carve up and
serve the big brass, the shop foreman, and the
stenographer with fine impartiality.
(Referring to the office 'grapevine'.)
Joseph K Shephard, journalist and contributing author,
Leadership in the Office, **AMACOM 1963**
'

SATAJTA (for those of you who like acronyms and tongue-twisters)

L EADERSHIP IS AN ETERNAL SUBJECT OF DISCUSSION. Academics often attempt to bring something new to the subject. In analysis, little is new, though terminology may suggest a new insight. Distinction has been made between styles of leadership, between leadership and management, between leadership of others and self-leadership, and leadership approaches for varying purposes and stages of organisational evolution.

The following are perennial constants:

1. **Know your self:** self-awareness and personal development are the foundations for great leadership. Understanding one's personality, articulating one's values, acquiring attitudinal competency—the ability to identify, select, generate, sustain and adapt one's attitude to the 'now'—are crucial, placing the leader in a position to *firstly lead by example*.

2. **Know your purpose:** there can be no leadership without a purpose, articulated as a vision that leadership serves. Our common purpose is to serve each other and unify. Every great leader has held *a compelling vision* that has captured hearts, minds and actions.

3. **Distinguish between power and force:** use of authority or position so that followers comply is forceful. Use of value-based persuasion, influence and encouragement so that there is a willing choice to follow is powerful. Great leaders know when to *choose* to use force and power.

4. **Walk in another's shoes:** by understanding the perception of others, a leader can determine how to approach them. The primary method of achieving this is by *effective listening and effective open-ended questions* that encourage thinking and problem solving.

5. **Speak their language:** effective leadership ensures *all communication is understood*, with clarity and relevance to the purpose, and is timely, complete and congruent with the shared values.

6. **Be a master learner:** by being open to the new and innovative, ensuring usefulness and congruence with values and purpose, *perpetual improvement and sustainability* becomes a consistent outcome.

7. **Develop your people:** people are the most important component of any organisation and an effective leader honours this by *ensuring*

the people have optimum development, not only vocationally, but for the whole of life. Additionally, this relates to ensuring there is a viable leadership succession plan.

8. **Share the load:** effective leaders can *delegate and empower others* to take responsibility. Remaining aware of the situation without unnecessary interference is the key.

9. **Be humble:** this is a *common characteristic of all truly great leaders*, and is an endearing aspect that attracts followers. Humility is not a weakness.

10. **Be decisive:** decision making requires practice. *Effective leaders make more effective decisions*. Doing nothing can also be a decision, if well considered.

I encourage everyone, especially leaders, to adopt a SATAJTA way of being:

Self-Awareness: be aware of yourself, your personality, your habits, values and purpose.

Truthful expression: always speak truthfully.

Assume nothing: observe and listen carefully, then ask questions.

Judge nobody: otherwise you are judging yourself. However, do not accept unacceptable behaviour.

Take nothing personally: nobody knows you that well.

Always stay on 'manual': automatic reactions cause most accidents and pain.

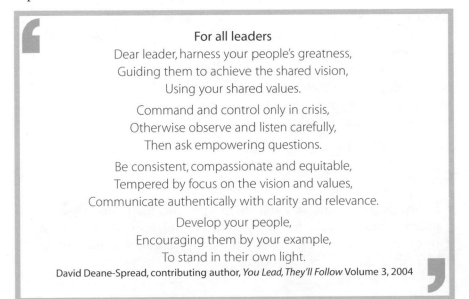

For all leaders
Dear leader, harness your people's greatness,
Guiding them to achieve the shared vision,
Using your shared values.

Command and control only in crisis,
Otherwise observe and listen carefully,
Then ask empowering questions.

Be consistent, compassionate and equitable,
Tempered by focus on the vision and values,
Communicate authentically with clarity and relevance.

Develop your people,
Encouraging them by your example,
To stand in their own light.

David Deane-Spread, contributing author, *You Lead, They'll Follow* Volume 3, 2004

Here's how we want it done

'WHAT'S THE POLICY ON …?' Who wouldn't like a dollar for every time that question has been asked? It is asked because people are seeking a clear direction for decision making.

Without policy you are open to inconsistency, subjectivity, manipulation and corruption. All the things that can make life unpleasant particularly when you are the point where 'the buck stops'.

Policy provides a firm set of parameters by which we can operate. Quite often the policy is supported by a set of guidelines that provides the rationale behind it. These guidelines also provide the detail that help with policy implementation.

When developing policy make it relevant, current, valid, practical, acceptable to the stakeholders and able to be resourced adequately and then inform everyone about it. It will be very useful to seek input from the people who will have to implement the policy.

Guidelines for developing policy:

- Check that the planned policy is relevant to the needs of the organisation.
- Establish the reasons for, and the purpose of, the policy. By having a policy, what can be achieved or what are the desirable outcomes?
- Inform staff of the reasons why the policy is going to be developed.
- Identify stakeholders likely to be affected by the policy.

- Form a reference group made up of people who are familiar with the current situation and work in that area or are in some way affected by the decisions made.
- Identify the key issues related to the policy development.
- Discuss policy issues with stakeholders.
- Prepare a draft policy document.
- Establish a consultation strategy after the draft has been written.
- Ask for feedback on the draft policy from key stakeholders.
- Discuss and define a clear purpose of the policy.
- Identify the situations or scenarios that the policy will address.
- Write guidelines that clarify policy and provide the rationale behind it.
- Check that policy is clear, unambiguous and concise.
- Determine a policy format that is consistent with the format of other organisation policies.
- Consult with informed staff during the policy development process.
- Identify procedures that need to be developed as part of the policy.
- Consider the need to be flexible in 'exception to the rule' situations.
- Consider statutory requirements during policy formulation.
- Establish regular communication briefing sessions.
- Establish an implementation strategy.
- Inform all stakeholders of the final policy statement.
- Include the following in the policy:
  - an introduction
  - a description of the policy
  - the rationale for policy statements
  - definitions of key concepts
  - guidelines which provide more information about the policy
  - a clarification of roles and responsibilities.

Ask the question—what has to happen to ensure that the people who will have to implement the policy have the skill and the will to do that?

Do unto others …

> If there is any one secret of success, it lies in the ability to get the other person's point of view and see things from his angle as well as from your own.
>
> Henry Ford (1863–1947), American industrialist

OFTEN, WHEN MANAGING OUR PEOPLE, we are uncertain how to approach discussion of a difficult issue. It can be advisable to think for a while what it would be like if 'the shoe were on the other foot', and you were the one receiving the news or instruction. How would you like to be approached/told/treated? Use this as your guide on how you should communicate with others, especially your staff, but also your peers and even your boss and those at their level and above.

If you find you are still struggling with how to approach the issue, think of someone whom you really respect, and try to imagine how they would handle the issue. Then, provided you are comfortable with that imagined approach, try to emulate it.

By treating others as you would like to be treated yourself, you will almost certainly be courteous, considerate and respectful, but still get the message across. In this way you will retain the respect and understanding of the person you are communicating with, despite any unpleasantness in the content of the communication.

This same philosophy should be used when dealing with customers, suppliers and any others you deal with in business.

In your position as manager, your staff look to you for an example of how to behave. You will find they will copy you in many small ways. This makes it doubly important that you act in the way you would like others to act.

Some guidelines to follow:

- ☐ If effort significantly beyond what could be considered normal is required of your staff on a particular issue, then lead by example and put in at least that much extra effort yourself.
- ☐ Do not ask any person to do something you would not be willing to do yourself, provided you were technically competent to do so.
- ☐ With all persons, be as honest and open as you possibly can whilst still bearing in mind good business practice.
- ☐ Share good news and achievements with all. Be willing to praise publicly.
- ☐ Do not ridicule in public, especially your staff.
- ☐ If you see one of your staff ridiculing one of their staff, find an opportunity to have a quiet word with them, and explain they ought not to do so, or they will drag themselves down in the eyes of their own people, especially that staff member. They may find the staff member no longer as willing to accept their directives because of this reduction in respect. The loss of immediate opportunity for a laugh is a small price to pay in the longer term. This can be particularly important for someone who has just been promoted from within the group. The new boss will still want to remain on friendly terms with his former peers. They can still laugh with them, but not at the expense of one of them any more. They must move beyond this.
- ☐ Do not talk behind the back of others—don't discuss negative things about any person with their peers. Take a moment to ask yourself whether you would be happy for what you are saying to be repeated to them, and if not, then don't say it.
- ☐ Do not engage in gossip about others.
- ☐ Recognise and acknowledge what is fact.
- ☐ If you are expressing an opinion or engaging in conjecture, say that is what it is. Never portray conjecture as fact.
- ☐ Do not engage in hollow flattery.
- ☐ Coach on areas requiring improvement of one particular person or group of persons in private.

Converting strategy into reality

I AM ALWAYS ANXIOUS TO LEARN from experienced people who have established a proven track record in the practical application of management concepts. One such person was a CEO who, in his mid-sixties, was responsible for the profitability of fifty major manufacturing facilities in Canada, North America and South America.

What intrigued me was how he and his immediate team had managed to convert a business strategy into a working reality given the complexities of geographic location, different manufacturing processes, language and many other salient factors.

I decided to pursue my curiosity by asking him how it felt to be placed in such a difficult position. His response was as mature and memorable as it was enlightening. He smiled as he pondered my question for a minute and said, 'You know, I felt so damn important in my big posh office on the top floor with my army of assistants and private jet. I likened myself to the captain on a giant liner standing on the bridge with a helm and line of levers that I could turn or pull to direct the course and destination of the vessel. After a while, however, I realised that my ship was not responding to my instructions and so I decided to investigate. I went down to the floor below and to my horror discovered that my precious helm and levers were not connected to anything, it was then that I realised just how difficult the job really was.'

As amusing as this true story may seem it does convey the difficulty of actually converting strategy into reality. It made me consider how many organisations have floundered, not because of management's inability to see the approaching rocks but because of its inability to connect the levers and take timely evasive action.

Business alignment

A proven basis for connecting the levers, particularly in a larger organisation, is to ensure that the business strategy, once defined, is effectively communicated/cascaded through all levels of the business and thereafter converted into a series of measurable actions that are in direct alignment with the overall strategy.

The following recommendations are based on a highly successful and proven formula:

1. **Determine a strategy—what is the destination and ETA?** Defining strategy is invariably the role of the CEO and his executive team. Obviously it is vital to have a clear indication of where the business needs to go in order to produce the required projected return. It is also essential to set an estimated time of arrival.

2. **Communicate and challenge—why it is necessary?** People inevitably respond more positively when they are fully aware of the reasons for change. They also react better when implicated in a situation of challenge. It is essential, therefore, to place considerable emphasis on the process of initial and progressive communications.

3. **Identify the major hurdles—what will impede progress?** Examine the critical issues that must be overcome in order to achieve a successful and timely outcome. Involving people in the early stages will reduce the possibility of unforeseen events.

4. **Devolve the responsibility for change—who will do what?** Having defined a detailed program for implementing a strategy, together with deadlines, it is essential to break the process down into manageable, measurable components. Once these components have been identified it is essential to formally agree who will be accountable for their progress.

5. **Maintaining focus—who is responsible?** Evidently the impetus of the implementation program will be directly influenced by the ability of senior management to sustain interest and maintain focus. With this in mind it is beneficial to allocate the responsibility for the change program to a specific individual who will monitor and report progress (against target) at prescribed intervals. They will also recommend expediting actions where required.

Self assessment

'
> Successful strategies flow like water; they are shaped by the
> circumstances of the conflict. When water flows, it avoids
> the high ground and seeks the low ground. Successful strategies
> likewise avoid difficult methods and find easy ones.
> The best strategy is to make a competitor's products obsolete
> through innovation. The next best strategy is to better ways
> of providing your products. The next best strategy is
> to market yourself more effectively. The worst strategy
> is to attack a competitor's reputation or products directly.
> This sort of strategy is a matter of desperation. It often
> results in the destruction of all involved.
>
> Adapted from Donald G Krause *Sun Tzu:*
> *The Art of War for Executives,* Berkley, 1995
'

N THE TIME OF SUN TZU, strategy was understood to be 'the art of planning and directing the movement of large military units and the operations of war'. In the business world of today, a strategy maps out the future directions of the company, determines which products and services will be taken to the market, how they will be taken and what resources are necessary to achieve the long-term objectives of the company.

The ability to think strategically is a skill that can be developed and heightened in most managers. Test your strategic thinking quotient by indicating how frequently you undertake these actions. For each action, circle 1 for *rarely*, 3 for *sometimes* and 5 for *always*.

Action	Score
1. I have a long-term plan (two–five years) for my area of business responsibility.	1 3 5
2. I discuss the strategy with all people involved.	1 3 5
3. I talk to people about their roles and responsibilities relevant to the strategy.	1 3 5
4. I confer with other managers about my strategy.	1 3 5
5. I understand where members of my team need to make improvements.	1 3 5

Action	Score
6. I ensure that my strategy is consistent with that of other managers and the company.	1 3 5
7. I take steps to ensure my team operates within the strategy guidelines.	1 3 5
8. I ensure that everyone involved in my strategy is kept up-to-date with the progress.	1 3 5
9. I understand my product or service advantages and disadvantages.	1 3 5
10. I understand my competitor's advantages and disadvantages.	1 3 5
11. I know the contents of my competitor's web site.	1 3 5
12. I am able to gain benefits from new technology.	1 3 5
13. I know what my customer's future (forecast) requirements are for my products.	1 3 5
14. I understand my customer's business imperatives and philosophies.	1 3 5
15. I am sure that I am ahead of my competition.	1 3 5
16. I have established product priorities for different market segments.	1 3 5
17. I measure my actual sales against budget and historical results.	1 3 5
18. I review and update my strategy as external circumstances change.	1 3 5
19. I have accurate and up-to-date costings of all elements of my strategy.	1 3 5
20. I have all the background information necessary to make informed decisions.	1 3 5
TOTAL	

Analysis: The total of all your scores that you circled indicates whether you perform the actions that are required and desired of the best strategic thinkers.

20–45   You are reactive and spend most of your time attending to operational issues in the business. Perhaps the nature of your business or the lack of resources impacts on the time you can devote to strategic thinking.

46–75   You are able to devote some of your time to strategic thinking but there are some areas of weakness that should be addressed. Perhaps the greatest impediment to your strategic thinking is the fact that operational issues are often given a higher priority.

76–100   You are in a minority of managers that has a balance between operational aspects and strategic thinking and you are therefore very competent in strategic thinking.

Swots up, Doc?

FOR THE UNINITIATED, SWOT analysis has been around for many decades. It is a tool used in the early part of an initiative to create sustainable improvement. It can be used from an organisation-wide perspective (macro level) or a manager can use it with their own work group (micro level). It can be used to help organisations/work groups decide, plan and implement strategies for change and sustainable improvement.

A SWOT analysis answers this question: What are our strengths, weaknesses, opportunities and threats?

- Strengths are our present advantages we have over our competition or the competencies and values that exist within the group that work well.
- Weaknesses are areas of our operation where we are out-performed by the competition or aspects of the way we work that lessen our efficiency and effectiveness.
- Opportunities are things that are happening or are predicted to happen in the environment in which we operate (both internally and externally) that present possibilities for gaining a competitive advantage or for sustainable improvement.
- Threats are things that are happening or are predicted to happen in the environment in which we operate (both internally and externally) that could be disadvantageous to the organisation or work group.

Why SWOT?

This is a smart 'heads up' exercise to do every one to two years—this period should be determined by the pace of change in the environment in which we operate. Identification of our strengths, weaknesses, opportunities and threats enables us to maintain our competitive advantage and to sustain improvement and be proactive in dealing with changing circumstances. We do this so as to optimise our strengths, correct or modify our weaknesses, take best advantage of opportunities and plan to remove or lessen the impact of threats.

The accepted practice is to conduct this analysis in the order S, W, O then T. But I reckon that it makes more sense to conduct the analysis in the order O, T, S then W. Why? I was hoping you wouldn't ask. No, because by doing the O and T first, we then have a context for doing the S and W. Effectively we are asking, 'In dealing with these opportunities and threats, what are our strengths and weaknesses?'

SWOT analysis

Opportunities: based on analysis of the external environment.

Threats: based on analysis of the external environment.

Strengths: based on analysis of the internal environment. In being able to deal with these opportunities and threats, what are our current strengths?

Weaknesses: based on analysis of the internal environment. In being able to deal with these opportunities and threats, what are our current weaknesses?

Summary

Reflecting on the issues identified in the SWOT analysis, what are the critical actions that we must initiate or undertake from now and over the next two years?

Improving. communication

Don't blame us, we weren't asked

THE PURPOSE OF CONSULTATION is twofold. One is to seek ideas to remove obstacles and to assist with implementation. The other is to keep people 'on side'.

If you are planning to introduce a new project or to make a significant change to the way you do things, a consultative process may help. Some managers hold the view that consultation is not necessary. Intelligent logic suggests that it makes good sense to incorporate into the planning process the perceptions of the people who will have to implement the new initiative or change. The act of consultation is nearly as important as the value of the views expressed. Be warned, however. If you don't show how the information obtained through consultation has been used, then be sure to explain the reasons why.

Part of the explanations about why you have not incorporated their views may require you to change inaccurate perceptions by giving people more context, more information, different perspectives and different interpretations.

Human beings at every level in the organisation like to feel worthwhile, that they matter, that their work life has some significance. Taking the time to ask a person for their opinion or perception is a simple but powerful act that enhances the self-worth of people. Importantly, it enhances cooperation.

You will get some mischief makers who will use consultation as an opportunity to shout their vested interests. But most people will respond reasonably and usefully.

A checklist for consultation:

- [ ] Discuss the purpose and benefits of consultation during the planning and decision-making stages of a project.
- [ ] Identify staff expectations and perceptions about consultation.
- [ ] Provide a context around which consultation will take place.
- [ ] Agree the amount of consultation that will take place.
- [ ] Discuss what is meant by consultation.
- [ ] Identify the stakeholders to be consulted.
- [ ] Discuss and agree outcomes, key result areas, major activities and the priorities for what we are aiming to achieve.
- [ ] Identify what information is vital for consultative planning and decision making.

- ☐ Explain to those people you consulted with the reasons for not implementing the suggestions they put forward.
- ☐ Agree the roles of stakeholders in the consultation process.
- ☐ Inform staff of what these roles are.
- ☐ Check that our sources of information are informed.
- ☐ Check that the people with whom consultation will take place have the best interests of the project at heart.
- ☐ Agree the sorts of information that will be required from stakeholders.
- ☐ Identify the areas where most value will be obtained during the consultation process.
- ☐ Provide a clear statement of what the intended project outcomes are before embarking on the consultation process.
- ☐ Discuss the timeframe for implementation of plans.
- ☐ Review regularly the progress of the implementation of the plan.
- ☐ Agree the sequence of activities for the implementation of the plan.
- ☐ Explain to those stakeholders not involved in the consultation process the reasons why they are not to be consulted.
- ☐ Check that people involved in implementation are consulted in the planning phase.
- ☐ Explain how information and data gathered will be used during the project.
- ☐ Reward those people involved in the consultation process when their involvement has been above and beyond the call of duty.

> ❝ Once you decide to make a change in a particular area,
> it often means a change in people, and that's most often
> where things bog down.
> T Wiles, turnaround operations consultant,
> *Inc. Magazine*, February 1988 ❞

Ping pong

HOW WELL DO YOU CONVERSE WITH OTHERS? How well do the members of your work group converse with each other? Your skill at conversation sets you apart. If it is not already, the 'art and practice of conversation' should be a mandatory subject taught at schools (along with 'ways to develop self-esteem', 'how to enjoy life without drugs and crime', 'the concept of choices and consequences on your life' and 'parenting').

I am not talking about debating skills. That's part of the problem. Debating teaches students how to use the adversarial approach—how to score points and beat the opponent. Conversations should be like a tapestry woven together with threads of context, information, perspectives and interpretations until we have the completed article—the full story for that situation. You have your parts to build the tapestry. I have my parts to build the tapestry. Some of our parts are similar, some overlap and some are different.

Conversations in society and in the workplace take place at such superficial levels. More stuff of substance gets said in the bar or the corridors after a meeting than during the meeting.

I express my view about the subject. You express your view about the subject. If we are in agreement, we think that we have had a successful conversation. And it may well be, but we have probably just missed an opportunity to get to a deeper level of awareness, understanding and commitment. If we are not in agreement, I defend my view. You defend your view. You put your point. I put my point. And so on back and forth. Verbal ping pong. Neither person really gains from this style of conversation, especially when they are listening to their own 'noise'.

When you enter a serious conversation, you should emerge changed, better informed, in some small, or even large, way. A conversation should be an exchange—an interchange—of information, ideas, context, assumptions, inferences, perspectives, interpretations. My intention in a conversation can be to dominate, to win, to subjugate, to show my knowledge, to show the superiority of my thinking, the inferiority of your thinking. Or it can be to arrive at a deeper level of awareness and understanding and, ultimately, commitment. Your intention or goal is very important because that will dictate your strategy. Be clear on your intention.

Here are some things to say that will improve conversations:

- Let's not agree to disagree. Let's agree to find the best argument—not to see who can win or lose the argument.
- These are the assumptions I have made … I would like to hear any assumptions that you may have made.
- I am going to tell you what I think and why I think that way. And then I would be very interested to find out what you think and why you think that way. Is that fair?
- I came to this conclusion because …
- To try and explain where I am coming from, imagine this situation …
- My intention in this discussion is to … What is your intention in this discussion?
- I am sure that I don't have the full picture yet. I hope that you can add to it.
- I have listened to what you have to say and there are still a few things that don't make sense to me. For instance, I am missing the connection between … and … Could you help me out on this?
- I don't see things the way you do. Why is that so? What things are forming your opinion and what things are forming my opinion?
- That's a strong view you hold there. What experiences have led you to that view?
- I'd like you to tell me how you think my reasoning would have to change to get a better understanding of this situation. And then I would like to do the same with you.
- We are talking about the same experience but our interpretations are different. Why is that so?

- What could be other ways to think about this situation that could apply and be true?
- What could be other ways to think about this situation that could serve both of us better?
- What could be other interpretations that could also be true?
- Let's separate facts from opinions and check out the basis of those opinions.
- What are the things that neither of us know about this situation?
- What information or perspective would we both need to add or take to change our positions on this issue?
- I feel that we are not making any ground here and that we may miss an opportunity to get to a better place than we are. Would you try this approach with me? I will describe what I perceive as your concerns and the basis for your reasoning. I would like you to do the same with your perception of my concerns and the basis for my reasoning. How about it? We have nothing to lose—we can only win or break even.

(Some points adapted from Peter Senge, *The Fifth Discipline Fieldbook*, Nicholas Brealey Publishing, London, 1998)

Warning: email can harm your relationships

From: Me
To: You
Subject: Project Status

I do not understand what you meant by 'it's about time'. Why did you respond so tersely?
Regards
Me

From: You
To: Me
Subject: Project Status

I'm concerned you don't understand. We are behind schedule. I'm not being terse just economical. Isn't that what emails are for?
Regards
You

THE PROLIFERATION OF THE EMAIL has created an interesting situation. Its benefits are many, such as rapid transmission of documents, information transfer, reminders, agreements to meet etc., to a person, or many people simultaneously. However, the email system, when overused or abused, can lead to the breakdown of meaning and intentions and can cause relationships to deteriorate.

Many of us (those who can remember them) treat emails like telegrams (yesterday's version of today's email) and attempt to compose them in the same way as if we had to pay by the word. This makes the message terse. This is one reason why the tone of many emails causes more disengagement than engagement.

Here are some common reasons behind email misuse:

• avoiding personal contact,
• avoiding confrontation,
• avoiding explanation,
• avoiding responsibility,
• 'getting them on paper',

- passing time and socialising, particularly when personal contact is easy,
- copying irrelevant or unnecessary material to too many people because it is so easy to do,
- not responding to the points in the email to which the sender wants a response,
- no clear direction from the sender as to which points require a response,
- no level of urgency in relation to a response individualised by the sender.

I was asked to intervene in one office of seventeen members where, despite being located in adjoining offices, they insisted upon communicating with each other by email for all transfer of information, queries, requests and responses. I was asked to intervene because they all felt a lack of team spirit and dysfunctional relationships.

Whilst there were other factors that influenced their situation, their overuse of emails proved to be the major factor. By following some basic guidelines, relationships improved, misunderstandings didn't arise or were resolved more simply, and greater efficiency in the workplace resulted.

Building relationships and effective communication between humans requires personal contact where voice and eye contact can be exchanged. This is because only twenty per cent of effective communication relies on words. Eighty per cent of effective communication relies upon body language, volume, tonality and the ability to immediately clarify and correct meanings exchanged in conversation. Email does not provide for this.

In protracted email exchanges over a particular subject, too many assumptions are possible about the meaning of specific words, possible emotions, possible intentions and the meaning of brevity, or verbosity. Even innocent typographical errors can cause misunderstanding. Also, there are occasions when humour is mistaken for sarcasm or worse, and seriousness is mistaken for anger.

Email conversations, whether on-line or not, don't provide the efficiency that direct human contact, in person or via telephone, can provide.

Some people are now using 'happy face' icons or such other graphic assistants to 'enliven' emails. Whilst this can be fun, I suggest it is a poor second to real human contact.

Judgement needs to be exercised about when to talk live or when to email. The need to develop or bolster relationships and 'cut through' ambiguity must prevail if we are to effectively use email.

Here are some basic guidelines for the effective use of email:

- One telephone or in-person contact for every four email contacts with any person or group.
- Restrict emails to brief and single issue information exchanges, such as agreeing meeting times, or transferring documents.
- Do not rely on email for detailed explanations, back it up with personal contact.
- Do not use email for any sensitive or complex issues.
- Consider the tone of your message and the possible impact at the other end.
- Take extra time to compose your message thoughtfully knowing that your words have the potential to create the wrong impression and damage the relationship.
- Include a clear request such as, 'Please respond to the following points …' This will help to focus the email.

> Nothing can replace the magic and pleasure of direct human contact. Nothing can create or heal relationships better than direct human contact.
> David Deane-Spread, contributing author,
> *You Lead, They'll Follow,* Volume 3, 2004

Listen up

ERE I GO AGAIN. For the fourth time in this book series I'm banging on about listening. Why? Because I continue to experience the consequences of breakdowns in communication because one or both parties wasn't listening. From my experience it may well be the single biggest cause of problems; of wasted time, money and resources.

Take notice. Count the number of times each week that you hear comments similar to these:

- 'I thought you said…'
- 'I thought you meant…'
- 'I didn't hear you say that'
- 'That's not what you told me'
- 'I didn't say that, I said …'
- 'You didn't say that, you said …'
- 'I asked you that last week'
- 'I thought that we had already had a conversation about this'
- 'We discussed this during our last conversation'
- 'This is what I thought that we had agreed'

Some symptoms of poor listening are:

- A person asks you the same question they asked you a week or so ago for the second or third time.
- Your recall of a previous conversation is different from the other person's recall.
- Things that you recall vividly as being said are denied by the other party.
- Things that were supposed to happen didn't because the other person or you 'forgot'.

So, big deal, you say. No-one died. That's true, but the consequences of people not listening are severe. And it would not be too far-fetched to suggest that people have died because someone didn't listen.

Let me be blunt. You are not a good listener. Yes, you. But don't slash your wrists. You are not alone. Look around you. Ineffective listeners are everywhere. And don't confuse hearing with listening. First, you hear. Then, you listen. Or not. More likely, not.

I have been noticing how well and poorly people listen for years. I don't know why, but I have made it into a bit of a crusade. Actually, I do know why. Through years of experience and observation, I have come to the conclusion that none of us (I'm in there too) are naturally good at listening. In fact, you'll become better at it the moment you accept that you are no good at it.

In my own case, I have noticed that when I am aware that I really must listen, I'm bloody good at it. Relax. Keep reading. I know this because I amaze people (and alienate some) when I reiterate the detail about things they said to me in previous conversations. Now consider this. I have spent over twenty-five years facilitating groups where your listening skills are on display constantly. Your credibility (and your effectiveness) suffers if you show the group that you weren't listening. So it's a case of listen, or else. No matter the duration of the workshop—eight, sixteen, even up to forty hours, you have to be actively listening every minute of every hour. I figure that I was forced to practise listening (read focusing on the words and meaning of the speaker) for over twenty-five years so something had to rub off.

Notwithstanding the above, there are occasions during conversations where I know I am listening to my inner dialogue (the voice in my head—the same one that you are listening to right now, except it's your head, your voice) instead of the voice of the other person. That is, I am focusing on my reaction to their words, tone and body language rather than the meanings and intentions of their words. I'm still hearing, however, just not listening.

It gets a bit tricky. I have a close friend who is a psychologist who is an excellent listener. One of the best that I have met. She spends a large chunk of her time listening to people trying to deal with life's problems. Again, to be effective, her job demands that she be a good listener. On the other hand, I have another friend who also spends a lot of time counselling and coaching people in life skills, who, outside that environment, is a poor listener.

One good indicator that someone is not listening is that they will frequently interrupt. This is a sign that they have switched from listening to your voice to listening to their inner voice.

I know that, for me, I stop listening effectively when I become internally focused (on me) rather than staying externally focused on the speaker. And again, I repeat, I can still hear them. You can't and don't want to eliminate your inner voice. It will always be there. But notice this. When you are listening effectively, your inner voice fades into the background of your consciousness and the voice of the speaker is in the foreground of your consciousness. When you are listening ineffectively, your inner voice moves into the foreground of your consciousness and the speaker's voice fades into the background. So the trick is to be eternally vigilant and notice whose voice you are primarily listening to. (See *You Lead, They'll Follow* Vol 1). When you notice that you are primarily listening to your inner voice, refocus back to the speaker. But you have to do this constantly. With practice, you'll get better at it. And you will be amazed at how your memory seems to have suddenly improved.

Start from the premise that none of us are naturally good listeners. To be a good listener takes a conscious act to listen. You have to go into manual, be totally present in the moment, stay with what the person is saying and not what you are thinking, and stay focused on their voice and not your inner voice. Most poor listeners are listening to themselves, not to the speaker.

Back to the future

A RECENT SURVEY REVEALED THAT, on average, over sixty per cent of the time spent in meetings or conferences was devoted to analysis and explanation (sometimes rationalisation) of results, twenty per cent on administration and less than twenty per cent to the future activities of the company. This alarming figure confirms the fact that many people leave such sessions wondering what was actually achieved during the meeting.

Most managers are well aware of the fact that when a company is experiencing growth, staff is usually too busy moving forward to spend time examining the past. The anomaly is that a company, faced with results that are below expectation, will often require an in-depth analysis and explanation of past results, rather than a comprehensive plan of positive, future interventions. In such a circumstance, the company should devote time to identifying the issues that are impacting the business so that corrective action can be taken. The focus should be on managing activities, strategies, promotions, business processes and management systems that will lead to improved company performance.

Studying the past often results in recriminations and may create an atmosphere that is not conducive to the freethinking creativity often needed to resolve issues. This does not imply that the past should be ignored; it does, however, imply that far too much time is frequently spent in examining the minutiae of results, to the detriment of determining future opportunities.

There have been many instances when a company has failed to address critical issues because they have been hidden behind graphs, spreadsheets, market surveys and the omnipresent 'war stories'. A good result does not require complex charts or graphs to be understood. A poor result, however, can be made to appear better through the creative use of charting techniques and clever data projection.

It is axiomatic that an issue is difficult to resolve until it has been clearly identified. One way of avoiding the 'paralysis by analysis' syndrome is to use a process that will allow rapid identification of the issues faced by a company rather than dwelling on history. The key to identification is to force people at the meeting to concentrate on the core issues and avoid being distracted by peripheral matters.

There are some simple process guidelines that a company can follow when conducting a strategic plan development or business review meeting, to ensure that the core issues, critical to the business, are uncovered:

☐ Establish a simple 'statement of intent' for the meeting and ensure that all participants understand the reason for the meeting. This will allow them to undertake whatever preparation is necessary for their participation.

☐ Allocate sufficient time (usually ten to fifteen per cent of the total) for succinct, quantitative reports of past performance. These should deal only with facts; not assumptions, interpretations or conclusions, and should be presented in a predetermined format.

☐ Avoid 'generalities'; insist on 'specifics' during the reporting session.

☐ Pinpoint the issues that are central to the statement of intent. This should be done in a manner that permits everyone to identify issues from their own perspective without criticism from others. In essence, this should be a brainstorming session. It should not be open-ended as the pressure of a deadline can be a useful tool in clarifying thoughts.

☐ Categorise and prioritise all issues through a risk assessment process that considers both probability of occurrence and impact on the business. The weightings, leading to prioritisation, should be done using a simple mathematical process.

☐ Have task centric groups develop action plan outlines with the whole group being involved in ratification/refinement/rejection of the intervention. This should be an iterative process until the entire group agrees with, and is committed to, the intervention(s).

☐ Subject the action plan outlines to tests for consistency against company constraints, competencies, budgets, resources and market reaction. This process may help prevent the group devote time to the development of an intervention that can never be implemented.

☐ Determine an implementation schedule noting individual and group responsibilities.

☐ Communicate the intervention(s) to key stakeholders within the company.

Following these guidelines will increase the possibility of achieving a beneficial outcome; a plan for the future. A well-balanced plan is one that recognises the past and is focused on actions or processes that will positively influence the future results of the company. If evolution of a strategy is the intent of the meeting, it is rather simple logic that there should be significantly more time devoted to planning the future rather than analysing history. To plan effectively, learn from the past but get 'back to the future'.

What to do when no-one talks

IMAGINE A SITUATION where you have called your reports together for one of your usual meetings. It could be the weekly, fortnightly or monthly management meeting. The meeting has been in progress for about fifteen minutes. The tone is flat and even if someone does speak they provide minimal information. The communication does not flow and you become more frustrated by the minute because you are not getting the information you need. The meeting drags on in this way, and finally ends with you walking out exhausted.

Use the following as a first checkpoint:

- Are people clear about the meeting's purpose?
- Is there an agenda?
- Are the people at the meeting able to contribute to eighty per cent of the agenda items?
- Are people actively involved or passively listening to historical data?

The second checkpoint should be:

- Is it you, the leader?
- Is it the team?
- Is it one or two members of the team?
- Is it the weather or lack of air conditioning?
- Are there unresolved issues, past 'baggage' or tensions/conflicts between some group members?

If you get past the first checkpoint, then consider whether the answer to the minimal participation lies in the dynamics of the group. Understanding group dynamics involves thinking about, and responding to, what is going on in the relationships between all the team members, not just on the surface but underneath. Reluctance to contribute is a symptom that occurs when a team or group is not functioning optimally.

To assess the extent of problems in your team ask the following questions:

- Do people typically arrive late or on time?
- Do some people habitually arrive late or does everyone arrive at once?
- What is the atmosphere or climate of the meetings?
- Do one or two people speak, while the others remain silent?
- Is conflict between team members resolved openly?
- Are people satisfied with decisions that the team makes?
- Do people agree and then resolve to do something different once they leave the meeting?
- What is the effect of the physical setting on participation? Is the room cramped or are people seated a long way from each other?
- Do people listen attentively while others speak or do they interrupt each other?
- Are people who are normally outspoken outside the meeting staying silent on the issue?

People arriving late, uneven contribution, talking over each other rather than listening, inability to resolve conflict, dissatisfaction with decision making and poor problem solving are all characteristics of ineffective teams.

A team in difficulty

The senior management team is due to meet. All bar one manager and the MD are present. Those present are seated around a huge boardroom table. The distance between the managers, particularly those on opposite sides of the table, is between two and three metres. Managers stand in small groups talking until the MD arrives. Once he walks in, everyone falls silent and moves to their seats. He starts to speak, addressing the agenda items. The missing manager finally turns up with great fanfare. The other managers turn to talk to him as he takes his seat. There is chatter and laughter but this quickly dissipates and silence returns. The MD continues with the agenda. There is a pause in the conversation as a manager goes to adjust the room temperature. Some think it is getting too hot. The meeting continues in much the same vein. Despite the MD's question on various issues, there is little response from his managers. One even cleans his nails.

Meeting analysis

Physical setting

The physical distance between people is a problem, but not the whole problem. The large boardroom table and the distance between managers makes conversation difficult. Participation would be helped with a less-formal setting and closer seating without the managers being shoulder to shoulder.

When there are issues in a group, people will often complain of the room being too hot or stuffy. This may be legitimate, but also consider what issues are on the table at the time. Is there conflict between members that is not being addressed?

Time of arrival

People blame the traffic, their kids, cats, dogs, the weather, talking to a client and all manner of things for their lateness. Look for patterns of behaviour and exceptions to these patterns. Do the same people habitually arrive late? Or are meetings characterised by a straggly beginning (by this I mean people arrive one after the other after the scheduled start time so that the meeting does not have time to get going without the next interruption)?

Consider the manager who arrived late in our example. He has a reputation for never turning up to meetings on time, legitimised by his role, where he is primarily relating to clients. This manager has power and status in the team due to his success, so his lateness is tolerated. He is also able to bring relief to the team by his humour. However, in doing so he trivialises the meeting. His lateness is actually due to the fact that he finds the meeting uninteresting.

Airtime

In an effective team, everyone contributes according to their experience or expertise. Everyone has an opportunity to express ideas and opinions. Airtime in this meeting is monopolised by the MD. He keeps talking even when he asks questions, so there are few opportunities for managers to speak. The questions asked are not directed at any one person and are posed in such a way as to require agreement, rather than discussion.

Communication style and conflict

Whenever someone ventures a comment the MD is mostly critical and quick to challenge that person's ideas. He is obviously impatient when the talker does not express their opinion succinctly. By responding in this manner, on a consistent basis, the MD creates a climate of fear or apprehension. Managers do not speak because they are afraid of being criticised and of being seen as stupid or ill informed. No-one wants to be criticised or belittled, especially not in front of their peers. In this environment, team members are unlikely to take the risk of censure to participate. Worse still, they may well replicate this in their own teams.

Group problem solving and decision making

The team is conflicted and underperforming. Problems are not adequately discussed nor resolved and seldom are meaningful decisions made. Most would agree that the meeting is a waste of time in its current form but no-one is prepared to say this. The manager who arrived late is the only one who comes close to challenging the MD but he is not sufficiently confident to openly say what he thinks of the meetings; instead, he distracts members from their purpose and momentarily alleviates the tension. On the surface it looks like the team is having some fun; underneath are feelings of dissatisfaction at the way meetings are run.

Another aspect to the management team's dissatisfaction with the meetings is the content. More time is spent reviewing what has happened in the business. Much of what is presented could be circulated before the meeting.

Leadership

The MD maintains control over the proceedings but does not gain the input he needs in order to have managers tackle some of the more important issues that face the organisation. The meeting does not move beyond past or current issues.

Hard work?

If your meetings are hard work and characterised by some of the symptoms described above, try doing the following:

☐ Be clear about the purpose of the meeting. What is the group of people coming together to do? What are the desired outcomes?

☐ Circulate an agenda in advance and any relevant information. You can also specify what is expected of each person for each agenda item.

☐ Start meetings the way you want them to continue. Welcome people but keep your introduction short.

☐ Open the meeting with a brief statement of the purpose of the meeting. Then tackle the agenda.

☐ On important issues ensure that you hear from each person. Encourage people to state their opinions in their own words rather than just saying I agree with manager 'A' or 'Y'. Listen carefully as people state their agreement in their own words; this will enable you to hear subtle differences in perception. These differences may be critical to people acting or not acting on what is decided.

☐ Use meeting time primarily for exchange of ideas and perceptions, problem solving and decision making. This will create interest and increase participation.

☐ Keep presentations to a maximum of thirty minutes and have breaks if the meeting is to run for longer than two hours. Watch to ensure people are still attending to what is happening.

☐ Thank people for their contribution. Acknowledge arguments, ideas and suggestions that improve understanding.

☐ Ask questions or make statements in a way that invite discussion and input.
'I would like to hear your comments or ideas on …'
'Let us spend some time discussing the following …'
'What do you think about … ?'
'What are the pros and cons of … ?'

☐ Vary the way you collect information. Make statements about what you think as well as asking questions. Mix up your questions so that some are general while others can be directed to a specific person for an answer.

☐ Watch for non-verbal responses as well as listening to what is said.

☐ Encourage everyone to contribute. Ask for people to speak up as well as asking people to be silent. If people don't speak out, then others will speak to avoid the silence.

☐ Acknowledge conflict between team members. Determine whether time is spent resolving the conflict in an open forum, or that those involved set another meeting and report to the team once they have sorted the issue.

☐ Avoid criticism, particularly public criticism. This damages self-esteem and is ineffectual in changing behaviour.

☐ Use 'reflection time'. That is, pose an important question and state that you would like to hear each person's point of view. Say that you will allow three minutes for people to reflect on the question and to gather their thoughts. Encourage them to write their responses to the question.

☐ Select team members to answer questions rather than always answering them yourself. This will help members interact with each other. It also takes a lot of pressure from you so that you do not have to have the answer to every question or be responsible for solving every problem. This leaves room for team members to contribute. As a consequence they feel valued and are motivated to do more.

Meetings are more interesting when substantive issues are addressed and the collective problem-solving skills of the managers utilised. Having made these changes you will observe differences in the team climate and the way people contribute.

PART 3

Improving
your performance

Who is in control?

D ON'T BRING YOUR PROBLEMS TO WORK. Nice advice, if it was realistic, but we all carry 'baggage'. Everything entering your mind impacts on you and your interpretation of people and events. Anything that moves you from your natural, peaceful state will impact on your dealings with others.

Perceptions, meanings, beliefs, feelings, intentions, expectations and awareness

The above are the ingredients of 'attitude'. Actual performance is eighty-five per cent attitude and fifteen per cent skills. Every event is perceived in your own particular way. You also attach meanings to your perceptions that are heavily influenced by your own complex belief system. These beliefs, which are largely automatic and often subconscious, cause your feelings. Added to your intentions and expectations, these ingredients determine your behaviour and performance.

However, if you also practise awareness—being 'present' rather than stuck in another time—and responding 'on manual' rather than reacting automatically, you can adjust these factors to behave in a more suitable manner.

In every upsetting incident at work, remember that each person is doing their best in the moment according to their belief system. You may disagree with their belief system or think their belief system limiting, but their beliefs, not yours, are driving their behaviour. If you desire them to change their behaviour, you need them to change their beliefs.

A useful process for improving one's belief system is the practice of Attitudinal Competence or 'Att-C©', which addresses improving perceptions, meanings, beliefs, feelings, intentions, expectations and, most importantly, awareness.

Awareness in this context means being aware of:

- The fact that we should direct our mind and body, not the other way around.
- Our current time zone—not the past or future. Are we missing what's happening now?
- Our personality and its tendencies, strengths and limitations.

- The meaning we give to our perceptions of what is happening now.
- Our current operating beliefs that cause our feelings.
- The quality of our intentions and expectations.
- The quality of our actions.
- Whether we are thinking effectively.

The key awareness question

'Right here, right now, in this moment, what's happening, what's lacking, what's the problem?' Unless your safety is being threatened right now, or you are starving, experiencing unacceptable temperatures or need medical attention immediately, then your problem will be mainly in your thinking.

When we are not being aware, we are thinking about something other than what we are doing. We are elsewhere in our mind and are reacting automatically to the present.

Have you ever driven a car and not remembered much about the journey because your mind was elsewhere? What if a child had run out in front of you?

Responding automatically is useful, however many people have conditioned themselves to react automatically to non-emergency situations, for example:

- the automatic resistance to change,
- the automatic fear of spiders or heights,
- the automatic defence to criticism and authority.

Those who can be more aware often achieve their goals, prevent upsets and believe they are living life to the full.

People operating on automatic—and reacting habitually—less often achieve their goals, frequently get upset and most often ask the question, 'Why is this happening to me again?'

Imagine switching to being 'automatically on manual' for non-critical situations and 'manually on automatic' when most needed.

The next four articles focus on awareness and how to practise it.

> Any fact facing us is not as important as our attitude toward it,
> for that determines our success or failure.
> Norman Vincent Peale (1898–1993), American clergyman and author

We have a mind, but we are not our mind

REALISE THAT, WHILST WE HAVE A MIND AND BODY, we are much more than just the two. Our mind has an amazing capability and learns automatically, although we can relearn anything, providing the brain and body are not damaged or impaired.

Separate from our mind is a higher self, which observes our thoughts and directs our mind. However, we can direct our mind, which is our servant. This is important to grasp—you have a mind, but you are not your mind.

The Australian Nobel prize-winning neurophysicist Sir John Eccles concludes that our mind is controlled by an individual self that resides beyond the quantum threshold. In his book *How the Self Controls its Brain* (Springer-Verlag, 1994), Eccles shows how human will emanates from quantum activity. The self that I am and the self that you are are sourced beyond the ten per cent of 'baryonic' matter, or that which we call reality. It is part of the ninety per cent of the universe that is mainly unknown.

This non-physical and constant self from the quantum threshold is similar to being a car driver. When driving, do you become the car? Of course not; you remain the driver. Similarly, you are in your body and mind, but remain more than just the two.

If you were just your mind, it would stop when you stopped. Ask your mind, 'What will you think next?' It may have gone momentarily blank, but you were still observing it. So, you must be more than just your mind. You are your mind's driver, but whether you drive in manual or automatic is dependent upon your awareness.

Meditators observe their mind and train it to break from constant thinking—they seek to experience again that they are more than their mind and body. Stress is caused by negative, hyperactive mental activity. Meditation is a proven method for de-stressing, with excellent benefits.

Awareness comes through your mind and body, not from it—but your thoughts come from your mind and body.

Awareness of your breathing

Whilst reading, you have been breathing automatically, but by gaining awareness—focusing on your breathing—your breathing becomes altered. Right now you are breathing on manual—much differently to how you were. Later your breathing will become automatic again and revert to being shallower. This is the simple difference between being on automatic or manual.

By gaining awareness of your breathing, you will discover how to extend awareness to your body. This will give you more energy and assist your thinking processes. Keep focusing on your breathing until you attain a heightened level of awareness, enabling you to become more alert.

Practise awareness of your breathing by sitting comfortably with a straight back and closing your eyes. Every time a thought enters your mind, notice it, without holding it, and then focus back to your breathing. This is easy and gives immediate benefits. Initially you may only do this momentarily but, as you continue, you will enjoy it more and choose to stay longer.

It's a great break from study or work of any kind!

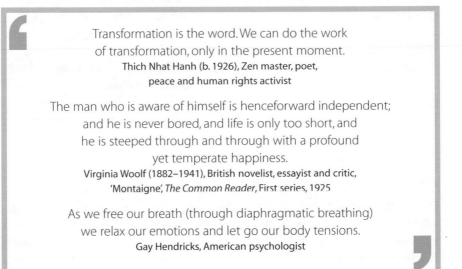

Transformation is the word. We can do the work
of transformation, only in the present moment.
Thich Nhat Hanh (b. 1926), Zen master, poet,
peace and human rights activist

The man who is aware of himself is henceforward independent;
and he is never bored, and life is only too short, and
he is steeped through and through with a profound
yet temperate happiness.
Virginia Woolf (1882–1941), British novelist, essayist and critic,
'Montaigne', *The Common Reader*, First series, 1925

As we free our breath (through diaphragmatic breathing)
we relax our emotions and let go our body tensions.
Gay Hendricks, American psychologist

Awareness of your body

RIGHT NOW, PLEASE DIRECT YOUR ATTENTION TO YOUR KNEES, without looking at them, or moving them or touching them. With your attention, notice their position, notice what they feel like from inside. Let your attention stay there for now. Notice what you feel. Now direct your attention to your nose, without looking, moving or touching it. Notice that you are now very aware of its presence. Don't make any judgment about it, just notice that it exists.

Most of us only bring attention to our body when it feels different or we experience a sudden sensation.

Right now, allow your attention to scan, like a wave, from the top of your head steadily through your body, down to your hips, legs and feet, and finally focus on your toes. Now do the same from your toes to the top of your head. Notice that your body has a slight tingle through it—it seems more alive. Nothing has happened, except that you have deliberately given attention to your body and yet the response is immediate, albeit slight.

As with your breathing, if you practise this frequently, your body will respond and benefit from the attention, in a manner that you will directly experience and enjoy. Very soon, and with little effort, you will have heightened awareness of your breathing, body and mind, automatically. The benefits you experience will encourage you to continue.

Awareness of your thoughts

Have you noticed that your mind keeps a running commentary about what you have just done, thought, experienced or noticed? Have you acknowledged that it makes judgments, sometimes positive, often negative? This is self-talk, or the continuous talking to ourselves that we all do.

Our self-talk is usually automatic thinking, reacting to our deeply held beliefs and learned or programmed behaviour in certain situations. What if we were able to be more aware of those thoughts and direct them to be more useful, positive, creative, truthful and caring? Most people have superb innate intelligence, but have not learned thinking skills.

Please notice your automatic reaction to my last statement. What did you think? What did you feel? Why did you think and feel that?

Was it what was said, or the meaning you gave it? Is there another more useful way of thinking about that last statement?

Notice how quickly you were able to answer the questions. You have just become more aware of your thoughts, instead of just having them and reacting to them. Notice that it didn't take much time at all, and that you did it at the speed of thought.

By directing your attention to your thoughts, you can increase your mind-directing skills, resulting in better quality thoughts and certainly more useful and less stressful thinking. And thus better decision-making and more effectiveness in leading and managing people.

Again, as with directing your attention to breathing and your body, by practising awareness of thought frequently, you will naturally choose to do so more often.

Similarly, you can discover that this practice does not hinder you and results in experiences that you can enjoy and benefit from.

> You are today where your thoughts have brought you;
> you will be tomorrow where your thoughts take you.
> **James Allen (1864–1912), British-born American essayist**
>
> The Law of Attraction attracts to you everything you need,
> according to the nature of your thought life. Your environment
> and financial condition are the perfect reflection of
> your habitual thinking. Thought rules the world.
> **Joseph Edward Murphy (1898–1981), author**

Awareness of your current time zone

IN THE CONTEXT OF AWARENESS OF YOUR CURRENT TIME ZONE, I don't mean the time relative to Greenwich Mean Time (GMT). I mean are you living in the past, present or future? Are your thoughts often about the past? Do you revisit and feel things, like they are happening again?

It's like rerunning a movie—you get the same feelings each time. Sometimes the movies are great, sometimes they aren't. You experience the feelings again because your mind, particularly your unconscious mind, cannot distinguish between reality and imagination.

Have you also noticed that your thoughts are sometimes in the future? Sometimes you imagine what it could be like in ideal circumstances and sometimes you think that it may be similar to your past. At times, particularly when you are active, you will be focused on the right now, not the past or future.

Awareness of your time zone is an answer to all problems

Consider this famous Zen question: 'Right here, right now, in this moment, what is your problem?' If you answer, 'I'm regretful about what's happened', you are speaking of the past. If you answer, 'I worry about how things will eventuate', you are speaking of the future.

Unless you are in immediate danger (real—not imagined), or lack something vital immediately, then you have *no* problems right here, right now, in this moment.

If we've trained our mind to regret the past, running the old movies over and over, and getting all the corresponding feelings, then we are missing the peace and beauty or excitement and joy of the now. Our bodies are poisoned with chemicals that cause guilt, regret, shame, anger and frustration.

If we've trained our minds to project the past into our future, then we are missing the peace and beauty or excitement and joy of the now. Our bodies are poisoned with unwanted chemicals that cause fear and worry.

If your response is, 'But what about the future?' or 'I feel this about the past', I would say, 'So what? What can you do about the past or the future?' The truth is you can do nothing, except think, feel, speak, act and be your best now.

With the past, you can only change the meaning of what happened, along with your feelings. You change the meaning by considering all the facts, not just some of them, and not just your distortions, deletions, generalisations, assumptions and judgments about them.

As for the future, that depends upon what actually happens then and what you do when the future becomes the now—not on what has already happened and what you have done in the past. And remember, 'some people are making such thorough preparation for rainy days that they aren't enjoying today's sunshine' (William Feather, 1889–1981).

You have always handled situations in the moment the best you can. When you are in the moment you have no problems—because you are focusing on what is happening right now. Realise you are alive and here right now. You have made it into the present moment. That means you can be your best right here, right now, simply by choosing to.

Train your mind to be present, only looking to the past to learn lessons from the facts, not your feelings about partial facts, and only looking to the future to plan and take appropriate action now. Persistent correct practice is all it takes.

> Remember, today is the tomorrow you worried about yesterday.
> Dale Carnegie (1888–1955), American author and public speaker
>
> A loser seldom lives in the present, but instead destroys the present by focusing on past memories or future expectations.
> Muriel James, author, *Born to Win*, Addison-Wesley, 1971

Practising awareness in everyday life

THE PRACTICE OF AWARENESS, I believe, is the most important skill to acquire. Awareness can prevent accidents, trauma and upsets. Most importantly, awareness is the foundation of, and central to, acquiring attitudinal competence.

Here are some steps on how to practise awareness every day:

1. Concentrate on your breathing whenever you have time. This gives you more energy, improves your immune system and aids your thinking.

2. As you wake and before going to sleep, scan your deep attention through your body, imagining you are holding that part of your body in your attention's hands. Start from the top of your skull and scan down to your toes slowly to the count of ten, and back up to the count of ten, three times. This helps your body heal and improves your immune system.

3. Whenever you seek a break, practise points one and two to decrease stress and refresh your body and mind.

4. During simple routines, such as eating, cleaning your teeth, or driving, be fully attentive. Don't let your mind wander, for it can only wander into the past or future, neither of which exist. In these cases, your digestion will improve, your driving will be safer and your teeth cleaning more effective!

5. Frequently, particularly before making decisions, pay attention to what you are thinking, feeling, saying or doing. Don't allow yourself to operate automatically during routine experiences.

6. Practise being the silent observer of yourself—your thoughts, feelings, words and actions. Don't get caught up in anything.

7. Spend at least fifteen minutes daily walking in nature and paying attention only to what your five senses perceive. Don't let your mind think about the past or future. Don't judge what you experience, just observe and notice. This is very refreshing.

8. Allocate time to review the lessons from the fully truthful past day, without feelings attached, perhaps writing your review in a journal. Balanced reflection is essential for improvement. But undisciplined and flawed emotional running of 'old part-fiction movies' is insanity.

9. Plan your future, making sure it is specific, measurable, action-oriented, realistic and timed, so you can take action now. Ensure your plans are well formed, and be clear about your actions—when, how, why and what the outcomes will be. Be clear about how you will feel when the goal is achieved. Again, it is useful to write these in a journal. Thinking about an unclear target is 'pinning the tail on the donkey'—great for a child's party, but insanity in reality.

The greatest challenge we all face

I believe our greatest challenge is to practise awareness until we can operate 'automatically on manual', so we can choose to 'manually go to automatic'. Most of us operate the other way around. As stated earlier, all that's required is correct practice.

Here are a few suggestions to help you do this:

- Frequently stop and ask yourself the key awareness question: 'Right here, right now, what is happening, internally and externally?'
- Every half-hour stop whatever you are doing and ask the key awareness question.
- Every time you change direction, whether walking, turning your head or moving differently, ask yourself the key awareness question.
- Constantly practise being your own silent non-judgmental observer or witness.

> The more deeply the path is etched, the more it is used,
> and the more it is used, the more deeply it is etched.
> Jo Coudert, author, *Seven Cats and the Art of Living*, Warner Books, 1998
>
> The easier it is to do, the harder it is to change.
> Eng's Principle
>
> A nail is driven out by another nail. Habit is overcome by habit.
> Desiderius Erasmus (1466–1536), Dutch humanist and theologian

What are your values, purpose and goals?

IS YOUR LIFE OUT OF CONTROL or missing something? Are you working too hard? Do you have everything but remain unhappy? Today's stress levels are enormous and skew our life balance: working too hard, financially strapped, undernourished, unfit, dysfunctional relationships, unnecessary wants and desires.

Regain control by reviewing the eight areas of life—your values, purpose and goals in each of them—regardless of your age or circumstances. By following the suggestions below you will be on track and balanced very quickly.

The eight core life areas

The eight core life areas are spiritual, mental, physical, relationships, vocation, material/finance, leisure/recreation and environment.

We demand satisfaction in many life areas to remain happy and healthy. Today, we give attention to too few, effectively starving ourselves of variety. The following are the core aspects that, by attaining a dynamic balance between them all, give us the essential nourishment for a successful life:

1. **Spiritual:** understanding yourself. Spiritual development is why we are here. How could you develop your spirituality to be happy, at your best and of most use? What's important to you about your spirituality? What goals could you set?
2. **Mental:** your mind is powerful and mental health is essential for success. We need to exercise it! What would it take to enjoy mental wellbeing? What goals could you have?
3. **Physical:** like your mind, your body requires exercise. What is important about your physicality? What do you want to achieve? What are your physical goals?
4. **Relationships:** aside from personal wellbeing, relationships are vital to humans. Beginning with family and extending to everyone we know, what do you most desire in your relationships? What are your goals?
5. **Vocation:** are you doing what you desire? How could you enhance your effectiveness? If you don't love it, how can you excel? What do you want vocationally? What goals are essential for the vocation of your dreams?

6. **Financial/material:** we live in a material world. Material things are neither good nor bad, it's our attitudes about them that make the difference. What are your needs? What is important financially and materially? And what are your desires? What goals could you have, making sure that your needs are being fulfilled?

7. **Leisure/recreational:** we all need time to recharge, to acquire energy for our life journey. What do you desire here? What are your goals and plans for this vital part of life?

8. **Environmental:** destruction of our environment is a reality. Not just the natural world, but the very space that you occupy is threatened by toxicity in all forms. What is important to your environment? What can you do to enhance your space? What goals could enhance your own environment?

Read on to establish your values, purpose and goals in each life area.

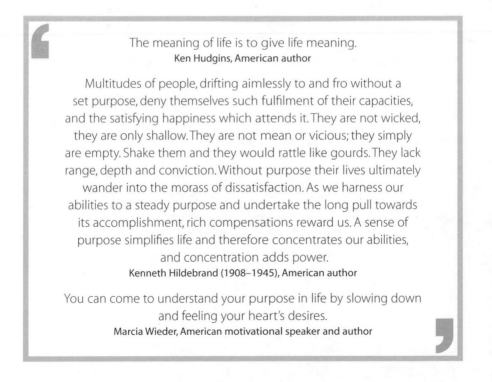

The meaning of life is to give life meaning.
Ken Hudgins, American author

Multitudes of people, drifting aimlessly to and fro without a set purpose, deny themselves such fulfilment of their capacities, and the satisfying happiness which attends it. They are not wicked, they are only shallow. They are not mean or vicious; they simply are empty. Shake them and they would rattle like gourds. They lack range, depth and conviction. Without purpose their lives ultimately wander into the morass of dissatisfaction. As we harness our abilities to a steady purpose and undertake the long pull towards its accomplishment, rich compensations reward us. A sense of purpose simplifies life and therefore concentrates our abilities, and concentration adds power.
Kenneth Hildebrand (1908–1945), American author

You can come to understand your purpose in life by slowing down and feeling your heart's desires.
Marcia Wieder, American motivational speaker and author

Your core values in each life area

OUR CORE VALUES—THOSE PRINCIPLES WE HOLD IMPORTANT—are the guiding principles by which we live. They are the navigation tools that determine decisions. To be effective as a leader and manager, you need to have balance in all your life areas.

Most people never articulate their values. We can do this by examining each life area and asking, 'What is most important?' For example, the most important financial values to me are responsibility, freedom and abundance.

Below, list your three most important values in each life area, in order of importance. To help, I have listed mine first.

Life areas

Spiritual: Unconditional love, fearlessness, joy.
1. _____
2. _____
3. _____

Mental: Attitudinal competence, challenge, creativity.
1. _____
2. _____
3. _____

Physical: Flexibility, strength, endurance.
1. _____
2. _____
3. _____

Relationships: Unconditional love, service, expression.
1. _____
2. _____
3. _____

Vocation: Integrity, service, discipline.
1. _____
2. _____
3. _____

Finance/material: Responsibility, freedom, abundance.
1. _____
2. _____
3. _____

Leisure/recreational: Creativity, humour, freedom.
1. _____
2. _____
3. _____

Environment: Unconditional love, responsibility, joy.
1. _____
2. _____
3. _____

Examples of values

adventure	fairness	love
authenticity	freedom	mastery
autonomy	fun	order
beauty	grace	passion
challenge	happiness	perseverance
comfort	harmony	playfulness
courage	health	safety
creativity	honesty	security
dignity	humour	self-reliance
diligence	innovation	service
elegance	integrity	simplicity
enthusiasm	joy	unconditional love
equity	justice	vitality
excellence	leadership	wisdom
excitement	learning	

Your purpose in each life area

Your purpose is the other guidance tool, which together with your core values, controls your life's journey. Without both, you cannot steer your life.

Knowing our 'life purpose' and what we are 'meant to do' is difficult. It usually comes after doing many things, although some people know from an early age. My life purpose arrived at forty-nine, suddenly, even though I was already doing it, and after years of doing different things.

When you discover your purpose, it will be clear and will involve all your skills, passion and experiences. Nothing will be wasted—everything that happened was necessary.

In the meantime determine your purpose in each life area. These are best characterised by your goals in each area. Using a page for each life area, fill each with your desires, needs and wildest dreams. If you need more than one page, don't hold back. Have fun and take your time.

Then, using your core values as your guide, decide up to the sixteen most desired goals for each area. Remember to keep your original lists so you can focus on the other goals later.

Next, list each of them on a life area 'elimination' page similar to the following. Using your core values, follow the elimination process by choosing the one most important to you. At the end of this exercise you will have a most important goal for each life area. You can attend to eliminated goals later, after you have achieved the most necessary.

Diarise their completion, reminding yourself of their importance and using your values to keep on track. If you get confused, remind yourself of your goals and that completing them is your current purpose. Never give up!

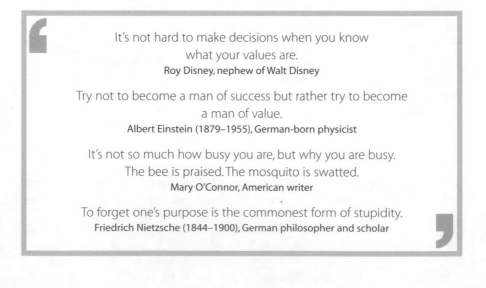

It's not hard to make decisions when you know
what your values are.
Roy Disney, nephew of Walt Disney

Try not to become a man of success but rather try to become
a man of value.
Albert Einstein (1879–1955), German-born physicist

It's not so much how busy you are, but why you are busy.
The bee is praised. The mosquito is swatted.
Mary O'Connor, American writer

To forget one's purpose is the commonest form of stupidity.
Friedrich Nietzsche (1844–1900), German philosopher and scholar

Life area: _____

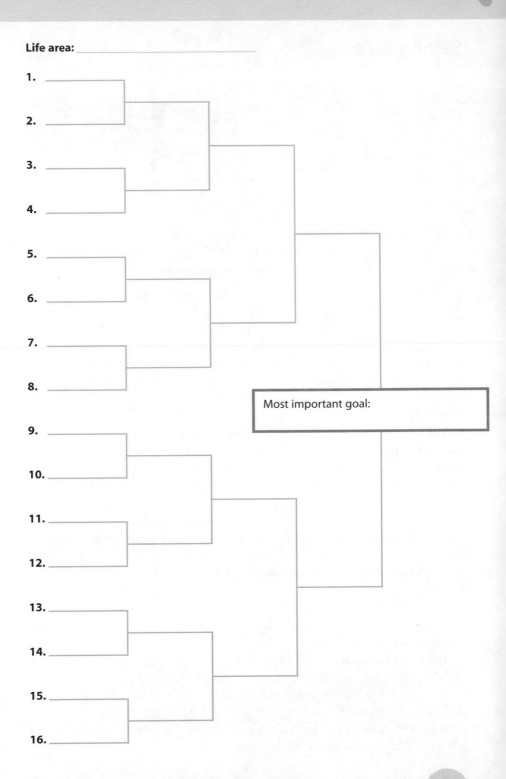

1. _____
2. _____
3. _____
4. _____
5. _____
6. _____
7. _____
8. _____

Most important goal:

9. _____
10. _____
11. _____
12. _____
13. _____
14. _____
15. _____
16. _____

Saving face

I T IS SAID THAT IT IS IMPORTANT in Asian cultures to 'save face'. I think that it is important in all cultures. Shame and embarrassment are very powerful emotions that we like to avoid. The desire to 'save face' is one reason that many of us respond poorly to criticism. Whose face are we saving? The face that we think we present? Or the face that others see that we have. We are trying to save the wrong face. The face we are trying to save is an illusion held only by us. So you see how stupid the whole thing is?

I've met very few people who like receiving criticism. Many of us react defensively or angrily. Some will later reflect on the criticism, possibly losing a few zzzs, and take it 'on board' if we see it as valid. Unfortunately, we don't always incorporate it into our normal behaviour.

Criticism that causes you to react defensively may be digging into something that is unresolved and buried deep in your psyche. It may be revealing something about you that you try to keep hidden from others or that you pretend doesn't exist. It might be highlighting a weakness or a flaw in your approach. It might be striking at deeper feelings of insecurity or inferiority. It might be threatening your delicately balanced self-image. Or it might be highlighting the reality for all of us—imperfection.

All of us have assets and liabilities to our personal style, to our way of being. We are usually more aware of our assets than our liabilities. Some of us don't even countenance that we have any liabilities. We don't see, or refuse to accept, our liabilities. But the reality is that the people with whom we interact are often very aware of our liabilities because they are on the receiving end.

A first step in dealing with criticism is accepting that it is quite okay, quite normal, quite human to have flaws, imperfections or liabilities in our personal style. Can you think, objectively, of one individual that you know well who doesn't? It is part of the human condition. It creates the challenge and reward of living and working harmoniously. It is part of the journey of life to seek enlightenment and the getting of wisdom.

A second step is to not see criticism as an attack on your whole being as a person. It is just suggesting that on this occasion, in this instance, something you did could have been done better. The person levelling the criticism is not saying that because of this one piece of your behaviour that you are a failure as a human being, that you have let people down, that you are incompetent, that they don't like or respect you. It is only you who can take it to a deeper level and relate it to your whole being and see it as an attack on you as a person.

Think about times when you are critical of someone else. Does the flaw or imperfection that you have observed really alter your perception of that person? Do you go from generally liking or respecting the person to generally disliking or not respecting the person? Do you ignore all the other bits of information you have about that person's behaviour and form an entirely new perception of the person based on this one incident? Unless it is something that really violates your values as a human being, of course you don't. To do so would show you as unbalanced.

When someone is criticising you and you feel angry or defensive, try this approach:

- Take your focus off the actual words used for a moment. You can come back to them.
- Observe or feel your reaction. Note what has changed about how you are feeling. Note where the feeling is located in your body. Feel your emotional temperature rising and use this feeling as a warning to say nothing in response at this moment.
- Focus on that feeling and ask yourself why is this happening? What am I letting happen here?
- Accept that someone has seen a flaw in your approach. If it wasn't there, they would not have seen it. Admit to yourself that in reality it could have been better to do this or that.
- Acknowledge the comment with something like, 'That's a fair comment. At the time I did not do that or think to do that. I guess that there's a lesson for me. My focus was on …'
- And leave it at that. Stop the thought demons at this point that want you to react angrily or defensively.

Standing in your own light

OTHER ARTICLES HAVE DISCUSSED ATTITUDE, awareness, mind control, values, purpose and goals. Those who have flexibility in these areas achieve a fulfilling life. These people stand in their own light. They are unafraid of being their best and showing the simple self-discipline of consistent correct practice.

The skills they practise are thorough listening, great questioning and useful thinking. They don't make judgments, assumptions or display undue emotion. They listen carefully, realising that observing leads to fuller comprehension. They ask great questions, knowing they'll receive great answers and direct their mind in a particular way.

And their greatest ability? They ask the great questions of themselves first! They know their behaviour creates their life and their attitude is the primary determinant of their behaviour. That's why they become skilled at listening to themselves, asking themselves questions and thinking usefully. They become aware of themselves and are able to select the best attitude for the situation.

So how do they listen? What questions do they ask? How do they direct their thinking?

Listen to yourself

You can observe what you think, feel, say and do just by paying attention. This is also a primary principle of awareness.

The listening takes place without question, judgment, preparation for, or attention to anything else. It is pure observation. Your unconscious mind remembers everything and you can then retrieve the knowledge.

Ask yourself these great questions that successful people ask:

- **What am I perceiving?** Ensure your perceptions embrace everything. See all the positive, negative and neutral aspects so you can choose which to focus upon.
- **What meaning am I giving my perceptions?** Ensure your meanings are based on facts.
- **What beliefs are operating now?** Ensure your beliefs are not limiting, fearful or unrealistic. Know your values and learn to articulate them. What beliefs would you prefer?
- **What feelings do I have?** Terminate unwanted feelings by deep breathing and positive questions. What feelings would you prefer and what beliefs cause those feelings?

- **What intentions do I have?** Ensure they are in accordance with your values and purpose.
- **What expectations do I have?** Let them go anyway.
- **What am I doing?** Act with your highest values and purpose.
- **Who am I being?** Be your highest self.

Directing your way of thinking

Direct your thoughts, listening and questions to the qualities of thought that I describe as the PUCCICT (pronounced 'pu-ch-ict') way of thinking:

- **Positive:** we ascribe three values to everything—positive, neutral and negative. Your focus will determine your response. Choose wisely!
- **Useful:** by remaining aware we can choose responses related to our higher values. On automatic, we may choose others.
- **Creative:** creativity can be strengthened through practice. Always consider a creative approach.
- **Caring:** responding in a caring way doesn't mean weakness or agreement to lesser values. But remember we all intend our best—subject to our beliefs.
- **Inspiring:** seek that which inspires you and inspire yourself and others by being your best.
- **Competent:** you become competent through correct practice.
- **Truthful:** selective truths are destructive. Strive for the fullest truth!

Underpinning these skills is consistent correct practice. It's up to you to consistently practise this.

> It's up to you to stand in your own light, or not.
> David Deane-Spread, contributing author, *You Lead, They'll Follow* Volume 3
>
> Listen, or your tongues will keep you deaf.
> Native American proverb
>
> It is the province of knowledge to speak and it is the privilege of wisdom to listen.
> Oliver Wendell Holmes (1809–1894), American physician and author
>
> Knowing is not enough, you must use it;
> Willing is not enough, you must do it.
> Bruce Lee (1940–1973), Chinese actor and martial artist

It goes with the territory

UM..SIR.. I DON'T AGREE WITH SAYING "HEIL HITLER."... IT'S ELITIST!

THE LAST TIME THEY SAW ERNST...

EVIATIONS FROM THE PLAN. Disruptive behaviour. Noncompliance with systems and procedures. Whingeing. Grievances. Complaints. Disputes. Unsafe work practices. Substandard performance. Damaged relationships. Conflict. Tension. Stress. Hurt feelings. No cooperation. And this is on a good day! It can drive you nuts. Just as you fix one problem and everything settles down and returns to normal, bang, something else happens. Who would want to be a manager?

This is the lot of the manager. This is why managers exist. If work groups engaged in none of the above behaviour, managers might become an extinct species. The manifestations of the human condition in the workplace creates the need for managers. Before you take on the job of manager, be aware of what you are taking on.

Your role is not to focus on the technical aspects of the work your group performs. That is why you have a work group of, hopefully, technically skilled people. Your main focus needs to be on the conceptual and human factors that affect performance. (See *You Lead, They'll Follow* Volume 2.)

Your primary purpose as a manager is to deal with the above issues or, better still, put in strategies and actions that eliminate or modify the causes of these types of workplace behaviours. Apart from getting the technical aspects of your job down, you have to be an amateur therapist, counsellor, psychologist, arbitrator, mediator, bouncer, coach, guide, trainer, mentor, inspector, diplomat, negotiator, informant, peacekeeper, referee, confidant, advisor, politician, motivator, fugleman (don't ask me ask Dr Roget from *Roget's Thesaurus* fame) and a role model to boot. Phew! That's a hard ask. No wonder many of us struggle.

And as many an experienced manager will tell you, the behaviour of people in the workplace can be very exasperating at times. There will be times when you are attempting to introduce something which you genuinely believe is in the best interests of everybody and somebody will block it or complain or adopt a negative stance.

Be mindful too that the above manifestations of the human condition in the workplace may have little to do with you. You may not be the cause, but you still have to try and deal with the consequences.

It will be handy to remember the serenity prayer: '(God) grant me the serenity to accept the things I cannot change, courage to change the things I can and wisdom to know the difference'. Not to be confused with the senility prayer: 'God grant me the senility to forget the people I never liked anyway, the good fortune to run into the ones I do, and the eyesight to tell the difference'.

So don't get overstressed (just the right amount of stress will do) when things go awry because, as sure as politicians lie and lawyers overcharge, they will. Expect these things to happen. No matter how good you are as a manager, you will experience many of these behaviours—in varying degrees—during your career as a manager. That's why we have managers.

Now just before you all rush off and resign your commission as managers, let me add a little balance. When a manager is managing their people effectively, many of these things are replaced by the immense satisfaction of people working productively and well together. And that's a real buzz.

> It has long been an axiom of mine that the little things are infinitely the most important.
> Sherlock Holmes in Arthur Conan Doyle's 'A Case of Identity',
> *Adventures of Sherlock Holmes*, 1892

> Many people equate good management with perfection. This is a fallacy. If perfection could be achieved, there would be no need for management.
> James L Hayes, President and CEO, American Management Association,
> *Memos for Management: Leadership*, AMACOM, 1983

> Put your personnel work first because it is the most important.
> Robert E Wood (1879–1969), President and Chairman, Sears Roebuck and Co.,
> in 'Memo to territorial officers', December 1931

Beware of false prophets

TAKE A NEW BOOK ON LEADERSHIP AND MANAGEMENT, any book, this one included, and read it with a view to distilling the substance of the text. What is it really saying? Does it actually describe actions that are useful and useable and that a real manager in real time with real people would apply? Is it saying something new about better ways to lead and manage people? Or is it regurgitating fundamentals of leadership and management that have been with us for centuries and will be with us for centuries?

Is it moving us forward in our ways of thinking and doing as leaders and managers? Is it contributing to the evolution of our understanding of the human condition and the ways to optimise human performance though leadership and management? Or is it just new constructs, new words, new jargon, new ways to describe age-old wisdom? Are you learning new ways of leading and managing or are you learning a new set of words and phrases about leadership and management?

Because of my line of work, I read a fair number of books and magazines that focus on leadership and management of humans at work. Infrequently I come across one that really does give the reader some new ways of thinking and doing in relation to leadership and management. Every now and then there is a breakthrough that gives us new insight, new perspectives, that adds to the evolution of our understanding about human behaviour at work. But they are few and far between.

Beware of new age psychobabble—there's a lot of it about. The litmus test or the reality check is to always refer to the reality of the workplace. Employees judge leadership and management effectiveness on two things only—what managers say and what managers do. All new theories, models and concepts eventually have to translate into words and actions in the real workplace to be effective.

In my past, when I was delivering traditional leadership and management training, I would get excited about some new leadership or management concept and develop a training session around that concept to present to practising managers working in real time. Stumbling to get the concept accepted for application in the real workplace, I would often hear myself explaining it using simpler and more familiar words. When I did this both the participants and myself would too often come to the same conclusion. When you boil it all down there was really nothing 'new' in the concept except for the terminology.

Where do we stand? We don't even try to compete. We believe that there are fundamental ways of thinking and doing in relation to leadership and management which have been around since humankind put pen to paper and will still be around long after you and I have ceased to be.

This is why in the *You Lead, They'll Follow* series of books we deliberately avoid taking an academic or theoretical approach. We don't claim to have 'invented' what we are writing about—hopefully we have enhanced and perhaps crystallised it for easy digestion. We have concentrated on giving readers a range of useful and useable 'tools' to apply leadership and management actions in the workplace.

It will pay you well before launching the latest fad onto a silently protesting work force to ask two questions:

1. What are the fundamental things that drive successful organisation and individual performance?
2. How well do we do the fundamental things?

Get the fundamentals right and guess what? You may not need the latest fad.

> The ideas I stand for are not mine. I borrowed them from Socrates. I swiped them from Chesterfield. I stole them from Jesus. And I put them in a book. If you don't like their rules, whose would you use?
> Dale Carnegie (1888–1955), American author and public speaker,
> *Newsweek*, 8 August 1955

Your workplace is your palace

THE MEETING APPROACHES and you simply cannot find the papers. The mail arrives and you add it to the burgeoning in-tray. A telephone caller asks for some information. 'Now where did I put it?' as you desperately hunt through your mess and waste both of your time. More reading material and the pile is growing daily. Papers disappear in the clutter on your desk or attach themselves to material where they don't belong or you go through the same piles of paperwork for the third time trying to find that missing item.

The work place is winning but wait! Help is on the way. You can turn the tide today by taking some action to help yourself.

Try these simple tactics and sample the benefits:

- Trays: get yourself some—in, out, pending—one for each manager or project. For example, you may have an operations manager and a corporate services manager—give them a tray each.
- Drawers: organise them into portfolios and have a personal one for your lunchtime gear.
- Bookshelves: make them reachable and in an order that suits your work.
- Reference texts: these are your personal source of material—make sure you know what is where.
- Work Area: a cluttered desk is a cluttered mind. Don't kid yourself with the sucker excuse, 'I like it like this because I know where everything is'. That may be true but the time you waste and the stress you suffer does not justify the mess. Get the junk off. (This is one of the weakest excuses I have heard for a messy, cluttered work area. Consider the alternative. I wouldn't know where to find anything if everything was placed in a neat, organised and orderly system. For those with cluttered desks, get a grip on reality by checking out your daily stress levels. And listen to yourself as you cry your daily lament, 'I'm under the pump.'.)
- Reading material: have a place for the reading matter that descends on us by the truckload. And turn it over.
- Pathways: know where you go in your office or work area and make sure that you are not covering unnecessary kilometres in your daily travels grabbing at material.
- Decorate the place: it's your territory so decorate it how you like with plants, prints, trinkets etc.—in moderation, of course.

- Techno: get the phone and computer in-line so that the ergonomics are fine.
- Meeting spots: isolate the meeting territory so that others feel comfortable in your palace e.g. establish a meeting table that is separate from your desk area.
- Mail: examine at routine times, perhaps before your morning tea. And that includes the electronic version.
- Diary: get one that works—it doesn't need to be electronic. Organise the next day before you leave the office. Decide what 'chunks' your day comprises and allocate accordingly. Some examples are personal administration, projects, meetings and reading.
- Work periods: forty minutes is a balanced period and then take a break and stretch, walk or get a brew.
- Water: keep a bottle or mug close by and drink plenty during the day. It is a proven brain food.
- Focus: work on one thing at a time. When working on that job, keep your desk free of all material that has no relation to that job. Rearrange your work area so that you have storage space, benches, shelves, cabinets, cupboards, etc. at your side or at your back—out of your line of vision (distraction). Out of sight, out of mind.

Remember, it is your workplace and you are there for a big chunk of your time. And, in the words of Benjamin Franklin, 'A place for everything—everything in its place'.

Tips for presenters

ARE YOU STARTING TO THINK ABOUT that upcoming presentation? How will I start? How will I control my nerves? Here are a couple of tips to help you prepare for, and to start, your presentation.

Start at the finish

Arguably, the most important part of a presentation is the close. This is where you leave your final impression, where you want the audience to be thinking about certain things. Good questions to ask are, 'what are the most significant things I want the audience to take away from this presentation?' or 'what do I want the audience to do as a result of this presentation?'

Plan and design your close at the beginning of your preparation for your presentation. Once you are clear on your close, you are then better able to design the contents of your entire presentation. The contents of your close dictate the contents of the body of your presentation. The close provides answers to questions posed at the beginning of your presentation.

Answer these questions to design your close:

• What are the key things you would like them to remember? Summarise the central thoughts and the key points that support them.
• What are the key things you would like them to do as a result of this presentation?

Engaging the audience and reducing your nervous discomfort

If you had to give a presentation in an empty room by yourself, would you get nervous? If you answered yes, I suggest that you don't read any further. In fact, close the book now. Pick up the telephone book and look up therapists. Call and book weekly appointments for the next ten years.

The rest of you would have answered, 'No. Of course not.' You are not the focus of anyone's attention in an empty room. But fill that room with people and now what happens?

As you know, there are a number of reasons for your nervousness (see *You Lead, They'll Follow* Volume 2). One is that you have now become the focus of people's attention and all your imperfections will be on show.

How do you engage the audience, keep them interested, focused, actively participating in the presentation and increase your enjoyment by reducing your nervous discomfort? Here is a process to follow:

- ☐ Identify the keys points you want them to learn, know or do as a result of your presentation.
- ☐ Turn these into a series of questions with multiple-choice answers or a series of true or false statements. This will also help you place the content of your presentation in an easy-to-digest sequence.
- ☐ The body of your presentation should then elaborate on each of the questions or statements—also providing the correct answers. This will help you develop the actual content of your presentation.
- ☐ Start your presentation by handing out the questionnaire. Ask each person to complete the questionnaire during the course of your presentation. (Where do you reckon their focus is right now? Not on you!)
- ☐ Conduct the presentation elaborating on each of the issues related to the question.
- ☐ Close the presentation by going through each question and asking the audience for the answer. Ask people to mark their questionnaire and record the correct answer. You might consider a reward for the person with the most correct answers.

Not enough questions

URING PRESENTATIONS we generally provide a lot of information to the audience. How do we know if we have addressed the needs of the audience, if they have not fully understood something or whether we explained something in enough detail?

More often than not the presenter will ask, 'Are there any questions?' and when there is no response from the audience they pack up and go home. The question itself is next to useless. It does not stimulate thinking. Nor does it encourage the audience to confidently ask questions about topics on which they would like more information.

There are many ways to get the audience to ask questions:

- 'In relation to (the topic) on which points would you like me to elaborate?'
- 'How many of you are clearer about (the topic) now?' Wait for a show of hands. Where there is uncertainty hone in and ask, 'You seem a little hesitant. Was there anything specific that you would like more information about?'
- 'I am going to provide you with a piece of paper. On it I would like you to write down any questions you might have about the presentation. I will then collect them and go through each one.' Give them three minutes to write down any questions.
- 'Let me go through the key headings for you. When I mention them to you let me know if you have any questions.' List them and address questions as they arise.

The key is to provide a 'wait time'. People often need time to reflect before a question starts to crystallise.

Too many questions

What about the constant interrupter or the person who asks questions that you know you are going to address later in your presentation? How can we keep them happy and not destroy the flow and sequence of the presentation?

At the beginning of the presentation establish some clear ground rules for the audience. Here are some things you might say:

- 'There may be questions that spring to mind while I am presenting. If they relate directly to the point in question or you require a point of clarification, please feel free to ask.'
- 'If you have a question that is indirectly related to the topic you may find that I will cover it at a later stage during the presentation. I would encourage you to write your question down, so that you don't lose the thought, and, if I haven't addressed it by the end, please ask it then.'
- 'We will be having a question and answer session at the end. If questions spring to mind during the presentation, jot them down and we will address them during this session.'
- 'Thankyou for asking that question. If you don't mind I won't answer it now because it will be addressed at a later stage. If you still have queries at the end please ask me then. Is that okay?' Make a note of the question on the whiteboard.
- 'Please hold all questions until the end of the presentation. This will enable us to cover the content in the time available. I will be happy to answer any questions at the end.'
- 'If you have questions that spring to mind after the presentation my phone number is … Please feel free to contact me.'

One more check

> Advertising may be described as the science of arresting
> the human intelligence long enough to get money from it.
> **Stephen Leacock (1869–1944), Canadian humorist and economist**
>
> A thing may look specious in theory, and yet be ruinous in practice;
> a thing may look evil in theory and yet be in practice excellent.
> **Edmund Burke (1729–1797), English statesman, orator and writer, 19 February 1788**
>
> Do not think what you want to think until you know what
> you ought to know.
> **John Crow (1905–1970), British philosopher**

YOU HAVE BEEN THROUGH THE TEDIUM of precisely defining the job role, advertising, reviewing applications and interviewing. Finally, you have decided you have found the best possible candidate. You may well have checked written references that the candidate has provided and you want to proceed without delay to make an offer and get an acceptance.

Except in the most unusual of cases, it is of very great importance that you take the time to verbally check references. Don't be satisfied with written references. They can be carefully worded to avoid addressing some issues, and if they are unfavourable, the candidate will most likely not present them to you. You should always try for at least two referees.

The candidate will almost invariably put forward referees who will speak favourably. You should try to ensure that you speak to the candidate's immediate boss. Usually you will have to go back one employer prior to the present employer, because in many cases confidentiality will preclude you speaking with the candidate's present boss. In any case, the referee's knowledge of the person should be as recent as possible. The degree to which this can be achieved will vary from case to case. You should not approach a referee without the candidate's approval.

It is not uncommon for matters that were not obvious before to be revealed during reference checking. Often this will simply reinforce your decision. In such an instance you can go forward with even more confidence. However, in many instances, you may be quite surprised by what you are told, and it may cause you to pass to the next candidate.

It can happen that you receive a very negative reference from one referee, and this seems inconsistent with others. In such a case, try to check the matter out further with other referees. It may be that the referee is the faulty party ... but proceed with extreme caution if you still contemplate hiring.

Reference checking is so important that for very senior appointments it can be worthwhile to ask to visit the referee and discuss the matter face-to-face over a cup of coffee, if that is geographically possible. This may reveal matters which would not come forward during a telephone interview.

If psychological testing is contemplated, then reference checking should be completed first, so that any notable characteristics suggested by the reference checking can be checked by the testing.

Questions that you put to the referee should include the following:

- How well did you know them?
- What was your relationship to them?
- What was the job role? Title?
- What comments would you have in general?
- How well did they perform in the job?
- What would you consider to be their strengths?
- What would you consider to be their weaknesses?
- How well did they get along with the team? Peers? Seniors? Staff?
- Were they well liked? Why? Were they well respected? Why?
- Would you say they showed any special initiative on a particular matter? How? What?
- What risks does this person present for an employer?
- What are their assets and liabilities regarding personal style?
- What does this person need to change about themselves?
- Any punctuality or work absence problems?
- How would you rate their overall reliability?
- Did they always seem to be honest?
- We are considering them for the position of ... Do you consider they would be capable of that, or do you have any other comment?
- Were you aware of any personal problems?
- Do you know the reason for leaving?
- Would you reemploy them?
- Any other comments?

Be prepared to probe their responses for verification, clarification or elaboration.

Mixing it with the propeller heads

YOUR DEPARTMENT HAS STRUGGLED with its information system for years. As the system gets older, more problems occur and getting the job done gets tougher. At last, approval has been given to replace the source of much frustration and, as you use the system, you are on the project team.

A project team is made up of subject-matter experts and is normally quite a small group, around five people. A team leader will guide and ensure that all the responsibilities are being met. There will be one or two people who are directly involved in using the majority of the system, an IT person, and a representative from management to provide corporate input. Each member has an equally important role to play on delivering a system that works.

If you are on such a project team, what role do you play in making sure that the system being delivered is right for the job? Here are some hints:

☐ A system is designed and/or configured based on a set of requirements. These requirements are the foundations on which the system is built. If the foundations are wrong, it may be difficult to change the system. So when specifying what the system is supposed to do, be precise, and make sure that everything is covered (see 'Be careful what you wish for ...' pp. 238–9). Something minor, but mandatory, that may have been overlooked could be a real headache to include after the system has gone live. Changing a system is expensive. None more so than when the change is needed because the original design was wrong. Getting it right in the first place reduces effort and the long-term costs.

☐ The group dynamics are important. Listen and respect others' opinions as well as provide reason to your opinion. Debate will often occur, but it doesn't have to be heated. And remember, after the system is installed you have to go back to your normal job and continue working with those on the team.

☐ Beware of techno babble. IT is well known for using acronyms and complex labels for even the most simple things. Get to know the terminology being used in this project. And do not hesitate to interrupt and ask what an acronym stands for as chances are everybody else is wanting to ask the same question.

☐ Read what is to be presented prior to the meeting. This simple given is not often adhered to as normal work duties will often still need to be performed. Ensure you allocate the extra time needed to keep up-to-date.

☐ There will be work you will need to do as part of the project team outside of the meetings. Delays in delivering this work may have an effect on the overall time taken to complete the system. Quality and timeliness is the key. If you are struggling with your piece of work, let the team leader know early. A surprise at the eleventh hour when all is critical may not be well received.

☐ An important aspect to remember is there will be change in the way people do their work with a new system. Implementing a new system is an opportunity to improve the work process and this often involves change that may be seen as good and bad. If you hear the words 'but it's not like that in the old system' too often, there may be reluctance to change. For the new system to do everything that the old system did, there would have been no need to replace it! And putting in a new system is a great time to fix some flawed practices promoted by the old system. If the reluctance is running high on the team during the analysis and design, seek change management expertise.

☐ After the system has gone live, the project team will need to sign off that the system deliverable has been met. In other words, has the system delivered all that has been asked for? Take the time and ensure it has. A common mistake is, with a sigh of relief, to sign the system off without properly checking the system against the original requirements. All that hard work putting the requirements together is undone. Check the system against the requirements and keep the system architects honest.

☐ Finally, project teams can be as fun as they can be hard work. Start and end the meetings lightly. Reward yourselves for achieving milestones along the way with a treat, such as cake or special biscuits at the meeting. Have a party at the end of the project. Being a member of an IT project team is a rewarding experience. Being on a team that had fun delivering a successful system is even more memorable.

I just did it

THE FAMOUS NIKE SLOGAN, 'Just do it', is a simple and commendable philosophy for certain people and when certain conditions exist. There are many of us who never do it and many of us who wish we never had done it. Some of us are undisputed champions of the world when it comes to procrastination. Some of us fail to think through all the choices available to us and the consequences of all those choices, and regret our actions later.

And slightly digressing, if fear of failure is one of the reasons for your procrastination, you may need to change your mindset about failure. Try seeing failure as an event that happens along the journey of life. If you want that journey to be risk-free, predictable, with no bumps along the way, if you want to tread a conservative, safe path, where the routine of your life is consistent, where the emotional highs and lows feel much the same, then, don't do much. Don't take chances, don't take risks. The less things you do, the less chances you take, the less the likelihood of failure.

If, on the other hand, you want that journey to be exciting, challenging, creative, innovative, full of a wide variety of experiences with highs and lows, be prepared to accept failure as the price you pay for that journey. But remember to use each failure wisely, for the opportunity that it presents, for the learning that it holds. Success and failure go hand in hand. You probably can't have one without the other. The world is full of stories about successful people who had many failures along the way. Except these people probably don't think in terms of failure, they probably just see these as bumps in their journey.

So, be smart, don't set out to create failure, but don't be frightened to fail.

Before you jump in and just do it or to help you jump in and just do it, see if you can answer these questions:

- ☐ What are the things that have the potential to go wrong and what is the real likelihood that they will?
- ☐ How will you react to these if they occur? How will others react?
- ☐ Are you prepared to accept those reactions? Will those reactions make the situation better or worse?
- ☐ What could you do to prevent things from going wrong?
- ☐ How will you know if things are going wrong?

☐ What is blocking you from taking this action? What do you fear about taking this action? Are these fears real or imaginary?

☐ What is the worst consequence for you if what you fear comes true? Does it really make the current situation better or worse?

☐ If what you fear does come true, is it something others will feel or notice or is it something that only you will feel?

☐ Are you clear on what to do? Do you have all the knowledge or information that you need to be successful? Do you understand the broader context affecting the situation? Have you checked out your perspective and interpretation of the situation with knowledgeable others?

☐ Are you clear on why you want to do this? Are you convinced that this is the right thing to do?

☐ Do you know what precautions you need to take?

☐ What unpleasant but necessary actions are you likely to avoid?

Okay. Now, just do it or just drop it.

> Fear makes come true that which one is afraid of.
> Victor Frankl (1905–1997), neurologist, psychologist, author
>
> While one person hesitates because he feels inferior,
> the other is busy making mistakes and becoming superior.
> Henry C Link, American author

Transparently hopeless

EVER SAT THROUGH A PRESENTATION where you were more fascinated with how the presenter was using (or abusing) the overhead projector than the subject itself? Ever found your mind wandering off the topic as you pondered what they would do next to demonstrate their incompetence? The overhead projector is meant to enhance the delivery of information not detract from it. And while the data projector has tended to supersede the overhead projector, it is still used by many.

Here are some ways to improve your use of transparencies and overhead projectors:

- Make rough drafts of transparencies on paper to produce bold, uncluttered designs. Keep the content simple and make illustrations uncomplicated.
- Leave adequate margins around the edges of the transparency so that all the information can be seen without having to move it.
- Use cardboard transparency mounts or plastic transparency holders and print or label each transparency with a number in sequence and the topic of that transparency.
- Don't put the full text of what you want to say, just key points for you to elaborate on.
- Use a minimum of 16-point font size.

- Before the presentation, switch on the projector and focus with the first transparency before the audience arrives.
- Check that the projected image is visible from every position in the room. Darken the room if needed to obtain a sharp image. Check sight lines to avoid standing where you block someone's view.
- Before displaying a transparency, verbally introduce the information to be displayed. Check that the transparency is straight, within the projected area, right way up and then switch on.
- Keep quiet (very hard to do) while the audience absorbs the information and then begin to elaborate on each key point. Don't talk when they're reading.
- Switch off the projector when changing transparencies. Practise changing transparencies beforehand so that you will do it smoothly and correctly during the presentation.
- Have a small table within reach to place used transparencies neatly, face down so that if you need to refer back to a previous transparency you can do this quickly.
- It is usually best to present information bit by bit. This way the audience is focusing on the key point you are making, not reading ahead and thinking about other things and missing your points. Place a sheet of paper between the projector glass and the transparency and reveal each point as you need it by pulling the sheet of paper towards you.
- Use this sheet of paper to write your notes on—prompt words to remind you of the key things on which you want to elaborate.
- When pointing to a feature, point on the transparency (use something flat and thin so it won't roll) so that you remain facing the audience.
- Switch the projector off when you have made all your points— leaving it on is distracting and irritating. The projector should only be on when the image is related to what you are talking about.

Do you see what I see?

I'M STILL SEARCHING FOR THE MANAGER who reckons that they have spare time on their hands. The pressure in most organisations is relentless. The demands on a manager's time are ever increasing and seemingly never ending. Many managers struggle to cope—the strain affecting their wellbeing, their family, their work relationships and their output. Workload overload is a fact of modern organisational life.

I was working with a group of managers introducing a new initiative to improve product quality. One manager, Rudi, protested that while he saw that this was an important initiative, he wanted to know how he was supposed to find the time to work on this project along with all the other projects he had on his plate. He said that he was already going home late at the end of the day exhausted, too tired to spend quality time with his family. He also said that some things were slipping simply because he did not have enough time to do everything.

I felt that there were a couple of contributing factors to his plight. The efficiency of his self-organisation was questionable and he believed that he needed to be 'hands on' or he feared losing contact and communication with his people.

Nonetheless, he did have a heavy workload. He had discussed his workload with his manager whose essential message was 'manage it' because his manager suspected that Rudi was the real problem.

Rudi's not unfamiliar lament was, 'I am given one project, then another, then another. Which one has priority over the other? If I work on one, another one suffers and I get a kick in the pants from my boss.'

I asked him whether he and his boss had the same view on his priorities and his workload. He said that it wasn't clear. He agreed it would help if he and his boss had the same perception about his workload and the priorities of his workload.

He agreed to do the following analysis of his workload to give him some 'data' to show his boss:

☐ List all the projects and non-routine key tasks that you are involved in for the next three to six months—randomly, in any order.

☐ Under each project/key task, list all the elements that make up each project/key task—randomly, in any order.

☐ Allocate priorities to each of the projects/key tasks and to each of the elements. The format should look something like this:

Project/key task _____ **Priority** _____

Elements

- _____ A2
- _____ A1
- _____ B1
- _____ A3
- _____ C1
- _____ A4
- _____ B3
- _____ B4
- _____ B2
- _____ A5

Where   **A** = most important
           B = next most important
           C = least important.

☐ Now use your analysis as a basis for discussion with your boss to see if you can align expectations regarding your priorities.

Sort of

THIS IS A SIMPLE TECHNIQUE to use when you want to improve the layout, the sequence or the flow or the organisation of written ideas, text and statements. You can use it to sort text into a format easier for the reader to follow and absorb the message. It will help you present your information in a logical flow.

Your starting point may be:

- pages of random notes you have made in preparation for producing a report, memorandum or letter,
- a first draft for a report,
- an existing contract that needs to be renewed and updated,
- pages containing randomly ordered ideas and thoughts written in a bullet point format.

Before you start this exercise, write an answer to all or any of the following questions:

- What is the purpose of this report/document?
- What action do you want the reader to take as a result of reading this document? Or what do you want them to know?
- What do you want to accomplish by producing this document?

For longer documents, there will be several answers.

The process is as follows:

☐ Start with the first paragraph (in a longer document) or the first sentence (in a shorter document) or the first bullet point and allocate the letter A in the margin.

☐ Read the next idea, concept, point, sentence or paragraph and allocate the letter B if it contains a different point to that contained in A. If it is a separate but related point, allocate the letter A again.

☐ Read the next idea, concept, point, sentence or paragraph, and allocate the letter C if it contains a different point to that contained in A or B. If it is a separate but related point to either A or B, allocate the letter A or B again.

Continue this process either allocating:

1. New letters of the alphabet (in alphabetical sequence) for each new point, or
2. Letters used already if the idea or point is related to an earlier one.

When you have finished, your original notes or document will have a number of letters written in the margin, some repeated many times.

The next step in the process is to consider all the A items together and decide which of these is the logical starting point. That becomes A1. The next logical point in the sequence becomes A2 and so on. Then do the same for the B's, C's and D's etc.

Alternatively, you can reorder all the A items together (rewrite or use your word processor), the B items together and so on. Placing them all together can make it easier to compare them against each other to decide the numerical sequence.

Your original material will look something like this:

• Agree criteria for target organisations	A2
• Identify target organisations	A3
• Prepare covering letter	B1
• Make follow-up phone calls	C2
• Establish name and title of target person	A2
• Prepare key questions to ask	D1
• Prepare a script to follow	D2
• Send books, brochure and covering letter	E1
• Note details in marketing activity report	F1
• Arrange date and time for presentation	G1
• Prepare demonstration materials	G2
• Review a profile of the organisation	H2
• Obtain a copy of the annual report	H1
• Review articles about the target organisation on the Internet	H3
• Make phone calls	C1
• Obtain list of potential targets	A1

Now sort your material and rewrite in sequence A1, A2, A3, A4 …; B1, B2, B3, B4 …; C1, C2, C3, C4 …etc.

PART 4

Improving individual performance

When winning is losing

I N EVERY WORKPLACE THERE ARE A NUMBER OF MISFITS who go out of their way to be disruptive, upset people, do what they want to do instead of what is required, and generally act as an irritant to others. They can be a bit tricky, too, because they will often not do anything too obvious but will play their games in subtle ways, which makes it hard to pin anything on them.

As they play their immature games, they get a sense of smugness because they think that they are winning. They lack the awareness to see that in the bigger picture, the bigger scheme of things, they are actually losing. But they can't see the connection with the way they conduct themselves and the consequences they experience in their life—in or out of work.

Their 'whole of life' wheel will probably be out of whack. Something will be badly out of balance. There is a good chance that they will use alcohol or other drugs as a means to block out their frustrations, anger or unhappiness.

In the short-term, they will experience what they perceive as wins. They might think that that is as good as it gets. Because of their attitude and their behaviour, they may never have experienced anything better.

But they miss out on so much in terms of the relationships they could have, both in and out of the workplace, in terms of the immensely powerful buzz of achievement satisfaction they would experience by being accepted as one of the team and working in harmony with others.

They may satisfy their 'limited thinking' desires for revenge, for the short-lasting moments of false power they get or the false adulation from like-minded coworkers, which causes them to think that they are winning.

In reality, somewhere inside there will dwell an unhappy chappy— they will have unmet wants.

It is a vicious circle that they are usually ignorant of and don't even realise that they are creating their own consequences.

Here is an example drawn from real life. An operator, Peter, needed another operator, Joe, to finish a task so that he could get on with his job. Peter asked Joe, who was not busy at the time, if he would finish this task as he was waiting on him. Joe told Peter 'f... off. I'll do it when I'm ready.' Over the next half hour Peter asked Joe on three more occasions to finish the task, each time getting the same response. Joe thought this was great fun and he was letting Peter know that he would decide when he would finish this task, not Peter. He thought he was being really smart. To his warped way of thinking, Joe was 'winning' this little one-sided power play.

The real consequence for Joe? This lack of cooperation was observed by others (who Joe was playing up to anyway) and just added to Joe's reputation of not being part of the team, of being a troublemaker and of being difficult to work with. This just added further distance between Joe and the others. The others never went out of their way to help Joe. They didn't include him as much in their social interactions. They didn't give him any affection, appreciation or respect. It always took more effort to deal with Joe, so if they could avoid him, they did.

So Joe, instead of basking in the warmth of the human relations that the others shared in, lost out on those feelings of belonging and acceptance—so important to all human beings.

Naturally, Joe, lacking awareness and insight, looked to blame others for his situation. His belief system was limiting and counterproductive. He was driven by his need to fulfil his many unmet wants instead of adopting the belief that the treatment he received from others was directly related to his ways of behaving. He couldn't see the connection.

To try and turn Joe around, you could ask him these types of questions:

- [ ] Joe, how much do you really enjoy working here?
- [ ] How much do others enjoy working with you?
- [ ] When you say or do …, how do you think the others feel about you?
- [ ] How do you think it affects their attitude to you?
- [ ] How do you think it affects their desire to help you?
- [ ] How do you reckon you gain by doing these things? What's the pay off for you? Why do you do this?
- [ ] What would happen for you if you didn't do this?
- [ ] What would you lose? What would you gain?
- [ ] How would that make a difference?
- [ ] What's the connection between the vibes you put out and the vibes you get back?

☐ What could it be like for you to work here? How much happier could you be at work?

☐ When you do these things, who do you reckon loses? Who wins? How?

He will probably start by answering untruthfully with 'I don't know', or 'I don't care'. Don't accept these responses. Use silence and just repeat the questions or ask them in slightly different ways.

Counselling Jack (1)

ONCE AGAIN, Jack has fallen short of what you require in order to have a smoothly running ship. You have ensured he is properly trained and there are no genuine obstacles to satisfactory performance. You feel you may have to get rid of him. Stop! It is no longer acceptable legally, and increasingly frowned upon by society on moral grounds, to simply sack a worker without first engaging in a counselling session and following this with a series of warnings. The number of warnings can depend upon the cause.

Your employer may very well have set down procedures for such instances, and if so, you should follow these procedures. If, on the other hand, you are seeking some guidelines on what to do, then the following will help.

There are instances that can lead to immediate dismissal, such as serious or wilful misconduct, and these can be handled differently and quickly, some with no warning and some with only one warning and no counselling.

In this and the next three articles, however, we are considering the much less urgent, but more frequent, and still important, situation of someone who repeatedly falls short of desired standard.

Examples of issues that require counselling and can ultimately lead to dismissal include:

- unsatisfactory attendance
- unsatisfactory job performance
- unauthorised absence from the work area
- persistently bad time keeping
- refusal to obey a reasonable instruction from the manager or team leader
- doing personal work in company time without permission
- disregard of safety or quality procedures.

If the matter ultimately proceeds to dismissal, it is of fundamental importance that your organisation can demonstrate that due and fair process was adopted. You must be able to demonstrate that the employee was counselled about the shortcomings, and that the employee was warned of the consequences of further nonconformance to requirements. (Refer also to *You Lead, They'll Follow* Volumes 1 and 2 for further advice on ensuring you have an open mind and have given the employee every opportunity.)

Counselling and verbal warning

In the first instance, it is essential to engage in formal counselling. This can be by the employee's immediate supervisor or their delegated representative. The person has to be made aware that it is a formal counselling session and that the consequences of not improving/meeting standards will be termination. The individual should be offered the right to be represented by either a union representative, or other colleague of their choice, both at this and any subsequent meetings. The courts will not look favourably if they suspect a language problem, intimidation, or some other such lack of balance in the meeting. For your own protection, you may like to have a second management person with you as a witness also.

The counselling session is intended to advise employees of their shortcomings and help them to improve. Consideration should also be given to whether the shortcomings are due to misunderstanding or lack of clear direction.

Don't conduct the session in informal surroundings—conduct it in the office or in private on the work site. This avoids the situation, 'I didn't realise that the first session was a formal warning. I thought we were just having a bit of a casual chat.'

If the issue relates to unsatisfactory job performance, then it is advisable to relate this to KPI's and/or job description. In this first discussion you should stipulate a time limit within which a second failure could lead to further action and, ultimately, dismissal.

You should enter the meeting with an open mind and try to discover the causes of the shortcomings from the employee's perspective.

A record of this counselling should be made as described later.

Before the counselling session you should:

- Investigate the matter thoroughly.
- Review any notes made about past performance.
- List the major points you want to cover at the meeting.
- Arrange a mutually convenient time so both parties can focus on the issues.
- Inform the employee that they may have someone (e.g. union representative or colleague) accompany them for help or support.

Now refer to 'Counselling Jack (2)', on the following page for details on how to conduct the meeting.

> It was a pity he couldna be hatched o'er again,
> an' hatched different.
> George Eliot (1819–1880), English novelist,
> essayist and editor, *Adam Bede*, 1859

Counselling Jack (2)

> If it becomes necessary to discipline employees, they should
> be told why and be given every chance to be heard.
> Johnson & Johnson Co., *The Employee Relations Manual*, 1932

YOU HAVE DECIDED to formally counsel Jack about his unacceptable performance and you have done your preparation (see previous article).

Approach to the counselling and verbal warning meeting

Things you can say at the meeting include:
- 'We are here to discuss the fact that I perceive there has been a repeated shortfall in your ... The standard we require is ... whereas your actual performance/behaviour has been ...'
- 'From the organisation's point of view this is unsatisfactory for the following reasons ...'
- 'Is that a fair assessment?'
- 'What do you see as the reasons for your behaviour?'
- Outline the behaviour the organisation is seeking. 'Do you have a clear picture of the standard that we require and what is expected of you?'
- 'What would be required to change the situation and bring your performance to an acceptable level?'
- 'Do you have the resources you require to meet the standard?'
- 'Do you agree you have the skills and knowledge required to meet the standard?'
- 'Is there some other impediment to your achieving the required standard?'
- 'Is there a personal problem that is affecting your work?'
- 'We need you to meet our required standard from now on/immediately after ...'
- 'Is that fair?'
- 'Do you agree to try to achieve this?'
- 'Have we covered all aspects from your viewpoint?'

- 'This is a verbal warning and we need to meet again in ... weeks (say two to six weeks) to further review the matter. Let's set a date now.'
- 'Do you confirm that you understand that this has been a formal counselling session?'

You will need to tailor the questions to the situation. The above is only a general guide. Ensure that the atmosphere is not intimidating. If it becomes unpleasant, terminate the discussions and resume later. Or put in a strategy to deal with it so that the person doesn't curtail further discussion and go off on sick leave claiming stress. Invite them, but do not compel them, to sign your notes.

If a dispute was ever to arise about the way the dismissal was conducted and it was taken to an independent body for arbitration, you want to be sure that the arbitrators would see the process as fair and not demeaning of the person. It will most likely be a stressful situation for the person anyway without adding other factors that will contribute to their stress. You may not like what this person has done, but you still need to conduct yourself in a dignified manner and allow the employee to maintain their dignity as best they can under the circumstances.

Make sure that there are no bonuses paid or salary increases given while the review is in place. Also make sure that words of encouragement are not interpreted as acceptance that a satisfactory standard has been achieved and the need for a formal warning negated.

Records

A written record of the interview should be made after the meeting and placed in the employee's file, including:
- an outline of the problem
- details of the required performance
- any explanations offered by the employee
- any other relevant information
- the time frame for the review period and any measures to be implemented during this period.

Use the following as an example of a record sheet.

Record of counselling session

Employee: _____ Date: _____

Time session started: _____ time session concluded: _____

1. Purpose of discussion (specifics of performance/behaviour issue):
   _____
   _____
   _____

2. Outline of employer's perspective (including required performance/ behaviour):
   _____
   _____
   _____

3. What does the employee see as the reasons?
   _____
   _____
   _____

4. Employer's further comments (including agreed actions):
   _____
   _____
   _____

5. Any other matters of relevance:
   _____
   _____
   _____

6. Date for future meeting:
   _____

7. Persons in attendance:
   Name _____ Signature _____
   Name _____ Signature _____
   Name _____ Signature _____

Formally warning Jack

> There is, however, a limit at which forbearance ceases to be a virtue.
> Edmund Burke (1729–1797), English statesman, orator and writer,
> *Observations on Late Publication on the Present State of the Nation*, Volume 1, 1769

YOU HAVE COUNSELLED JACK (see previous two articles). Performance continues to be unsatisfactory. You believe the only sensible course is for him to no longer be employed by the organisation, but you hesitate because of all the laws surrounding dismissal. There is the ever-present possibility that your organisation, and perhaps even yourself, will end up in a court hearing on unfair dismissal. What can you do?

If your organisation has procedures for this, then follow them. Otherwise the steps set out below can be used.

Once again, we are considering someone who simply falls short of desired standard, not someone who has committed serious or wilful misconduct.

It is of fundamental importance that your organisation can demonstrate that due and fair process was adopted. You must be able to demonstrate that the employee was counselled about the shortcomings, and that the employee was warned of the consequences of further nonconformance to requirements.

First written warning

If, during the review period following the counselling session, there is a subsequent failure to meet the accepted standard of conduct or work, a further meeting followed by a written warning, including a brief account of the incident, is necessary.

Before the meeting you should:

- Advise the employee you need to meet again to discuss the issue.
- Ask if they want another person (union representative or colleague) to also be present at the meeting to support them.
- Consider whether you should have a second person from management to accompany you at the meeting as a witness.

- Set the time and place for the meeting so both parties can focus on the issues.

At the meeting:

- Review the previous discussion at the counselling session.
- Discuss the employee's performance during the review period.
- Ask if there is any explanation.
- Outline the specific change in performance that is expected.
- Ask the employee to confirm this is understood.
- Explain that they will receive a written warning and that continued behaviour of this type could lead to dismissal. (This is a very important part of the process.)
- Set a specific period for the next review.
- Make a record of the meeting. (The following record sheet may be of assistance.)

After the meeting:

- Write a memo or letter to the employee that includes a summary of the meeting. (Attaching a copy of the record of the meeting mentioned above may be useful.)
- Ensure there is a clear statement in writing that if the employee fails to produce the required change in behaviour or performance, dismissal may follow.
- Issue the document to the employee, with a copy to the employee's file.
- During the review period, monitor performance, noting any developments.

Final written warning

At the end of the review period following the first written warning, a further failure to meet the required standard will justify a further meeting, followed by a final written warning. This document should be a memo or letter and state in clear terms the reason for the warning, the nature of the shortcomings and that if at the end of a specific review period the employee's performance has not improved to the required standard, then employment will be terminated.

Guidelines for the meeting are similar to those outlined above.

Dismissal

If the employee still fails to meet the required standard, they may be dismissed. (See 'The final act', pp. 122–3.)

Record of written warning session

Employee: _____ Date: _____

1. Review of previous discussion (dated _____ / _____ / _____):
   _____
   _____

2. Employer's perspective of behaviour during review period:
   _____
   _____
   _____

3. Response/comments from employee:
   _____
   _____
   _____

4. Specific changes required in performance/behaviour:
   _____
   _____
   _____

5. Employee agrees understanding of the above:
   _____

6. Confirmation that a written warning will be issued (failure to remedy the matter may lead to dismissal):
   _____

7. Any other matters of relevance:
   _____
   _____
   _____
   _____

8. Date for future review meeting:
   _____

9. Persons in attendance:
   Name _____ Signature _____
   Name _____ Signature _____
   Name _____ Signature _____

The final act

O NLY AFTER COUNSELLING AND WARNING THE EMPLOYEE as set out in the articles 'Counselling Jack (1)', 'Counselling Jack (2)', and 'Formally warning Jack' can you proceed to this next step. Those articles and the following can be taken as a general guide to good practice, but you should check legal requirements in your own area before finally proceeding with dismissal, including a check to ensure actions taken already are adequate.

Final review

At this meeting, all concerned parties should be present. If performance has improved, tell the employee and set a date for further review. If performance continues to be unsatisfactory, state that this is the final meeting and it is the last opportunity to ensure all information is available. Present your facts and explain you are considering termination. Ask the employee (or their representative) to present their side of the case, including any facts which management should consider before making a final decision.

Dismissal

After considering the information provided by the employee, you can now proceed to dismissal. This may be at the same meeting or at another meeting held shortly afterwards, perhaps after you have had time to review the proposed dismissal with senior management.

During the dismissal meeting, explain the reasons for the dismissal, reviewing all previous steps. Ensure you give the employee the opportunity to respond and, if appropriate, confirm the decision to terminate. Provide all information on entitlements in writing, either now or shortly afterwards, and place a summary of the meeting in the employee's file.

Make sure that the dismissal minimises emotional trauma—that the employee is not dismissed in front of others and not marched out of the office or off the work site.

Outplacement

It is a very good policy to offer to assist the dismissed employee to find new employment. After all, the organisation has probably made an error of judgement in slotting the employee into the role where they did not fit. If you are having doubts or misgivings about providing such assistance, then reference to the quotation on page 115 may help you to feel more supportive.

A suggested approach is:

- If you know of somewhere that the employee may have some likelihood of gaining a position, then offer to make enquiries on their behalf.
- Phone some labour hire companies and explain the situation and ask would they be willing to interview the person.
- Ask your employee if they will agree to formal outplacement assistance through an outplacement firm. Not only is the foregoing a socially desirable thing to do, it makes the separation less harsh and it will improve the morale of those work mates who remain.
- The employee may refuse certain types of assistance, or even all of it, but it is highly desirable to offer.

Disclaimer: Whilst the above can be taken as a general guide, you should check the legal requirements in your own local state/area before proceeding. No responsibility can be accepted by the authors for failing to check and follow your legal requirements.

Great expectations

GENCIES SET UP TO RESOLVE DISPUTES related to labour and industrial relations deal with a multiplicity of disputes in relation to employment. There is a view held by the professionals who work in these agencies that a large proportion of these disputes could be avoided if all contracts of employment were in writing. Both parties should have a clear understanding of their respective duties, obligations and entitlements. A contract in writing should minimise misunderstandings and disagreements about the terms and conditions of employment.

Apart from standard provisions regulating wages/salary, hours of work, the title and duties of the position, and leave, the contract may address matters such as:

- ☐ The duty of the employee to maintain their skill levels and the employer's obligation to ensure that the employee has the opportunity to practise and develop those skills.

- ☐ An acceptance by the employee that they may, from time to time, be required to perform a range of duties, some outside the scope of their normal work, to assist the business.

- ☐ An acceptance by the employee that they will cooperate in the development of policies and adhere to policies designed to promote the business, customer services and harmony in the workplace.

☐ That the employer will consult with the employee in the development of these policies.

☐ Any arrangements and conditions for incentive payments (which are to be included as a term of the contract) will be clearly and comprehensively set out.

☐ If the employer chooses to implement a bonus scheme (which is not part of the contract) it should be made clear that it is discretionary and is not a contractual entitlement.

☐ That the employee understands and accepts that the employer may introduce particular performance assessments but that the employee will be informed of the basis of assessment and will be afforded the opportunity to discuss outcomes.

☐ That both the employer and the employee understand the terms on which either party is able to bring the contract to an end.

The employment relationship is regulated not only by the terms of the contract entered into between the parties but there are duties and obligations on the employer and employee implied under law. Managers should be familiar with the scope of the employment environment when employment relationships are being considered.

Examples of duties and obligations implied in a contract of employment by law:

• Employee's Duty of Obedience/Cooperation—obey lawful reasonable orders.
• Employee's Duty of Fidelity:
  – act honestly dealing with employer's property,
  – no secret commissions to be accepted,
  – not to abuse or disclose confidential information,
  – recognise employer's right to retain property in inventions.
• Employee's Duty of Care and Competence.
• Employer's Duty of Care.
• Employer's Duty to Indemnify—cover expenses incurred in the course of employment.
• Employer's Duty to Act Reasonably e.g. not to harshly or unfairly dismiss.

Ask great questions

A S MY FRIEND AND COLLEAGUE, David Deane-Spread, is fond of saying, 'Ask great questions and you will get great answers.' One of my many faults that David has pointed out to me is that when commenting on someone's performance I tend to make statements that are perceived as judgemental and critical—even when I don't intend them to be. This immediately gets the other person on the back foot— on the defensive. Their focus may now be on protecting their self-image or their sense of self-worth. So we are off on the wrong foot to begin with. Not conducive to a productive discussion about a person's performance.

A far better way is to not make statements, but rather to ask questions. This is more likely to lead the person to the awareness that they need to resolve the problem.

Here are some examples of questions to ask of somebody whose performance could be better, assuming that you have set the scene with some preliminary remarks and created an environment suitable for this discussion. Pick ones that suit you, the other person and the situation:

☐ How do you feel about the outcome here for you and others?

☐ How do other people see your behaviour?

☐ What were your intentions?

- [ ] How do you feel about your level of overall performance? How do you feel about your performance in relation to ...?
- [ ] If there are any areas of your performance that could be improved, what, in your opinion, would they be?
- [ ] What would you say are the main reasons for this lack of performance?
- [ ] What's your perception of the issues here?
- [ ] What could be other perceptions?
- [ ] How could your perceptions differ from others?
- [ ] Which of all these perceptions are facts?
- [ ] What may be the assumptions you and others are making?
- [ ] What information are you using in this situation?
- [ ] What other information could be useful?
- [ ] What does this situation mean for you?
- [ ] What's the meaning of your actions here?
- [ ] How could your actions be interpreted?
- [ ] If you had the chance to do or say ... again (be specific), what would you like to do or say differently?
- [ ] What beliefs do you hold about this situation?
- [ ] What beliefs could others hold?
- [ ] What other beliefs could also be used by you?
- [ ] Which of your beliefs are facts?
- [ ] What interpretations have you placed on this issue?
- [ ] What are other interpretations that could also be placed on this issue?
- [ ] What are other ways that this situation could have been handled?
- [ ] What could have worked better for you and for others?
- [ ] How would you have to change your thinking to enable you to act in a better way? What would need to happen to cause that change to your way of thinking?

Remember, our intentions are usually honourable. It is our execution that may be flawed.

Fair and balanced

A WASTE AND RECYCLING FACILITY was using our M•A•P•P™ System to improve a number of things on the site. We had two groups operating with about nine people in each. The newish CEO was an enlightened, progressive thinker who had made a number of improvements to the performance of the facility and to the quality of the work life of the employees. His operations manager was a 'hands on' type, who had been there many years and employed more of the 'old school' style of management. He was struggling a bit making the transition to a management style more consistent with modern times although he was very dedicated, hard working, and very competent at most parts of his job. It was mainly his communication style that alienated people. As with most of us, this was unintentional.

I had noticed that the M•A•P•P™ groups in which the operations manager participated had less constructive and productive discussions than the ones in which the CEO participated. People were not as forthcoming when the operations manager was present. This was having a detrimental effect on the effectiveness of his M•A•P•P™ group.

The operations manager came in for a bit of flak, which came to the attention of the CEO who passed on some of the criticisms. The operations manager was feeling a bit bruised and exasperated because, to his way of thinking, he had done nothing wrong. In an initial discussion I had with him, he was understandably defensive and refuted the criticisms.

We set up a meeting with the operations manager and representatives of the four operational areas of the facility—five people in total. While each person provided feedback to each other person, the real purpose of this meeting was to provide feedback to the operations manager on his style of communicating with his people.

A key concern of mine was to ensure that the feedback session was fair, balanced, two-way and focused only on specific actions that a person could change or modify. It was important to establish the right climate.

To do this, I discussed the following points at the start of this session:

- Issues or conflict between people can only be resolved by bringing them out into the open.
- Every person on this site believes in their own minds that they do a good job.
- Each person can identify things that other people do which they wish they didn't.
- Not one of us is perfect. Each of us has personality characteristics that attract and repel other people. Each one of us has things we do well and things we could do better. Each one of us has assets and liabilities to our personality, to our style and to our approach to workplace relationships.
- Most people act in good faith according to how they perceive things and according to the demands and pressures on them. Most people on this site do not maliciously set out to make life harder for others.
- We are not going to like all the people we have to work with, but if we are smart we can work out ways to work with the strengths and weaknesses of others. Relationships are a two-way street—each person is responsible for their fifty per cent of the relationship.
- Most people find it easier to criticise others than to accept criticism of themselves.
- All of us on site have the right to be treated with dignity even if some things we do are not liked by others.
- People have differing levels of self-awareness—from the very aware to the very unaware. I can't change or modify anything about myself until I become aware of it and how it affects other people.
- Feedback that is unfair and unbalanced is likely to cause most people to become defensive.
- Acknowledgment is a powerful act in reconciling the differences between two parties at odds with each other. It takes a strong person to acknowledge that they may have got some things wrong in the past.

Discussing these issues before we started the feedback exchange seemed to help the process.

Men in shorts

A FEW YEARS AGO I was conducting a training program for senior managers to refine their skills in providing performance feedback. Confrontation skills were on the agenda for the second day. This segment was to provide managers with the opportunity to apply what they had learned about giving feedback and the principles of confrontation. Managers were asked to think of situations from their workplace where they would need to use confrontation skills. Several situations were raised but the one that was of interest to all was how to confront another manager about the appropriateness of his attire during summer.

The problem was how to address the issue of a manager, let's call him Rob, wearing shorts (and tight ones at that), when a business suit was required. Rob it seems had regularly worn shorts to work, but now that he was in a role that involved client visits this was no longer appropriate. A visit to a major client was scheduled, but despite hints and some jokes at Rob's expense, there had been no change in his attire. Rob was left out of the meeting, on a thin excuse, but the problem remained. All agreed that something had to be said but what, by whom, when and where?

This scenario might appear easy to some readers, but there was a catch. The approach managers used had to meet the following criteria:

- preserve the person's self-worth,
- maintain the relationship,
- result in the person's agreement to change their behaviour.

There are other similar situations in the workplace that might necessitate feedback or confrontation skills. A member of your team or a colleague may relay tasteless jokes, abuse facilities or resources, interact with other team members in an aggressive manner or talk to clients with indifference. Giving feedback to people about these behaviours can be difficult. How would you tackle these situations?

In the workplace, the choice exists for you to confront or not confront. Think through the consequences and benefits of so doing and ensure that your approach meets the three criteria listed above. It might be that you decide that it is all too hard, but what about the consequences of not doing anything? The person remains unaware of the impact of their behaviour on others. The consequences may be career limiting with the person missing out on valuable opportunities for development and promotion. In Rob's case, it is easy to see that being excluded from client meetings will have negative consequences in terms of performance in his new role and promotion is unlikely. Without feedback, he will never know the reason for his exclusion from client meetings. His relationships with people might become strained as he tries to work out the reason for missing out on assignments or promotions.

Another way in which such problems are dealt with is to subject the person to ridicule. They become the brunt of jokes or continued criticism. However, this approach is ineffective in changing behaviour and is damaging to the person's self-esteem.

The acid test for confronting rather than say nothing is:

- ☐ You express your frustration or dissatisfaction about the person to friends, family and anyone who will listen—except the person.
- ☐ The person's behaviour has a negative impact on the wellbeing or performance of other people in your team.
- ☐ Your feelings towards the person are altered because of their behaviour. You avoid them or spend less time with them than other people.
- ☐ They miss out on opportunities to develop and learn because of your unexpressed opinions about their behaviour.
- ☐ The person is the subject of jokes or ridicule on a regular basis.

If you tick more than one of these boxes raise the issue with the person using the following as a guide.

Confrontation skills

The aim is to outline the person's behaviour and their impact on other people so that they are able to listen to and hear what you have to say. Once the person understands their impact on others, let them come up with possible solutions. This is more likely to result in them acting constructively. You can modify their solutions once they have been put forward. You can also refuse a solution that is offered if it does not address the problem.

In preparation:

- Decide how it will benefit the person to receive the feedback. A change in behaviour could make it easier for a person to gain a promotion, relate better to their colleagues or be less stressed. Think of yourself as a provider of information rather than judge or critic.
- Write down what you want to say and then review your choice of words. Instead of using words that are 'labels' describe the person's behaviour in terms of what they do or do not do, what they say or do not say.
- Phrase what you say in such a way that the person is able to hear you instead of becoming instantly defensive. If you are unsure, test what you intend to say on someone who is impartial. Watch how they react.
- Wait until you can talk to the person in a calm and informative manner. If you are angry or frustrated, this will only create defensiveness.
- Make sure you can talk the issues through without interruption.
- Build the confrontation into a coaching or development meeting.
- Arrange the meeting as soon after the incident as possible.

Remember the criteria: gain agreement for behaviour change while maintaining the person's self-esteem and your relationship with them.

The discussion:

- Greet the person.
- Outline the purpose of the meeting in general terms. For example you could say, 'The purpose of the meeting is to discuss your performance and your client relationships', or 'The purpose of the meeting is to discuss the company's dress code'.
- Provide a context for the discussion. You might want to let the person know that everything about their performance is great except for the fact that their standard of dress is inappropriate. If you do make positive statements make sure they are genuine.
- Raise the issue directly and in a matter-of-fact manner. It can make it easier to determine whether the person is aware of their behaviour by outlining the situation you want to talk about.
- Pause and watch carefully to assess the impact of what you have said. Does the person view their behaviour as problematic for others and do they understand the degree to which it is a problem? Their reaction is the best guide for what you need to say or do next.

It is preferable to be direct so the person knows what you mean, rather than going around the point where they will just end up confused.

Five possible reactions and responses to your feedback are:

1. **Reaction:** The person may have been unaware and responds with enthusiasm at your honest feedback. Rob may be grateful at knowing that the shorts are inappropriate in his new management role. It may never have occurred to him that the shorts were a problem. He agrees to go shopping and purchase a suit.
   Response: You don't need to do any more. Your confrontation was successful. You can now talk about what client visits and further opportunities are coming up.

2. **Reaction:** The person may have been unaware but is also defensive about the feedback. They may need time to come to terms with the feedback. Rob may be upset at the thought that his shorts are inappropriate. He may tell you that he has worn shorts in the past so why not now.
   Response: Listen to what the person says. Check to see whether it would be useful to continue the conversation later. Give them time to absorb the information. Plan another meeting.

3. **Reaction:** The person may deny the truth of what you say. Rob may tell you that other managers have never pointed out this problem and that the shorts will not have any negative impact on his clients.
   Response: As a rule of thumb, there is no point arguing over differences in perception. If the person is unable to hear what you have to say because of their defensiveness, then leave it. However, if it is important to work performance, focus the discussion on their ability to achieve set objectives. Reinforce the standards that are needed for business success.

4. **Reaction:** The person may be aware but for some reason be unable to change or chooses not to change but without being hostile. Rob responds by telling you that he has a skin disorder that means he is more comfortable wearing shorts. He is disappointed to hear that wearing shorts will make it harder for him to meet all his objectives in his new role.
   Response: Identify ways to work around the situation. It might be possible to assign Rob clients whose code of dress is similarly informal. If this is not possible, then other opportunities within the company may need to be considered. This situation requires listening skills and responding with empathy.

5. **Reaction:** The person may be aware of the impact of their behaviour but not wish to change anyway. It does not concern them. Their response indicates that there is a degree of hostility towards you or others. Rob refuses point blank to wear anything different. He thinks that the dress code for men is ridiculous and accuses you of being a snob. He thinks that he should be recognised on his merits, not on his clothing. He is not concerned that it is a problem.

   Response: Point out the consequences of the person choosing to continue with their old behaviour. Show that you understand their perspective without necessarily agreeing with them. You might say, 'Rob, it is your right to wear shorts. However, in the interest of client relationships, it would be preferable for you to wear a suit.'

If you acknowledge the person's position it helps them to give some ground. Having acknowledged that Rob might find shorts more comfortable, you may be able to gain his agreement to change into trousers for meetings with clients. If he does not want to change, then reiterate the consequences of not attending client meetings.

If your response meets with an 'I don't care' attitude, then it is possible that your message was evaluative or judgemental and therefore precipitated the resistance. Try again at a later date having thought more about it from their point of view. Ask yourself, 'what could be the benefit to them of behaving this way?'

Conflicting values are the source of many of the frustrations in relationships. Yet they can be difficult to confront and resolve. The greater the difference between two people in terms of their values, the greater the chance of conflict. People are unlikely to change their values overnight, but they might just change their behaviour. In a work environment it is important to manage and utilise difference and diversity rather than striving to have everyone the same. Diversity brings richness, resilience and opportunities for learning.

I'll take 'pleasant', thanks

Y OU CAN'T MOTIVATE YOUR PEOPLE—only they can do that. However, you can remove or add factors that detract or enhance motivation. And keep this simple concept in mind—people act to seek pleasant circumstances and act to avoid unpleasant circumstances.

Guidelines for motivating people

What can you do as a manager to motivate your staff more effectively?
1. Identify and understand the needs and personal goals of your staff. Ask them rather than making assumptions which may be incorrect and misleading.
2. Remember that money is not the only motivator. Many other rewards may be more effective than money in getting your staff to work better.
3. Set your staff targets that are realistic and achievable but also stretch ability. If possible, involve people in setting their own targets.
4. Always recognise significant achievement by praise or some other reward.
5. Do not alter targets without consulting with the staff concerned. If changes are necessary these should be agreed jointly.
6. Harness the strength of the group. Group pressures can affect motivation positively and negatively. Involving your staff as a group in making decisions and determining implementation strategy will strengthen commitment.
7. Keep your staff informed about what is going on in the organisation.

Alternative approach

Focus on somebody whose motivation is low. The reasons for their poor levels of motivation could be:
• They don't believe that they have the skills and knowledge to do the job.
• They believe that the task or outcome is too difficult.
• They believe that they probably won't do it successfully.
• They place no value on doing the task or in achieving the outcome.

Using the table below, list some of the key tasks in which they show least motivation. Then using the scale, rate your perception of how they would rate themselves for perceived level of skill and knowledge (PLSK), perceived ease of successful outcome (PESO), etc. This will give you the focus for a counselling session designed to raise their level of motivation.

Better still, involve the person and ask them to rate themselves. Then compare your rating with theirs as the basis for a discussion to identify what needs to happen to lift their level of motivation.

Least motivated tasks	PLSK	PESO	PPSO	PVSO	TOTAL
Counselling poor performers	6	2	2	9	19

PLSK: perceived level of skill and knowledge
PESO: perceived ease of successful outcome
PPSO: perceived probability of success
PVSO: perceived value of successful outcome

Rating scale

PLSK	Very low skill and knowledge	1 2 3 4 5 6 7 8 9 10	Very high skill and knowledge
PESO	Very difficult	1 2 3 4 5 6 7 8 9 10	Very easy
PPSO	Very unlikely	1 2 3 4 5 6 7 8 9 10	Very likely
PVSO	No value	1 2 3 4 5 6 7 8 9 10	High value

Scores:

34+   Extremely high level of motivation.
29–33   Good level of motivation.
24–28   Adequate, but needs some coaching.
19–23   Just plodding along. Some perception changing/skill development required here.
14–18   Phew! Serious perception changing/major skill development here.
9–13   Oh no! Nearly a basket case.
4–8   If not a new recruit, check for rigor mortis.

Take an inventory

IF YOU EVER STOPPED TO ASK, you might be very surprised at the breadth, extent and quality of skills that are possessed by members of your staff outside their work responsibilities. I was once surprised to learn that one of the migrant process workers on the shop floor was in fact a qualified architect. Being an immigrant with limited English and perhaps with qualifications not necessarily recognised in his new country, this fact was not known to us.

It can be a useful exercise to informally and formally speak with every member of your staff and seek to find hidden talents. They can be as simple as having won or participated in the local garden competition, being skilled in calligraphy, being fluent to some extent in another language, being competent at building and maintaining a web site or, perhaps more significantly, having some first-aid skills.

Once these skills are identified and recorded, they can prove useful to the organisation in areas that had not been anticipated before. For example, you may need a quick interpretation of a foreign language document, you may need an interpreter for foreign visitors, your office garden may look a bit neglected, you may need some temporary signage or you may discover a nil cost means of creating and maintaining your web site.

You might find it beneficial to either seek advice or even delegate responsibility for that area to the person. If you are considering the latter, be careful to define carefully how much time they should spend on the matter. You do not want to find they neglect their primary role.

You can take the following approach:

- Start with the personnel files and check for clues there. If the person's original job application is present, there may be a list of qualifications, experience and extracurricula interests. These will provide leads for you.
- Meet with each person, preferably informally and in their area or a casual meeting place, and explore their background more fully. You may need to explain you want to make a list of skills beyond what is obvious from their work role, but be careful not to make it all seem threatening.
- Ask about their previous training—both job related and non-job related.
- Ask about their previous experience. Are there issues and experiences that are not immediately obvious?
- Ask about their hobbies, what they do in their recreation time, if they play any sport, etc.
- Ask are they doing any night-time or weekend training at present, and if so, what?
- Ask if they perceive that they have any special skills or experiences, which may be of benefit to the organisation beyond what is obvious.
- Ask would they be willing to assist in the future if a need for one of their skills arose for the organisation.
- If a need subsequently arises, then discuss how they could assist in that area, while still maintaining agreed performance in their principal job role. If the need is expected to be ongoing, explain that the revised role is to be undertaken on a trial basis.
- Set down a date for a review meeting on the issue after the revised responsibility has started.
- Before the review meeting, note down any issues you have, including those raised by other staff on the matter.
- At the meeting congratulate the person on taking on the extra responsibility and ask how the person feels about it so far.
- Raise any areas of concern you may have, and discuss possible solutions.

- Discuss whether the revised role should continue (from the person's viewpoint as well as your own).
- Finish by acknowledging again the extra effort being put in and thank the employee once again.

> There is probably no man living, though ever so great a fool,
> that cannot do something or other well.
> Samuel Warren (1807–1877), English author and lawyer

A positive KISS approach

HOW ARE YOUR TEAM MEMBERS TRAVELLING? Need something a bit more robust than the old, 'You've had a good week, Bill' approach? Having trouble getting a system started? Not too sure about whether performance reviews might well be opening a Pandora's box in your otherwise comfortable business world?

Then ease the pain. Here is a simple, workable, five-step system for reviewing the performance of your staff from the front-line operators to the managers.

Establish the review schedule

An acceptable approach in a number of organisations is to identify when people started with the team and establish that as the 'anniversary' for that individual. Reviews can be conducted annually using this anniversary as a target date to commence the process. Space people out so that you are not overloaded with a batch in a short space of time. Publish the schedule to the staff so that there are no surprises when their day looms.

Collect the staff view

One successful approach is to issue the staff member due for review with a form which contains a number of 'what do you think' questions. Some examples are as follows:
- What tasks do you like to do?
- What has caused you frustration or disappointment over the last year?
- Do you consider you are generally given sufficient information to carry out your role properly?
- Have you developed any new skills over the last year?
- Did you have sufficient resources to carry out your tasks?
- How have your duties altered over the last year?
- Is there any other equipment that you feel that we should have in your workplace?
- What additional training do you feel that you need?

Prepare your view

As the reviewer, gather and document your information in a structured way. Develop a balanced appraisal over the whole report period. Some aspects of your summary might be:

- How did the staff member perform against the relevant position description?
- What have been the strengths and weaknesses of the person?
- How has the person related to others?
- Has the person been enthusiastic in the position?
- What training has been undertaken?
- What approach has the person had to teamwork?
- Is the person's personal character satisfactory i.e. reliability, honesty, etc.

Conduct the performance discussion

Use the documentation as a framework. Some agenda items might be:
- your points
- the person's points
- a gap analysis
- agreement on strengths and weaknesses
- some targets for the forthcoming year
- training needs.

Action plan

Confirm the 'way ahead' in terms of work targets, performance criteria for these targets and what training plans you have. Some examples are:
- Submission of monthly operations reports by the end of the fifth working day of each month.
- Conduct of documented staff meetings with subordinates on a weekly basis.
- Attendance at a minimum of three software courses in the next year.
And the result? A simple, workable system that everybody understands and accepts.

> If you can't measure output, then measure input.
> Anonymous
>
> If you can't measure it, you can't manage it.
> Anonymous
>
> She is efficient in doing things right and effective in doing the right thing.
> Anonymous
>
> Understanding should precede judging.
> Louis Dembitz Brandeis (1856–1941), US Supreme Court Justice,
> *Burns Bakery Co. v Bryan,* 1923

You can help

MANY PEOPLE IN THE WORKPLACE suffer from low self-esteem. This will manifest itself in a number of different ways (see 'Worth your time', pp. 184–5).

Self-esteem is the opinion you have of yourself. It is based on your attitude to the following:

- Your value as a person.
- The job you do.
- Your achievements.
- How you think others see you.
- Your purpose in life.
- Your place in the world.
- Your potential for success.
- Your strengths and weaknesses.
- Your social status and how you relate to others.
- Your independence or ability to stand on your own feet. (See www.more-selfesteem.com.)

If you have people working for you whose performance and relationships with others suffers because of low self-esteem, here are some guidelines to help you help those people develop better self-esteem:

- Engage in learning about self-esteem—what it is, how we use it, how we lose it, how we get it. Read books and attend seminars or courses, which relate specifically to self-esteem.

- Discuss with your colleagues and friends the concept of self-esteem.
- Research issues related to the development and maintenance of self-esteem. (Use the resources of the World Wide Web by keying in self-esteem. For example, have a look at www.more-selfesteem.com.)
- Identify which staff members may need assistance with improving their self-esteem. Assess what the benefits will be to them, you, your work area and the organisation if their self-esteem can be improved.
- Actively listen to these staff members to gauge their feelings about themselves and others through the attitudes that might be expressed.
- Offer, discreetly, to arrange help for staff members who are obviously having problems in this area. Do this by offering them articles to read, suggesting they take up leisure activities in areas you know they are interested in or good at, or suggest books or videos that might touch on the topic.
- Plan tasks for the person that are success oriented.
- Plan activities that promote cooperation of all participants.
- Let the person know that you value them for who they are. Be specific about their strong points.
- Provide the opportunity for staff members with low self-esteem to assume leadership roles, with discrete support from you.
- Discuss with other staff members the impact that teasing has on those with low self-esteem.
- Discuss with staff members the importance of their cooperation.
- Recognise achievement towards desired behavioural outcomes by saying things such as, 'That's great so far. Keep it going', or 'You're almost there, well done', or 'This is great so far. It will be fantastic when you finish'.
- Recognise genuine effort by acknowledging what they have done. Take extra time with these people to acknowledge their efforts even if the results aren't quite there yet.
- Inform other management of your intended intervention strategies so that they can support your endeavours.

> If you know anything that will make a brother's heart glad, run quick and tell it: and if it is something that will only cause a sigh, bottle it up.
> Old Farmer's Almanac, 1854

> Those whom you can make like themselves better will,
> I promise you, like you very well.
> Lord Chesterfield (1694–1773), English politician, *Letters to His Son*

You can't always get what you want ...

WE WERE USING the M•A•P•P™ System with a group of managers and supervisors from a manufacturing company to improve internal communications. As part of the process, each manager agreed to seek feedback about their own style of communication from three people with whom they worked closely. One supervisor, Herman, was informed that sometimes he came across as a bit fiery and impatient so he decided to take a softer approach next time one of his workers transgressed.

An incident occurred ending with one of his men, Sam, telling him he was a 'f... wanker', storming off and giving Herman the one-finger salute. This happened within sight and sound of other people.

The workplace is a foundry that is hot, dirty and noisy, physically demanding, the work monotonous and where the pay for the unskilled jobs is not high. Because of this, attendance on the job is a problem. The background to this incident was that Sam had had two days off sick in the week leading up to Friday. He had already used his sick leave credits so he lost two days pay. He expected to top up his pay that week by working overtime on the weekend. Herman needed overtime to be worked but he allocated it to two other operators who had not had any days off that week. Overtime was offered as an incentive to those who worked the full week. Sam, who already knew that the other two guys had been allocated overtime, asked Herman for overtime and was refused. So he blew his top and started verbally abusing Herman who, trying to quell his sometimes-fiery temperament, did not react as he normally would.

Herman was bothered by this incident because he felt the way Sam spoke to him was unacceptable and that he would suffer in the eyes of others who witnessed or knew of the incident. He felt he was owed an apology from Sam—or at least an acknowledgment that he was way out of line.

These were some pointers I suggested to Herman as a guide to the conversation with Sam:

- 'Sam. I want to talk to you about what happened the other day. I'll go first and talk about what happened from my point of view. Then I would like you to put your point of view. Unless I ask questions, please don't interrupt—let me finish what I've got to say and I'll do the same with you. Is that fair?'
- 'You called me a "f... wanker". In the same situation, how would you feel about that?' (Pause) 'Is that what you really think or was it in the heat of the moment?' (Pause) 'Do you think that it is fair that I cop that sort of abuse?' (Pause) 'The other guys know about this. How do you reckon that affects me?'
- 'I know that you were pissed off because you wanted overtime. I can understand that. You also know the policy is to give overtime to the guys who attend all week. That's the standard practice.'
- 'Sam, I know that sometimes I get a bit fiery myself. I acknowledge that and it is something I am trying to curb. I have no problem with swearing at all, but when it is directed at me personally and in front of others, I have a real problem with that.'
- 'Whatever the reasons, it is totally unacceptable for you to speak to me the way you did. As the supervisor, I can't and won't tolerate it. As a person I find it insulting and unnecessary. Would you tolerate it if you were in my shoes?'
- 'What I would like is an acknowledgment from you that you went over the top and a commitment that it won't happen again. Is that fair?'
- 'I think you are a decent bloke and generally a good worker. I'd like to enjoy working with you, not be pissed off by something you said.'
- 'Okay, it's your turn. Over to you. I'll shut up and listen to your side of the story.'

PART 5

Facilitating group performance

Group bravado

THERE IS A SMALL MINORITY OF WORKERS who see that their prime mission in life is to make mischief. While small in number, they can do a lot of damage if they influence the 'fence sitters' in a work group. Often there is no rationale or balance to their viewpoint. They oppose management initiatives more for the sake of opposing them than for any justifiable reason.

They are usually vocal and forthright in a group setting. In fact, this is their stage. They nurture and feed off the 'us' versus 'them' divide. They tap into the common tendency for many people to resist any form of change because it upsets their routine and habit. Change threatens their comfort zone. Thus in a group setting, the mischief-makers can often elicit vocal support from the 'fence sitters' because it is easy to paint a picture of negativity. The negatives may be a reduction or elimination of a current occurrence, condition or benefit, which is easier to define. The positives are still unknown or unproven and therefore harder to define as probabilities. So it is easier to talk about what we may lose than what we may gain.

The mischief-maker will usually use sweeping generalisations and gross exaggerations to make their case. They will usually refer to history to cite examples of other failed management initiatives. It is easier to garner support with broad generalisations than with tight specifics, which are often missing from their argument. This support helps foster a certain group bravado in this group setting. The general feeling created is that there is a real, widely spread and deeply felt problem here. There is apparent consensus in the opposition to the initiative or proposal. The vocal minority set the tone in the absence of expressed opinions to the contrary from the silent majority.

Now here is a funny phenomenon I have experienced several times. When you get with the people in a one-on-one basis to explore the substance of the problem or issue, you find that there is often little substance. You will often hear the comment, 'Look. I don't actually have a problem with this myself, but I know some of the others do.'

When you push back in relation to the sweeping generalisations or exaggerations, you will often find that there is little basis of fact. Or that perceptions formed are inaccurate and show little awareness of the wider context, show a lack of information pertaining to the issue, narrow perspectives or narrow interpretations. It then becomes apparent that the real reason for the resistance or disgruntlement is simply because some people see this as an opportunity to make mischief.

There are two issues a manager needs to consider here. First, is there genuine substance to the opposition and people only feel comfortable in expressing their genuine concerns when they have the moral support of other workmates in a group setting? Second, in a one-on-one situation, are some individuals fearful of speaking truthfully because they fear repercussions?

> The eyes believe themselves; the ears believe other people.
> German proverb
>
> What some invent the rest enlarge (i.e. rumour).
> Jonathan Swift (1667–1775), Irish cleric and satirist,
> *Journal of a Modern Lady*, 1729
>
> It is impossible to defeat an ignorant man in argument.
> William McAdoo (1863–1941), railroad executive and US Senator,
> remark to President Woodrow Wilson
>
> Where there is no wood a fire goes out; and where there is
> no whisper a quarrel dies down.
> *Old Testament*, Proverbs 26:20

Overcoming shyness

IN ANY GROUP SITUATION there are often a number of people who don't contribute much of value to the discussion. That may not be a problem if they are happy to commit to the proposal or decision. However, if their contribution is necessary to the quality of the decision or outcome and to the implementation of the same, then we need to get their real thoughts and feelings.

Why don't people speak out in a group discussion? (See 'A meeting of minds?', pp. 176–7). Some of the reasons are:

- Fear of repercussions.
- A desire to 'cruise' through the discussion.
- Shyness or lack of confidence in public forums.
- Peer pressure—concern about reactions from their work mates.

We have discussed fear of repercussions in *You Lead, They'll Follow* Volumes 1 and 2, so I will focus only on the middle two of the above points.

'Cruisers' are those people who know that there are always a couple of people in the group who will happily dominate the discussion. So they let these people take over the ship while they sit back and cruise. They know that if they wait long enough one of these people will jump in and contribute their opinion. Once there are enough other opinions on the table, it is easy for the cruisers to back a point of view without really giving it deep thought, without really engaging with the proposal or the decision, and without really testing their true level of commitment to the outcome and the implementation of the outcome.

Shy people are possibly a little less secure in themselves. They find the public exposure of speaking out in a group too painful or embarrassing. In a group situation, shy people find it difficult to express themselves articulately and to their satisfaction because their mind is cluttered with other concerns. It helps if shy people have the time to reflect and you give them a little structure to follow. Doing this will cost you some time but the benefits will far outweigh the costs.

Take twenty to thirty minutes out of your time set aside to improve the quality of the discussion. Try these steps—they are simple and they work:

• Issue a one or two page handout to each participant.
• Number and list the critical issues or questions to which you want people to respond.
• Provide space under each issue or question—up to ten lines as a guide—to allow written responses.
• Allow two to three minutes reflection and writing time per issue or question.
• Randomly go around the group taking each person's response to each issue or question, one at a time. That is, take the first person's response to the first question. Then take the second person's response to the first question. And so on. Then deal with each response to the second question, selecting people in a different random order. (Selecting people at random helps keep everybody focused.)
• Nominate somebody, maybe yourself, to record the key points of each person's response on a whiteboard (preferably) or on a pad.

Now you will find that the shy people will be better able to contribute to the discussion and the cruisers will have to think about the questions and issues for themselves instead of jumping on to someone else's bandwagon.

Traps for young (and old) players

IT IS GENERALLY ACCEPTED THESE DAYS that it is good practice to involve your work group in solving problems. However, a group can still arrive at ineffectual solutions.

The outcome—the resolution to a problem—is most likely to be effective if you use the following steps:

1. Make sure all team members are clear about the issue. Ask people to express their perceptions of the issue and the causes of the problem. Explore differences of perception in a non-judgmental, non-critical and non-threatening manner.
2. Agree what is the desired resolution. Who are all the stakeholders, what are their needs and what are all the conditions that need to be met?
3. Analyse before solving—the obvious solution may not be the best solution. In fact, the best solutions are often not obvious, which is why there is a problem in the first place.
4. Brainstorm action ideas. Anything goes. Go for quantity, not quality. Sort out irrelevant or impractical ideas later.
5. Select action ideas. Consider the consequences of each action on the underlying causes and on all stakeholders.
6. Plan a strategy for implementation. List the key activities that will need to happen, in any order, and then sort them into a logical sequence. Consider also contingency plans for undesirable events occurring. Ask the question, 'What could go wrong with our plan?'
7. Monitor implementation and adjust strategy as necessary. Identify the key performance indicators for each key activity and decide how to monitor them—remember that the plan changes as soon as the battle commences.

Beware of the following traps:

1. Getting hung up on words, such as issue, goal, problem, etc. All goals reflect implicit problems, and all problems and issues reflect implicit goals. It doesn't matter what terminology you use as long as all of you agree the meaning you are all applying.
2. Arguing about the issue or goal. Instead, inquire into each team member's understanding and then either:
   – agree on a common issue, or
   – if you cannot agree, split into subgroups.

3. The premature suggestion of solutions before a careful analysis. Careful analysis takes effort and time, hence avoid the desire to quickly jump into solutions. Note for later analysis.
4. Arguing during the information gathering stage. Wait until you have the full story and then argue your heads off (if you must).
5. Endlessly discussing or arguing about unsolvable items or opinions without accurate data.
6. Ranking (first, second, third etc.) instead of choosing several forces that can be considered 'most' important, several that can be considered 'less' important, and several that can be considered 'least' important.
7. Working on a task as if you can avoid the maintenance of the team and still expect a good outcome. Focus on resolving the problem and keeping everybody 'onside' at the same time.

> I was never satisfied with a problem that I understood only partly.
> I wanted to understand it as completely as I could.
> David Sarnoff (1891–1971), Founder and President of RCA,
> *Wisdom of Sarnoff and the World of RCA*, 1967
>
> There is no situation that cannot be made more difficult with just a little bit of effort.
> David Gerrold (b. 1944), American author,
> *The Galactic Whirlpool*, Bantam, 1980
>
> How often have I said to you that when you have eliminated the impossible, whatever remains, however improbable, must be the truth.
> Sherlock Holmes in Arthur Conan Doyle, *The Sign of Four*, 1890

Au contraire

WHEN IT COMES TO THE BEST WAY to resolve a problem, disagreement is inevitable. It is neither desirable nor undesirable. Disagreement is important to the health of your team. Each of you is different. You will have different values, a different context, different knowledge and information, different perspectives, different interpretations, different needs and wants. You will be likely, therefore, to disagree.

However, a disagreement will be destructive if it is:

1. avoided, or
2. exclusively argumentative (as expressed in the attitude, 'I disagree and must convince you'). It will be constructive if it is done in an inquiry mode.

Inquiry mode

I disagree and want to find out:
1. Do I understand your viewpoint correctly?
2. What assumptions, opinions or facts do you have that cause you to take that point of view?
3. What information can be requested from available resources to help our inquiry?

In an inquiry mode:

1. I can paraphrase (repeat to you the meaning—not the exact words—that I received) and ask you to correct my understanding.
2. I can inquire about your assumptions, opinions or facts. I can invite you to do the same for me.

Restraining forces and supporting forces

Restraining forces are those things acting to create, drive or sustain the problem. Supporting forces are those things acting, or with the potential to act, to resolve the problem.

It is helpful to list restraining forces because these are frequently overlooked. Resolution or improvement will happen when the real restraining forces are reduced or eliminated. Remember that the forces you have listed are opinions and not necessarily facts. Keep asking, 'How can we know whether these forces are really operating?'

Do not assume that your forces are accurate. Check them out or acknowledge that they are private opinions, perhaps incorrect.

Consider a supporting force or forces pushing towards the goal you want. You may want to list such forces and suggest ways to use them to achieve your goal or resolve your issue successfully.

Ask each person in the group to list:

1. restraining forces
2. supporting forces.

Starting with restraining forces, write them on a whiteboard and ask the group to discuss what needs to happen to reduce or eliminate these restraining forces.

Then list supporting forces and get the group to discuss what needs to happen to optimise each supporting force.

Looking at process

The deeply personal and human feelings of being prized or ignored, whether they are influential or not, must be understood to increase the probability of success in a problem-solving situation.

If these feelings are not taken into account, creativity is stifled and problem solving is adversely affected.

You have a task to complete. You are working on the task in a certain way or with a certain process. The two questions you need to ask about the process are:

1. Are the contributions of individuals valued and seen to be valued?
2. Are we avoiding falling into common traps?

Warning: If you want action, do not leave the meeting until you know clearly who will do what, when, how and how you will know it has been done.

> Try several solutions at once. Maybe none of them, alone, would solve the problem, but in combination, they do the job.
> Ray Joseph, President, Ray Joseph Associates Inc. and contributing author, *Leadership in the Office*, AMACOM, 1963

Motivation—it's the name of the game

THE PURPOSE OF THIS GROUP EXERCISE is to identify ways you can improve the motivation of your people. You can do this on individuals or you can do it on the group. Perhaps a good starting point is to do this on the group as a whole, with the option of doing it later on individuals.

Seven basic factors

The following questions relate to some of the basic factors that contribute towards getting personal satisfaction from work. Think carefully about each question and circle the appropriate number.

Rating scale:

1 2 3 4 5 6 7
Definitely **No**   Definitely **Yes**

Do you/your people:

1. Understand and accept the purpose of the work
   you/they are doing?   1 2 3 4 5 6 7
2. Know the criteria that will be used to measure
   your/their performance?   1 2 3 4 5 6 7
3. Have an influence over the planning and
   organisation of your/their work?   1 2 3 4 5 6 7
4. Receive timely and accurate
   information about changes and developments
   in company policy and operations, and the
   rationale for those changes?   1 2 3 4 5 6 7
5. Have opportunities to feedback your/their
   thoughts and feelings regarding your/their work
   or relationship with the company?   1 2 3 4 5 6 7
6. Receive feedback on your/their performance?   1 2 3 4 5 6 7
7. Receive encouragement in the
   form of praise, recognition or tangible rewards
   for success?   1 2 3 4 5 6 7

Score:

Item	Individual scores													Average
1														
2														
3														
4														
5														
6														
7														

Use the following procedure:

☐ Give a copy of the questionnaire to each member of your group explaining that you would like to get everybody's opinion on these seven basic factors that can influence motivation. This will help you decide what needs to be done if people feel that any factors are deficient.

☐ You answer the questions from the perspective of the whole group.

☐ Your people answer the questions in relation to themselves.

☐ Collect the completed questionnaires and record the scores including your own score.

☐ Add the scores for each item, divide by the number of people to determine the average score and place the total in the **Average** column.

☐ Convene a session with the group (one hour to start with—you can always hold more sessions if required). Where the average score for you and the group is less than five, refer to the question for that item and ask the group to reflect on what could be done better in relation to this factor. Allow them three minutes to reflect and write their responses. Ask for responses and compile an action plan reflecting things you and others will do. Repeat this process for other relevant items.

After you ... no, after you

'YOU'VE GOT TO GET YOUR PRIORITIES RIGHT.' How many of us have heard that advice? Is it true? Most successful and effective people will tell you that it is.

How clear are you about your priorities in life? How clear are you about your priorities as a manager? How clear are your staff about their priorities? Is your perception of their priorities the same as their perception of their priorities? How do you know? How do you check this out?

Here's a simple way to do this. Do this with respect to each person. If more than one person has the same job function, then you only need to do this once for all these people. (Forget the duty statement or job description, unless it is up-to-date, relevant and accurate, and followed by the person in the job.)

Follow this procedure:

☐ Using a blank sheet of paper, make a list in random order of the key tasks for each position. Go for quantity—list the key tasks and then break them up into their elements. Consider the technical, conceptual and human aspects of their position. (See *You Lead, They'll Follow* Volume 2.) Prepare the table below with ten to fifteen rows.

Priority T	Key tasks	Elements	Priority E
1	☐	☐	B
		☐	A
		☐	B
		☐	C
		etc.	etc.
2	☐	☐	C
		☐	A
		☐	A
		☐	B
etc.	etc.	etc.	etc.

☐ Write the key tasks and elements onto this table. Now allocate a priority (Priority T) to the key tasks. Use 1 for the highest priority, 2 for the next highest priority, and so on.

☐ Now allocate a priority (Priority E) to each element of each key task using the following code:
A: Essential
B: Important
C: Desirable

☐ Ask each person to follow the same process with respect to how they see their key tasks, the elements making up each key task and their perception of the priorities.

☐ Compare the results with your analysis noting any differences.

☐ Compare the results of people doing the same job and note any differences.

☐ Meet with your work group or individually to compare any differences.

☐ Use the results as a basis for a constructive discussion about aligning our priorities. Request that all of us (including yourself) be prepared to change our position in the light of new information or new perspectives.

☐ Explore, in a non-threatening way, the reasons behind the differences. Ask why they perceive that something has a certain priority where it differs from you or somebody else doing the same job. Explain the reasoning behind your priorities.

☐ Check that the lists of key tasks and elements are also aligned. Explore the reasoning behind any differences.

Work towards an agreement on the key tasks, elements and priorities. During this discussion, always explain the context. (See *You Lead, They'll Follow* Volume 2.) When you have finished this exercise, state that you expect everybody to work toward these priorities. Review the lists every year to incorporate changing circumstances.

> The secret of success is constancy to purpose.
> Benjamin Disraeli (1804–1881), English Prime Minister
> and author, speech, 24 June 1872

I'll get you for that (later)

'SPEAK UP OPENLY AND HONESTLY? No thanks. I tried that once. Never again. Management don't want you to tell them the truth. They want you to tell them what they want to hear. They want you to tell them that you will unquestioningly go along with their plan or strategy or that you are doing it their way. And you'd be an idiot to do otherwise.'

This is the gist of a conversation I have heard many times in many different workplaces. Does it matter if people don't speak openly and honestly? After all, most people don't really speak their mind in wider society. Most of what we think is filtered before we say it. And that's probably a smart thing. Imagine if you could read everybody's mind—what they're really thinking. Could be very unsettling. Could be very titillating too.

So why this emphasis on openness and honesty in the workplace? People don't really want to know what you really think about them unless it is something positive. And most people don't really like you to disagree with them even when they invite you to express contrary opinions.

Back to the question. Does it matter? Yes! I've seen or heard of too many incidents of waste, inefficiency, counterproductive behaviours, damage to equipment or property, injury, damaged relationships, loss of trust, lowered motivation, loss of sales, withholding of important information, lost opportunities and even death, because people feared the repercussions or reprisals for speaking openly and honestly.

The reality is that you would be a mug to speak openly and honestly on all occasions. Unless you are so pure of mind that you have transcended all negativity. And even then that can be dangerous. Ask Socrates or Jesus. If what you really think is that your boss is an arsehole, it's probably not a good career move to share that with them.

But as a manager, if people can see a flaw in my plan, strategy, reasoning, instructions, proposal or request, or they can see a better way, then it is in my very best interests to know. But here's the rub. It is my reaction or response to the openness and honesty that dictates the degree to which my work group are open and honest. They won't be moved by what I tell them about being open and honest, but by what I do to them. Immediately or later.

Let's face it. If you have an over inflated or a fragile ego, or are a perfectionist, you will have difficulty dealing with openness and honesty.

As with most, if not all, problems in life and work, you can't do much about this issue until it is brought into the open. Here is a game plan to investigate the extent of, or to remove, psychological fear in your workplace. Do this with your people (this is a challenging exercise and will require a healthy self-esteem on your part):

- ☐ Discuss the concept of psychological fear in the workplace.
- ☐ Discuss the extent that people fear reprisals or repercussions for speaking openly and honestly.
- ☐ Discuss incidents that staff perceive as examples of reprisals or repercussions.
- ☐ Identify the consequences of people not speaking openly and honestly because of a perceived threat to them.
- ☐ Discuss the benefits of reducing psychological 'fear'.
- ☐ Identify the causes of psychological fear in the workplace.
- ☐ Identify and discuss what things currently happen in the workplace that prevent openness and honesty.
- ☐ Identify the commonly agreed major issues and resolve them first.
- ☐ Discuss the concept of an open environment.
- ☐ Establish communication sessions where staff can air their opinions without fear of consequences.
- ☐ Conduct a review to measure the perceptions of staff in relation to psychological fear in the workplace.
- ☐ Deal with the facts when discussing issues which pose a threat to staff.
- ☐ Identify situations where people will not speak openly and honestly, and discuss what can be done to reduce the perceived fear in each situation.
- ☐ Seek professional development for management in relation to handling this issue.
- ☐ Discuss the role of all stakeholders in reducing fear in the workplace.
- ☐ Discuss with senior management what they can do to help reduce fear in the workplace.
- ☐ Discuss how our 'organisational culture' contributes to psychological fear and what needs to be done to change it.
- ☐ Review regularly the progress of your 'workplace fear reduction' process.

Attitude, attitude, attitude

THERE ARE MANY CONSIDERATIONS when recruiting and building a team of people. The three requirements of 'can do, will do, will fit' are very important. We must look for someone who can do the job technically (this can be after training and a period on the job). We must ensure the person will want to do the tasks required. It is also very important to ensure the appointee will fit in with yourself, your existing team, and the culture of the organisation. These 'will do, will fit' requirements can both be included under the broader heading of attitude.

It has been borne out time and again that a positive attitude will generally overcome inadequacies in other areas. For example, if you recruit someone whose technical skills or experience is lacking, it is most often the case that a positive attitude and desire to succeed will ensure that the person acquires the skills very quickly. Once this has happened, then the positive attitude will ensure ongoing success well beyond what would be achieved with someone who was already skilled, but whose attitude was average or below par.

It is important to ensure you are happy with the chemistry between yourself and the prospective recruit. A team full of similar, positive chemistry will succeed.

Sadly, on the other hand, if there is a team member whose attitude is negative, it will drag down the morale of the whole group.

Productivity of the group will decline over time, and good people may leave when they would not otherwise.

For this reason, it is important for a manager to not only try to bring into the team only those people with a positive attitude, but also to change a situation where a poor attitude exists.

Changing a person's poor attitude can be done in many ways, some of which are listed below. If, however, the attitude seems to be too deeply embedded to allow change, then a way to remove the member from the team should be found. Whilst there will be some team mates who will initially regret such a change, there will shortly be a great improvement in the morale of the group and hence also in productivity.

Some guidelines:

- When recruiting, consider positive attitude to be one of the most important criteria to consider, perhaps the most important.
- Do not be afraid to recruit someone whose technical skills may be incomplete at this stage, but who has a very positive attitude.
- It is important that there is positive chemistry between yourself and every member of your team. If this is the case, then it is almost certain there will also be positive chemistry between team members.
- If you are confronted with a team member with negative attitude, then you must try improving this. Explain that you are keen to maximise the performance of the team and you perceive that they do not seem as motivated as you would like. (See *You Lead, They'll Follow* Volume 1.)

If you are confronted with 'damaged goods' which you seem unable to improve (see *You Lead, They'll Follow* Volume 2), then you have the choice of ignoring and moving on, or of removing the offender from the team. The latter is by far the best course of action if it can be achieved. There will be ongoing damage to the team's morale if the situation continues indefinitely. In following this course, you should refer to 'Counselling Jack (1) & (2)', pp. 113–8, 'Formally warning Jack', pp. 119–21, and 'The Final Act', pp. 122–3. Hopefully, you will be able to stop short of 'the final act'.

A good attitude will overcome shortcomings in many other areas.
Anon

Motivation will almost always beat mere talent.
Norman R. Augustine, President & CEO, Martin Marietta Corp.,
Augustine's Laws, Viking, New York, 1987

I don't care if his skills are weak and he's got no experience. Look at
that enthusiasm and energy level. He's going to be terrific.
Edgar Trenner, Director, Camp Arcady, July 1954

Eternal vigilance

KEEPING PEOPLE FOCUSED ON SAFETY, especially when there have been no serious incidents, takes continuous effort. Here is an exercise you can conduct with your group. Reproduce this making more space available for responses. Ask people to do this individually and then discuss it as a group.

Here are some reasons why we need to improve safety practices. Add others you can think of:

- Society no longer tolerates accidents and death in the workplace as part of the risk of working in the industry.
- Cost to the personal lives of those injured and the families of those injured comes in many forms:
  - constant pain
  - loss of limbs or senses
  - incapacitation
  - loss of income
  - bankruptcy
- Cost to employer comes in the form of:
  - lost time on job
  - loss of productivity
  - damage to plant and equipment
  - workers compensation
  - low staff morale
- Other costs (add your own)

Unsafe working environments

1. What are the consequences when people break Occupational Health and Safety rulcs?

2. Is it possible for workplaces to be totally free of incidents? Why/why not?

3. What do you consider to be the main causes of incidents?

Take a recent incident to use as a case study or use an example from an unrelated work site. (Contact your local Occupational Health and Safety authority to obtain examples of incidents.) Now complete the following:

1. In relation to this incident, list the direct and indirect causes of this incident.

2. What needs to happen to prevent this incident happening again?

Note the deliberate use of the word 'incident' rather than the word 'accident'. Avoid using the word accident in discussions about safety. Barring so called 'acts of God', accidents don't just happen. They happen for a reason—always.

> Early and provident fear is the mother of safety.
> Edmund Burke (1729–1797), English orator and writer, speech, 11 May 1792
>
> One is not exposed to danger who, even when in safety,
> is always on their guard.
> Publilius Syrus (c. 1st century BC), Roman writer

OOSE A?

DOES YOUR TEAM HAVE OOSE A? Now, if you have had any exposure to the military or to bureaucracy, you'll know that acronyms are essential to their survival. Hence my use of the above acronym as the title for this article in the hope that it will help it survive into the future.

I'm digressing—stay with me on this. One of the features of our book series that we like to tell those people who are prepared to listen is that our books are light on when it comes to theory. And some years ago I was informed by a critic that our books were not theoretical enough. So in the hope of turning that critic around, I present an article about teams that moves away from our action-based approach into the realm of theory. However, I think it provides some good 'food for thought'.

I have to also tell you that this article was not penned by me. I found it in my collection of material but with no source identified. If you are reading this and you recognise yourself as the author, I thank you and hope you won't mind it being adapted and brought to a wider audience.

So what does OOSE A stand for?

Output
Objectives
Structure
Energy
Atmosphere

Output

The test of a team is its capacity to deliver the goods and services. A team is capable of achieving results that the individuals who comprise it cannot do in isolation. Their diverse talents combine in the team to create an end product or service beyond their individual capability.

Objectives

A team needs a purpose that is understood, shared and felt to be worthwhile by its members. This purpose can be described as the team's 'mission'. In addition, there will be specific objectives that the team and each individual member have a commitment to achieve.

Structure

A mature team has dealt with thorny questions concerned with control, leadership, procedures, organisation and roles. The team's structure is finely attuned to tasks being undertaken and individual talents and contributions are utilised without confusion. Team members with a drive for leadership have learned to understand each other and to cope with any feelings of hostility, competitiveness or aggression. The team has managed to become flexible, responsive, orderly and directed.

Energy

Team members take strength from one another. Collectively, they feel more potent and find that team activities renew their vitality and enjoyment. The word synergy was coined to describe this special group energy. Synergy has been explained with the mathematically improbable, but psychologically accurate, equation: $2 + 2 = 5$. A team does have a character and capacity beyond the sum of its individual members. It has a capacity for synergy—a group energy that can be deliberately developed and utilised.

Atmosphere

A team develops a distinctive spirit. The team spirit allows for openness between the members and for their support and simple enjoyment of one another. Team members identify themselves with the team and its success or failure affects their feelings. They will extend themselves to serve the interests of the team. Such a team develops an atmosphere within which confidences can be shared, personal difficulties worked through and risks undertaken.

Now if this article has stimulated your thinking and you would like to assess the effectiveness of your team, check out *You Lead, They'll Follow* Volume 1.

Picking a winning combination

TEAMWORK IS AN ESSENTIAL PART of organisational life. The competitive advantage for an organisation lies not just in the quality of the people it employs but the capacity of these people to work together to produce outcomes for clients or customers. Some people adapt well to teamwork while others resist, preferring the satisfaction of doing things on their own.

High performance teams are those in which members are able to work together to achieve better-quality decisions and solutions to problems than if the individuals were working alone. The team's atmosphere or climate is created by the way in which the interpersonal style and qualities of each individual interact. There are usually mixed contributions with some members doing more than others and carrying the less-productive members.

The challenge for managers is that teams evolve and change. The demands on team members are often unpredictable and team members come and go. Any change will have an impact on the team's ability to perform. Keeping a team at peak performance is an art, much like the juggler who keeps all the plates twirling on sticks. The most critical time for a team is when one or more of the members change.

How do you go about finding a new member for your team when someone leaves or when a new role has been created? A team can jell and be extremely productive based on the unique qualities of one individual or equally it can grind to a virtual standstill because of a different set of unique qualities of another individual. The following steps will help you to select a new team member.

Step 1: Determine the qualities you want in a new team member

First consider the following:
- What was the contribution of the person who has left the team?
- What were their unique qualities?
- How did they help the team achieve its goals?
- How easy will it be for the team to achieve its goals without this person?
- What new challenges will the team face in the future?
- What as yet untapped talent do remaining team members have to meet these challenges?

Next consult existing team members:

- Does the vacant role create opportunities for other team member to contribute in a different way?
- Are there team members who want to take on new responsibilities?
- What qualities do they want in the new team member?
- What are the reasons for their choices?

Now finalise the new role and candidate qualities:

- Determine whether the replacement will be someone similar or different.
- Identify the qualities that are needed.
- Evaluate how current team members have responded to this review. What does this tell you about the individuals and the state of your team?
- Make final adjustments to the qualities and skills required of the new team member.

Step 2: Assess answers to your interview questions

The challenge of selection interviews is to determine which candidate meets the criteria that you have set. Listen for the use of 'I' or 'we' when each candidate answers questions. People who are used to working in teams often respond to questions in terms of 'we'. This is a good start, but remember, you want to know what attributes the individual will bring with them.

If you hear 'we' in response to your interview questions probe further:

- 'Who are you referring to when you say we?'
- 'What specifically did you do?'
- 'What role did you play?'
- 'What contribution did the other team members make?'

These questions will help you to determine specific capabilities of the person and how they work in a team. It will cause them to explain their relationship with their boss and work colleagues. If the person keeps their answer general and vague, this is not a positive sign.

Consider the following example:

Candidate: 'We implemented a new customer tracking system'.
Manager: 'Who was involved?'
Candidate: 'Oh, my boss and the rest of the team.'

Manager: 'What role did you play?'
Undesirable Candidate Response: 'Um, that's difficult to say, we all worked on it together.'
Desirable Candidate Response: 'I am good at organising people, so I acted as the coordinator. There were eight people working on the project.'

Avoid asking your candidate whether they are a team player because they will most likely answer 'yes' particularly if they know this is a criteria for selection.

Judgment

If a person cannot identify their contribution to a team to which they belonged, beware. It might indicate the lack of substantive contribution to the team effort and outputs. It might also be extreme modesty.

If you hear 'I' statements in response to your questions follow up by asking:

- What contribution did other people make?
- How did you gain acceptance for your idea to be implemented?
- What assistance did you receive from your manager?
- How successful was the project?
- How could you do things differently next time?

'I' statements are not bad in themselves, in fact psychologists encourage the use of 'I' statements because they help a person to 'own' their behaviour. However, if a candidate cannot acknowledge other people's contribution, they may prefer working alone or take credit that is not due.

Step 3: Make the best selection

Review your interview notes or checklist for each candidate. Look for people who can work in a team. Then look for the candidate who was able to do most or all of the following:
- Describe the role they played within the team.
- Give recognition to the contribution of other team members.
- Understand the importance of having clearly defined goals and roles.
- Provide evidence that they have led teams in the past.
- Demonstrate that they were able to gain buy-in from other team members for their ideas.

- Respond to interview questions with specific details of what they had done, not broad generalisations.
- Critique their own and other people's performance in a balanced way.
- Describe how they worked with other team members to solve a problem or make an important decision.
- Show enthusiasm for building on other people's ideas.

The more yes answers you get, the more likely the person will be able to fit into a new team.

Step 4: Introduce the new team member

This is very important in determining how quickly the new person fits in and is accepted. If you are introducing people individually, provide information about each person's role and watch how the introduction goes. Is the reception positive, lukewarm or negative?

Ideally bring the team together for a meeting as soon as practical. Here you can introduce the person. This is the time to restate the group's goals, review everyone's role and discuss any changes to procedures. With a team of five to six people this might only take thirty minutes, but it is time well spent.

You can watch the energy levels of team members increase as this process is completed.

PART 6

Understanding behaviour

A meeting of minds?

I'VE OFTEN SAT IN ON MEETINGS where the manager has stated that he would like a frank and open discussion about the topic of the meeting. I have heard managers say, 'I would like to know what you really think about this.' Do you think the ensuing discussions could be described as frank and open? Not really. A more accurate description would be guarded and limited.

Honest and open communications are often cited by members of work groups when they are compiling a list of desired values to govern their way of working together. But bring those people together in a meeting and this desired value is often missing in action.

In an idyllic world people may be open and honest, but in the imperfect world we live in it is a hard ask that people express themselves openly and honestly.

Here are some of the many reasons (both conscious or sub-conscious) why we don't express ourselves openly and honestly in meetings:

- If I really say what I think, I'll just be seen as negative and obstructing.
- I haven't really got a clue about this. But I'll keep that to myself.
- I think I'll just wait and see where this is going before I commit myself one way or the other.
- I know what is going to put me in the boss's good books. I'll say what I know they want to hear.

- I have no interest in this debate. The decision won't change anything I do. It won't be followed through properly and then it will just disappear.
- I'm not going to embarrass myself in front of the others.
- If I say what I really think the boss will just attack my views so why bother?
- It's obvious what the company policy is here so if I speak against it I'll suffer later.
- I won't say what I really think, but I will say something that makes me look good.
- The decision's been made. We're just going through the motions here.
- I have no strong view either way, but I am happy to go along with whatever the group decides.
- My gut feeling tells me that it is a dumb idea, but I'm not going to oppose it because I haven't really thought it through. If I try and explain why I don't like it, I'll look stupid.
- No-one wants to hear the truth. If I truly say what's on my mind, it will only upset others and I don't want to put up with the tension that creates.
- I know from past experience that if you contradict the boss he doesn't like it. He doesn't handle people challenging his point of view very well.
- I don't know whether this will work or not. I am 100% for it, but if I support this too enthusiastically and it doesn't work too well, that may be held against me.
- I'll try and think of something to say that sounds intelligent.
- If I'm asked to comment, I'll just reinforce what seems to be the popular sentiment.
- I haven't prepared myself for this discussion so I will just formulate some seemingly intelligent questions.
- I've got opinions on this, but I don't really know the facts. I'm not going to show my ignorance in front of others.
- The last time I spoke my real thoughts it was assumed that I was unwilling to go along with the proposal, but I didn't get the chance to explain myself fully. My comments were brought up later out of context and used against me. I'll keep my real thoughts to myself.

If you want to increase the degree of openness and honesty in your meetings, discuss this article with your group at your next meeting.

A rude awakening and what a relief

MANAGEMENT TEXTS TEND TO BE WRITTEN as if people in the workplace behave rationally, maturely and logically. Fortunately, many do. Some don't—which is why we need management texts, I guess. In any workplace, you will find examples of irrational, immature, illogical and downright childish behaviours. And at all levels. Consider the case of Charlie who took over as a supervisor of a group of bulldozer operators after filling the role of work site mechanic. He found going from being one of the boys to a position where he was accountable for their behaviour and performance a tough journey. He found that he had to now contend with a number of incidents.

The following is a sample of the incidents Charlie had to face:

- Allegations by one operator that another operator was taking drugs at work (not substantiated by the accuser), which incensed the accused (regardless of whether he was guilty of the allegation).
- Suspicions that one operator starting his shift was incapable of functioning safely due to excessive alcohol consumption the night before.
- Suggestions that an operator's car had been deliberately set on fire—the car was destroyed.
- Signs of tampering with an operator's lunch box.
- Abusive and obscene language being used over the two-way radio.

- One operator telling another to 'get f…' on five separate occasions in response to five requests to do something that needed to be done.
- Threats involving violence off-site and damage to property made by one operator to another through a third party known to both.
- Deliberately leaving jobs incomplete at handover from one shift to the next.
- Derogatory rumours being started by one operator about another.
- One operator telling another to 'piss off, maggot' in response to a request.
- Spreading lies about what one operator was purported to have said which then riled the other party.

Charlie was beginning to wonder what he had let himself in for and did he want this level of aggravation. Life was a lot less stressful when he was not the supervisor. He was thinking that this supervisor stuff wasn't much fun and feeling a bit overwhelmed by it all.

As part of his development, he attended a supervisory training program along with twenty other participants from a variety of private and public sector work sites. He was a mightily relieved man when he discovered that he was not alone in having to deal with this type of behaviour. Every other supervisor had their own stories to tell of equally disruptive incidents.

It didn't make his problems go away, but he was buoyed to know that his problems—or variations thereof—were commonplace in many work sites. Which is why I write about Charlie's situation so that if you are new to the game you will at least be armed with the knowledge that this happens. And not only to you or, necessarily, because of you.

> Take nothing on its looks; take everything on evidence.
> There's no better rule.
> Charles Dickens (1812–1870), English novelist, *Great Expectations*, 1860
>
> Men might be better if we better deemed of them.
> The worst way to improve the world is to condemn it.
> Philip James Bailey (1816–1902), English poet,
> 'A Mountain Sunrise', *Festus*

If you could only see it my way

W HO'S RIGHT AND WHO'S WRONG? Everybody. How many individual workers in a work group believe that their way of seeing and understanding the workplace is right? All of them. How many workers believe that management's way of seeing and understanding the workplace is more 'right' than their way? Not many, if any.

The same question and answer can also be applied to management in relation to workers. This condition of everybody believing that they are right is a major—the major—cause of frustration, friction, conflict, stress, 'us versus them' positions, damaged relationships and inefficiency in the workplace.

No-one likes to be wrong. It is very uncomfortable. Believing that they are right is something that people hang on to with tenacity. And the fun part is that, with few exceptions, no-one knows what the other person is really thinking—even when they say that they are being forthright and honest. Most of us filter our thoughts and feelings before expressing them. Silence is not compliance.

How do you convince somebody that your view is 'righter' than their view? Simple. Shout at them. If that doesn't work, shout louder and add a couple of personal insults. Maybe throw in a few swear words as well. You think I'm kidding? You're right, I am. But I've met plenty of people who seem to believe that the louder they shout, the more the other person is convinced to their point of view.

For most situations there is a 'best' view. But it is always debatable who holds the 'best' view. The 'best' view will usually, but not always, be a combination of integrated views.

How does a manager change the mindsets of people from a perceived 'wrong' view to a perceived 'right' view? Is it possible? Yes, but it is a real skill. To change people's mindsets, firstly you probably need to accept this concept of everybody believing that their view is right for them and that maintaining being in the right is important for their self-esteem and sense of dignity.

These are some of the things you can focus on. They need to believe that:

- They can trust you.
- You accept the 'rightness' of their view for them.
- You have listened to them and heard what they are saying.
- You understand what it is like to be in their place—what they are thinking and how they are feeling (or in hip speak—walked in their shoes. To which could be added—worn their underpants, gargled with their mouthwash, bathed in their bath, lain in their bed, chewed their fat!).
- You value their opinion and incorporate it in your response.
- You have explained your rationale for your thinking.
- You have clarified any assumptions upon which you have based your view.
- You have provided them with better context.
- You have given them better information and knowledge.
- You have shown them better perspectives and interpretations.
- You will acknowledge it if your view is inaccurate.

Some managers will dismiss the opinions of workers because the worker doesn't fully understand the situation. And if they knew all the facts, they would think otherwise. This is dangerous thinking on the part of the manager. Whatever people perceive about the situation—no matter how ill informed or lacking their perception may be—is the 'fact' of the matter for them.

Mind out!

YOU HAVE A MIND, YET YOU ARE NOT YOUR MIND. Most of us identify ourselves with our mind and behave as though we are our mind. We follow our thoughts and let them rule. We forget we have both our mind and body to fully experience life and instead, our mind can make us fearful and negative.

Collaboration between two eminent scientists, neurophysicist Sir John Eccles, an Australian Nobel prize winner, and quantum physicist Friedrich Beck has shown that we are not our mind and that we control our mind externally from our brain. (See 'Are you using your whole brain?', pp. 186–9.)

We are now being led to the possibility that we are, in essence, spiritual beings with control of our material form. This idea is gradually gaining acceptance—you can choose to accept, reject or remain open to it.

So, would you like to control your mind, instead of it ruling you? Why have we habits that we want to change, yet haven't? Why do we feel one thing, but would prefer to feel differently? How come we'd like to do something else, but haven't? Why does our mind think things we don't want it to?

If you want something different to your mind, then how can you be your mind? And who is dominant—you or your mind? Because you are not your mind, you can learn to control it. Indeed, you have already done so by your positive behaviour.

Some previous instructions you gave your mind have become habits that do not suit the present, and so it is beneficial to question your mind, particularly when stressed.

Controlling your mind is important to experience life fully. In its completeness, your mind is represented by your ego, which you often think is you. Your mind is so powerful that it can be mistaken to be you—yet it is not. This is because you are meant to experience *through* your mind, not *from* it. Your mind must learn to operate under your command!

You know when your mind is in control when you would prefer it not to be so negative. When your mind is being positive, it is under your control. But how should we communicate with it? Firstly *listen* to observe how it influences you. We do not let our mind run on automatic—we give it careful attention. For example, what happens when you make a mistake? Your mind may be automatically critical and judgmental. So, we can notice what our mind is saying and yet remain uninfluenced by its negativity.

Secondly, we direct it with *great questions*. Our mind is perfectly designed to seek answers to questions. For example, instead of letting our mind run its critical program, we could make it stop and ask, 'Okay, what can I learn from this mistake?' Now, instead of criticising, our mind must answer questions.

Great answers come from great questions. So ask your mind great questions. (See 'Standing in your own light', pp. 84–5, for additional questions.)

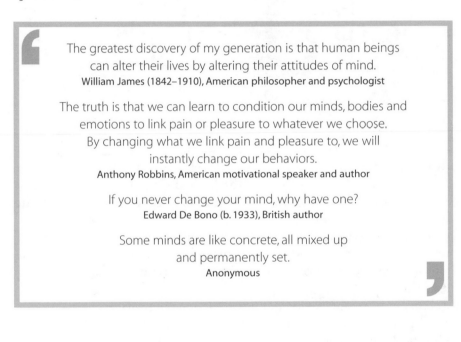

> The greatest discovery of my generation is that human beings can alter their lives by altering their attitudes of mind.
> **William James (1842–1910), American philosopher and psychologist**
>
> The truth is that we can learn to condition our minds, bodies and emotions to link pain or pleasure to whatever we choose. By changing what we link pain and pleasure to, we will instantly change our behaviors.
> **Anthony Robbins, American motivational speaker and author**
>
> If you never change your mind, why have one?
> **Edward De Bono (b. 1933), British author**
>
> Some minds are like concrete, all mixed up and permanently set.
> **Anonymous**

Worth your time

S ELF-ESTEEM AND A POSITIVE SELF IMAGE are largely established well before adulthood. You may ask, 'What can I do, as a manager, to help improve both of these in the limited time that I have with my staff member?' For that matter, is it your job at all to be worrying about developing self-esteem?

Yes, because the research shows that some of the benefits for you will be in the form of better performance, greater staff loyalty, respect, commitment, motivation and morale. This might be worth pursuing after all!

For many people work defines their life. It provides many things missing from their personal life. You may not be able to change their self-esteem, but at least in their workplace, you can show them that they are esteemed.

Managers who look for the positives in their staff really do help with the development of their self-esteem. Some people only need a taste of success to start blossoming. On the other hand, others need some firm foundations built before any growth can take place.

What are the indications that a person may have low self-esteem? Look for behaviours that indicate a perceived lack of selfworth such as:

• Constantly putting themselves down and being self-deprecating.

- Saying, 'I can't do it' without even having attempted the task.
- Refusing to take on new tasks.
- Taking excessive time to complete a task.
- Procrastinating on tasks.
- Holding their head down and avoiding eye contact.
- Making negative comments about things they don't understand.
- Refusing to attend staff functions and making excuses, which you know are not true, about not attending.
- Blaming others for their problems.
- Being overly defensive when an error is pointed out to them.
- Taking any comment about themselves as a personal attack. Unable to cope with anything seen as criticism.
- Being withdrawn in groups.
- Nervous mannerisms, such as constantly rubbing their thumb and forefinger together.
- Being overly critical of others and of events.
- Being overly apologetic and backing down quickly if something they have said contradicts another person's point of view.
- Speaking hesitantly and showing a lack of confidence in their point of view.

For actions to take to assist a person to improve their self-esteem, see 'You can help', pp. 142–3.

> Be a friend to thyself and others will be so, too.
> Thomas Fuller (1608–1661), English author
>
> Shyness has a strange element of narcissism, a belief that how we look, how we perform, is truly important to other people.
> André Dubus (1936–1999), American author, *Broken Vessels*, David R. Godine, 1991
>
> Happiness hates the timid! So does science!
> Eugene O'Neill (1888–1953), American playwright, *Strange Interlude*, 1927
>
> What is this self inside us, this silent observer,
> Severe and speechless critic, who can terrorise us,
> And urge us to futile activity,
> And in the end, judge us still more severely
> For the errors into which his own reproaches drove us?
> TS Eliot (1888–1865), American poet, critic and playwright,
> *The Elder Statesman*, Faber and Faber, 1958

Are you using your whole brain?

YOUR BRAIN CONTROLS YOUR MIND AND BODY. Your ability to use your whole brain is a key factor in maximising your life experience. Let's look at some useful facts.

Evolution of the human brain

1. The reptilian brain evolved first and is common in reptiles and mammals. It cannot think (noncognitive, non-verbal, nonlinear, non-logical, no sense of time) and acts instinctively. It is responsible for movement, basic body functions and survival.
2. The paleomammalian brain evolved next and is present in all mammals. It cannot think and is responsible for emotions and long-term memories.
3. The neocortex evolved last and is still evolving. It is most developed in humans. The neocortex is cognitive—capable of abstract thinking, creation and innovation. It is split into two hemispheres, right and left. The left hemisphere is responsible for reasoning and speech while the right hemisphere is responsible for receiving input from the lower parts, intuition, creation and the 'big picture'.

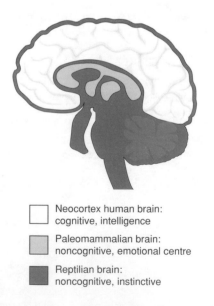

Neocortex human brain:
cognitive, intelligence

Paleomammalian brain:
noncognitive, emotional centre

Reptilian brain:
noncognitive, instinctive

Figure 6.5 The three parts of the human brain

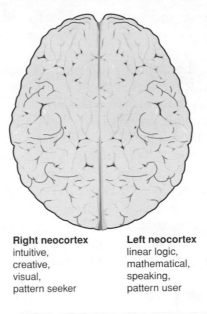

Right neocortex
intuitive,
creative,
visual,
pattern seeker

Left neocortex
linear logic,
mathematical,
speaking,
pattern user

Figure 6.6 The two hemispheres of the brain

What do you (your ego) favour?

When in survival mode, you are dominated by fear/anger—your reptilian brain is dominant. You are not thinking. When other emotions are triggered, old beliefs (many less than useful) are operating and you are dominated by the paleomammalian brain. You are also not thinking! When you are purely logical, you (ego) are being dominated by the left brain—ethics and others are not an issue. When you are purely creative and intuitive, you are not being logical and are right-brain dominated.

We use some parts of our mind more than others and this leads to dominance, which causes us to respond in more limited predictable patterns. Ideally, you will use your entire brain creating synergy between the parts.

Herrmann's whole brain model

Ned Herrmann developed a model showing the four dominant trends in brain use (see figure 6.7). Understanding these will help you to get more out of the functioning of your brain.

You can train your brain to be more balanced by 'cross-crawling' exercises—crossing your right and left limbs, causing both sides of your brain to function.

Finally consider this: Nobel prize-winning neurophysicist Sir John Eccles provided evidence that each human brain is controlled by its individual self which resides beyond the quantum threshold and not in the three brains defined by Paul MacLean (*The Tribune Brain in Evolution*, Plenum Press, 1990).

In his book, *How the Self Controls its Brain* (Springer-Verlag, 1994), Eccles demonstrates how human will emanates from quantum activity which he and quantum physicist Friedrich Beck trace to three of the six layers (laminae) in the human neocortex.

So, the self that I am and the self that you are are sourced beyond the ten per cent of baryonic matter, which we call reality. It is part of the ninety per cent of the universe of which we know very little.

Consider this: as discussed above, the physical brain has its three levels—the reptilian brain, the paleomammalian brain and the neocortex. The non-physical, ever-present fourth element is the self, emanating from quantum thresholds (similar to a movie director). At

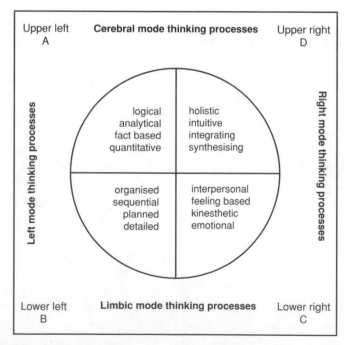

Figure 6.7 Whole brain model

the level of essence, the self is who we are individually and it is connected to the entire universe in an incomprehensible (for now) way. Scientifically, we don't know what lies beyond the quantum threshold. (Adapted from *The Creative Brain*, Ned Herrmann, Brain Books, 1988 and *Journal of Scientific Exploration*, 11:1, Spring 1997.)

> The intuitive mind is a sacred gift and the rational mind is a faithful servant. We have created a society that honours the servant and has forgotten the gift.
> Albert Einstein (1879–1955), German-born physicist
>
> If the brain were so simple we could understand it, we would be so simple we couldn't.
> Lyall Watson (b. 1939), South African anthropologist and philosopher

Beware, human beings at work

CONTENTIOUS ISSUES WILL OCCUR in every work group. It is the human condition at work—the foibles of human nature.

Here are some observations about the human condition in the workplace. You could use these to have an interesting discussion with your group to raise the collective consciousness about working in harmony:

☐ Every person in this group believes, of themselves, that they do a good job.

☐ Every person in this group believes that their personal style works for them. Every person believes that their approach is the 'best' approach for them.

☐ Each person can identify things that other people do which they wish they didn't.

☐ Not one of us is perfect. Each of us has personality characteristics that engage and disengage other people. Each one of us has things we do well and things we could do better. Each one of us has assets and liabilities to our personality, to our style and to our approach to workplace relationships.

☐ As much as we might try to hide our liabilities, they are evident to those with whom we work. In addition, all of us have our 'blind spots'—things about us that are known to others, but unknown to ourselves. Mostly, we act with good intentions but sometimes it is our execution that will let us down and diminishes our effectiveness. But we are not best placed to experience our execution first hand. It is the people with whom we work who experience our execution first hand. They are better placed to raise our awareness of when, and how, our execution is ineffectual. But some people would rather not know, than know.

☐ We act in good faith according to how we perceive things and according to the demands and pressures on us. Mostly, we do not maliciously set out to make life harder for others.

☐ We are not going to like all the people we have to work with, but when we are smart we can work out ways to work with the strengths and weaknesses of others. Relationships are a two-way street—each person is responsible for their fifty per cent of the relationship.

- [ ] Most people find it easier to criticise others than to accept criticism of themselves.
- [ ] All of us have the right to be treated with dignity even if some things we do are not liked by others.
- [ ] People have differing levels of self-awareness—from the very aware to the very unaware. I can't change or modify anything about myself until I become aware of it and how it affects other people.
- [ ] Criticism of only specific parts of a person's whole make-up and performance is unfair, unbalanced, irresponsible and likely to be counterproductive to what you think that you are achieving.
- [ ] Acknowledgment is a powerful act in reconciling the differences between two parties at odds with each other. It takes strength and courage to acknowledge that I may have got some things wrong in the past or my behaviour was inappropriate or counterproductive.
- [ ] Our behaviour is dictated by our perceptions which are based on:
  – our personal set of values,
  – our awareness of the context surrounding an issue,
  – the information/knowledge we possess about the issue,
  – the perspectives we choose to take about the issue,
  – the interpretations we choose to make about the issue,
  and all of the above are 'correct' or 'right' for each of us.
- [ ] All of our individual perspectives and interpretations make perfect sense to the person who holds and acts on those perspectives and interpretations.
- [ ] Each one of us does the best they can according to their operating belief system at that moment in time. I may not agree with your beliefs about the situation or I may think that your beliefs are limiting, but the reality is that you behave and function according to your beliefs, not my beliefs.
- [ ] It helps if our goal is to find the 'best' argument not to win the argument.
- [ ] In the resolution of every contentious issue, there can be other goals beyond the achievement of the obvious goal, i.e. in relation to relationships, sense of dignity, desire to work in concert with the other, mutual respect and trust, level of job satisfaction, enjoyment, etc.

☐ In the settlement of contentious issues, it helps if we can accommodate or incorporate, at least to some degree, the needs and wants and personal style of the other.

☐ Reflect on your last approach to a contentious issue. Was it to win the argument, to get it done your way, to score the point and ignore the consequences for others? Or was it to look for accommodation of needs and styles of others with your needs and style?

☐ Do you believe that the consequences on the relationship, the way the other person feels, the degree of cooperation you will get, the impact on the quality of work life and the impact on the person's dignity are as important as winning the argument? And does your intellectual belief transfer into your behaviour? What's more important? The goal? The journey? Or both the goal and the journey? When entering into a conversation about a contentious issue, what is your goal?

☐ It will sometimes pay us well to concede ground even when we know absolutely that we are right. But it is very hard to do. It is painful working with someone who is always right—in their mind.

☐ At any given moment in any contentious issue, each one of you is 'right' in your mind.

☐ No-one is expecting any of us to change who we are, but a focus on working to our assets, minimising our liabilities, operating with an awareness of the needs and rights of the other person will enhance the quality of work life for all. Importantly, it sets the tone for the rest of the work force.

☐ What we put out, we get back.

☐ Many people, when reading this article, will relate these points to others but not to themselves.

☐ Resolution of conflict, tension or damaged relationships becomes much easier if both people can let go of their egos and when they can let go of needing to be 'right'.

Food for thought: as I heard on the radio one day, if you don't like the harvest you are reaping, look at the seeds you are sowing. And as Abraham Lincoln once said, 'A man convinced against his will is of the same opinion still.'

> Good humour makes all things tolerable.
> **Henry Ward Beecher (1813–1887), American clergyman,**
> *Proverbs from Plymouth Pulpit*, compiled by William Drysdale, 1887

> Everyone thinks his sack is heaviest.
> **George Herbert (1593–1633), English clergyman and poet**

> Courtesy on one side only last not long.
> **George Herbert (1593–1633), English clergyman and poet**

> Mankind is made up of inconsistencies and no man acts invariably up to his predominant character. The wisest man sometimes acts weakly, and the weakest sometimes wisely.
> **Philip Stanhope (1694–1773), English Secretary of State,**
> **Letters from Lord Chesterfield to his son**

PART 7

Implementing change and improvement

Desirable attitudes come first

ORGANISATIONS ARE 'CHANGING', mostly due to undesirable statistical evidence, such as skewed profit-to-cost ratios. Sometimes it's a 'feeling', fuelled by low morale, staff turnover, encroaching competition and customer dissatisfaction. Prevailing rationale is 'bottom-line' focused.

Back in 65 AD, the Roman Petronius said, 'We tend to meet any new situation by reorganising; a wonderful method it can be for creating the illusion of progress while producing confusion, inefficiency and demoralisation'. In 1988, corporate USA spent US$48 billion on change management. And yet, a survey of 3300 executives and HR professionals, who had participated, believed only fifteen per cent of the investment was effective (R Lebow, Washington *CEO* magazine).

What happens is simply this: Costs are escalating, staff and clients are leaving, so let's make changes. In fact, let's trim all the fat! Immediately the figures improve, but staff become fearful of further down-sizing. Stress is rampant, survival paramount. Nobody is happy.

Sound familiar? What can we learn? Firstly, acknowledge that people are most important. People's attitude is the primary determinant of performance. People design and manipulate the processes and policies. Attitudinally competent people can better design and operate functional structures and systems.

So, let's get the people sorted. Then we can utilise them to improve the organisation because they have ownership and a positive attitude.

What about improving people's attitude?

- Treat the 'baggage'—those unspoken beliefs that hinder performance. Don't say, 'That's too hard!' or 'That's a personal issue'. You're kidding yourself—it's the *primary* problem in the company!
- Communicate all aspects of the company to all members. Uninformed people cannot be expected to make appropriate decisions. Informed people are more compelled to take appropriate action. If you don't believe that, see if you can change your belief!
- Ensure everybody knows the answers to these questions, operates from that knowledge and takes responsibility for the consequences of their choices:
  1. Who are we?
  2. What do we do?
  3. What don't we do?

4. Where are we headed in the future?
5. What are our immediate priorities?
6. What values govern our relationships?
7. What is my function and its relationship to the organisation and its purpose?
8. What is expected of me, and what is the most effective way to deliver those expectations?
9. How can I improve, and with whom should I interact to ensure improvements are accomplished congruent with the organisation?
10. To whom am I responsible and what is available to support me and communicate my progress? (From Peter R Scholtes, *The Leader's Handbook*, McGraw-Hill, 1998)

Leaders who don't provide these answers risk being incompetent. Team members who don't discover and abide by the answers risk being incompetent. Anyone who tolerates these issues is fearful, perhaps dysfunctional, and probably incompetent.

• Use a coaching system throughout the organisation. No champion in any field of endeavour ever got there without a coach, whose role is to observe. Our own eyes are made for looking externally and it's difficult to observe ourselves in action. An internal coaching system can be established that optimises external input.

If you attend to these issues first, the entire structure can improve concurrently and more effectively via *systems modelling*. Your investment in organisational improvement is ensured! You won't have to focus on the bottom-line—it is able to look after itself. You'll also discover there are enthusiastic coaches who specialise in facilitating organisations in achieving these objectives.

> Open your arms to change, but don't let go of your values.
> His Holiness, the Fourteenth Dalai Lama, 2000
>
> There is no master without a coach and no coach without a master.
> David Deane-Spread, contributing author,
> *You Lead, They'll Follow* Volume 3

Management by myth

I WAS ONCE ATTENDING A LECTURE ON MANAGEMENT by an eminent professor who had stated that such and such a concept was a myth. He then looked directly at me and asked, 'Do you understand that this is a myth?' Startled from my daydream I said 'Yeth.' As in wider society, there are a number of myths masquerading as truths that wander around the workplace.

Myth number one

'This (whatever the initiative or program is) won't work unless top management supports it.' I have heard this expression or variations of it numerous times when management have attempted to introduce some new initiative or program throughout the organisation.

This is a cop out. There is no doubt that the initiative will probably work better if top management do their bit. But the reality is that they seldom do actively support the initiative. Not because they are wanting to sabotage it, but because they are preoccupied with other demands on their time. And even if there are more sinister reasons why they are not doing their bit, it still doesn't matter.

You can still implement the initiative or variations of it with your work group. Cover yourself by explaining to your manager that you will be giving the initiative a high priority and that some other things (provide examples) will drop down in priority.

Myth number two

'We have to get maximum return on investment for shareholders.' This is the mantra of the boards of management and subsequently the executive management team. It is continuously cited as the driving force behind policy and strategy and for 'restructuring'. ('Restructuring' itself is an interesting term. It is a term used by politicians, executive management, management consultants and academics. It is not a term used by the work force. In the minds of the work force, restructuring simply translates as people losing jobs.)

Yes, the value of the organisation needs to be maintained and improved. Yes, the value of the shares needs to be kept healthy. But the shareholders are also members of the wider community and are subject to, either directly or indirectly, the widespread ramifications of the ways in which organisations operate. As organisations, especially the large corporations, conduct their business they impact on the social fabric of society and on the health of the biosphere on which we all depend for survival. No-one is immune from the policy and strategic decisions of the larger organisations that are based primarily on short-term material gain—on maximising return on investment for shareholders.

When profit is threatened, the easiest and simplest (but short-sighted) response is to cut costs by reducing the work force.

I recently came across a refreshing instance where the normal response to cutting costs in a depressed market—reduce the number of employees—was not chosen. The Legian Hotel at Seminyak in Bali was hit by a huge downturn in occupancy with the double whammy of the Bali bombings and SARS. The Indonesian owner would have been sorely tempted to cut staff drastically. He didn't. He has continued to employ all staff. Now there may be other contributing factors, such as the quality of training, but I wonder if there is a coincidence that the level of service is outstanding—the best I have experienced in twenty-five years of staying in some excellent hotels around the world.

In the interests of maintaining law and order in the societies of which they are part, shareholders may have to accept less returns on their investment. This would enable some funds now allocated as profits to be diverted into initiatives to improve performance and to maintain employment. Don't hold your breath waiting for this to happen. Meanwhile, the gap between rich and poor continues to widen as the crime rate escalates. Social problems caused by job loss continue to increase. The environment that supports life that we have polluted and destroyed for so long continues to deteriorate. And without getting too carried away, history shows us that you can oppress people through fear for only so long.

Dunphy et al. in *Organisational Change for Corporate Sustainability* (Routledge 2003) states, 'Shareholders must encourage organisations to ensure that their "return on their investment" also includes the organisations becoming major contributors to sustainability rather than social and environmental predators undermining a world fit to live in ... to ensure that all corporations are instruments of a broader social purpose than the generation of short-term wealth for shareholders—it is vital that corporations make profits—but not at the cost of destroying the future viability of society and the planet.'

Threat or opportunity?

COMMUNITIES EVERYWHERE ARE DEMANDING INVOLVEMENT in the processes and projects that are affecting their environment. We need look no further than the demise of the Berlin Wall or the change of government in the Philippines. People power abounds.

The catchcry all over the world and particularly in democratic countries such as Australia and the USA, is 'community engagement'.

Community engagement is about two-way communication, and the standards documentation strongly advocates, 'communication and consultation involve a two-way dialogue between stakeholders with efforts focused on consultation rather than a one-way flow of information from the decision maker to other stakeholders' (AS/NZA 4360: 1999 Risk Management).

Ignore this dimension to any project at your peril—address it poorly and the cost in terms of resources, particularly time and money, escalates. Conduct the process well and the benefits are massive in terms of outcomes, trust, image, and organisational and personal kudos.

Successful community engagement is about creating a win–win situation. Some key strategies exist to ensure this win–win situation and these are as follows:

Start early

- Recognise the need for community engagement early in a project.
- Build this dimension into your concepts, estimates and timelines.
- Collect information on various approaches, community leaders, specialists including public relations, and media helpers.
- Create an environment of trust in your community—clearly show and demonstrate that you are seeking and will, as far as is reasonable, act on community opinion.

Build your team

Teamwork is critical in engaging the community—you will need those who can design the engagement plan and those who can work on the plan—the technicians, the media, marketing, facilitators and worker bees. Remember, it is fine to say build an information display but someone has to put the thing up and pull it down.

Define the objective

What are we trying to achieve by engaging the community? Is it education, consultation or information? Or what? The community engagement ladder (Nolan, ITU, 2002) helps us define this: empower, partner, involve, consult, inform, influence. A mix of these strategies works well.

Selecting the strategies

- Understand the audience.
- Define your messages.
- Decide what delivery means you are going to use for these messages—TV, web, brochures.
- Work out your timeframes—remember, brochures have to be printed.
- Agree who is doing what in your team.

Underway

- Manage the activities carefully—sign off on each activity when completed.
- Expect the unexpected.
- Deal with the feedback thoroughly—people do not like to be forgotten.
- Organise the data—every piece is important and needs to have a place in this giant jigsaw.

Making sense of it

- What does it all mean? Report with rigour. The decision makers need to have the results presented clearly, concisely and accurately.
- How did you perform? Ensure that the process has been measured. Examples include percentage response rates and milestone checks.

An underlying philosophy

One successful project manager in Western Australia, after the introduction of an improved water treatment plant in Perth, on community engagement, summarises: 'Project leaders need to demonstrate consistent and continual presence in the community dimension—you, and not the consultant, are the face of the project and you need to show that face.'

The same old same old

STIFLING CREATIVITY...

NOW, BRING THE STICK TO ME, STUPID!.....

RIGHT...ALL YOU GET IS A DUMB STARE WITH MY HEAD ON ONE SIDE, CLEVER-DICK!

How do you transform an organisation, a department, a section or a work group? How do you create a culture that is empowered, future orientated, challenges current assumptions and beliefs about how to be better at what we do, is adaptive, creative, innovative, faster to respond to changing circumstances, moving with or ahead of the times? Buggered if I know. No, just joshing.

What is a good starting place for change/transformation? People's perceptions. Why? Because change/transformation requires people to adopt new or better behaviours—it requires a change in current behaviour. And, as we have pointed out many times, people's perceptions are a huge influence on their behaviour. So if you want to change your people, change their perceptions.

If you accept our premise that values/beliefs underlie perceptions and perceptions are based on context, information/knowledge, perspectives and interpretations, then you have a framework for change/transformation.

Here is a process that managers can use with their work groups. As an example let's say that you want to develop a more creative and innovative culture within your work group. Ask each person to write responses to all or any of the questions below. Bring the group together as a whole or in two halves to discuss their responses.

Values/beliefs

- [ ] What is it about being more creative and innovative that you would value?
- [ ] Why is it important that we apply more creativity and innovation as a work group?
- [ ] What do you believe about creativity and innovation in our workplace?
- [ ] Why is it important to you?
- [ ] How would we benefit? How would others benefit?

Context

- [ ] What's the 'big picture' here? The background? The rationale? The motives? The purpose? The changing circumstances? The needs? The contributing factors? The underlying forces? The new threats and opportunities?
- [ ] What are the connections between creativity and innovation, and productivity and the quality of our work life?
- [ ] What blockages would need to be overcome? What currently works against creativity and innovation? What training would we need? What support would we need both internally and externally?
- [ ] How would we have to think and act differently? What are the ramifications for us and others of being creative and innovative?

Information/knowledge

- [ ] What information or knowledge can you present to the group about creativity and innovation?
- [ ] What information/knowledge do we need to be more creative and innovative?
- [ ] In what areas and in what ways could we be more innovative/creative?
- [ ] What are the things that we do that would improve if we were to adopt a more creative and innovative approach?

Perspectives

- [ ] What are your current perspectives about the issue of creativity and innovation?

☐ What are the possible negative perspectives that people might hold?
☐ What are the possible positive perspectives that people might hold?
☐ What perspectives might need to be changed?
☐ What are the perspectives we need to take?

Interpretations

☐ What is your interpretation of creativity and innovation as applied to our work group?
☐ What interpretations are holding us back?
☐ What interpretations do we need to take?

Once this discussion has been held and everybody has contributed, meet again to agree actions we will now take to become more creative and innovative. See 'Create or perish' on the following page to help you with the next part of the process.

> Every man of genius sees the world at a different angle from his fellows.
> Havelock Ellis (1859–1939), English psychologist and author, *The Dance of Life*
>
> If you do not expect the unexpected, you will not find it.
> Heraclitus (535?–475? BC), Greek philosopher, *Fragments*, c. 500 BC

Create or perish

WOULD YOU LIKE YOUR PEOPLE TO SHOW a little more creativity and innovation in the way that they go about their work? There are many benefits to be gained for you, your people, your products and services, your customers, your market share, etc. by taking a focused look at increasing creativity and innovation in your work group.

Now before you start rushing around drunk on the idea of creativity and innovation, step back a moment and reflect. Consider the environment in which your group works. Is it an environment that encourages or blocks creativity and innovation? Is your own style—perceived in the eyes of your work group—one that encourages or blocks creativity and innovation? If 'fear and intimidation' are the key cornerstones of your leadership style, forget it. Okay, now that you have sobered up a little, here are some guidelines for increasing creativity and innovation within your work group.

Use these to stimulate discussion and to agree what needs to happen collectively and individually:

- ☐ Agree what is meant by creativity and innovation.
- ☐ Network with other areas and business units within the organisation to find out what they are doing which is creative and innovative.
- ☐ Identify specific practices that could be done in more creative and innovative ways.
- ☐ Encourage your team members to try different ways of doing things.
- ☐ Acknowledge and praise staff who are innovative and creative.
- ☐ Identify the possible risks from being creative or innovative.
- ☐ Discuss the benefits of being creative and innovative.
- ☐ Research new innovations in areas similar to that of your work area.
- ☐ Identify and discuss which things you do as a work group that could be done better.
- ☐ Take risks where the consequences of failure will not adversely affect the work that you do.

☐ Explain the benefits of ideas you have which you would like to implement.

☐ Allocate one hour each month to meet to discuss better ways to do things.

☐ Research, read and apply creative-thinking techniques.

☐ Look at a problem from the angle of 'how can we solve it?' rather than 'why it can't be done', i.e. think positively.

☐ Celebrate the successful implementation of new initiatives.

☐ Encourage ideas from 'out of left field'.

☐ Discuss and suggest new, different and better ways to do things.

☐ Consider the ramifications of new ways of doing things on all stakeholders.

☐ Implement ideas that are creative and innovative.

☐ Follow through on creative and innovative ideas to ensure that they are implemented.

☐ Provide training to ensure that all are capable and motivated to implement creative and innovative ideas.

☐ Brainstorm creative and innovative ways of solving problems or doing things better and then identify what needs to be done to implement each suggestion.

☐ Initiate actions to get management support for creativity and innovation.

☐ Identify and modify/eliminate blockages to creativity and innovation.

☐ Investigate what things your competitors or other organisations providing similar services are doing which are creative and innovative.

One way to start this discussion is to get your group to conduct a 'gap analysis' on the above items. Ask each person to rate the importance (I) of each item and then rate how effectively (E) they currently do this. Use a scale from 1 to 5 (1 being of low importance/effectiveness and 5 being of high importance/effectiveness). The gap (G) is I minus E. Total all gap scores and then get the group to focus on the highest gap scores. Ask the question, 'What can we do to move forward on this issue?'.

Never kill an idea, just deflect it.
3M company saying

Nothing is more dangerous than an idea
when it is the only one you have.
Emile Chartier (Alain) (1868–1951), French philosopher and essayist

New ideas are not born in a conforming environment.
Roger von Oech, American author, Founder and President of Creative Think,
A Whack on the Side of the Head, Warner, 1983

An innovator is not an opponent of the old;
he is a proponent of the new.
Lyle E Schaller, American priest and author,
The Change Agent, Abingdon, 1972

The amount a person uses his imagination is inversely proportional
to the amount of punishment he will receive for using it.
Anonymous participant, Roger von Oech, American author, Founder and
President of Creative Think, *A Whack on the Side of the Head*, Warner, 1983

Many of those who were ahead of their time had to wait
for it in not too comfortable circumstances.
Stanislaw J Lec (1909–1966), Polish writer and aphorist,
Unkempt Thoughts, St Martin's Press, 1962

The quality revolution

THE NEXT NINE ARTICLES ARE BASED on over twenty years experience in the creation and development of successful ideas management systems in major organisations. One such program has been successfully generating valuable ideas for over twenty years and has won several international awards from Europe, USA and the Middle East.

Cost benefits arising from these programs run into many millions of US dollars. However, the greatest advantage for introducing such programs is their positive impact on overall business culture.

In today's global business environment survival (let alone prosperity) will increasingly depend on the ability of organisations to implement continuous, rapid change more efficiently and comprehensively than their competitors.

Clearly management cannot just hope that such a situation will somehow evolve, it must create an environment that is conducive to change and which actively encourages everyone to get involved in a dynamic process of continuous improvement.

The quality revolution: today's competitive advantage—tomorrow's run of the mill

The Japanese have taught the consumers of the world that quality products and services (at a reasonable price) are an entitlement. To survive in this environment, organisations must learn to harness the full potential of their intellectual capability.

The dearth of products and services following the Second World War enabled manufacturers and service providers to focus entirely on volume. Product and service quality were irrelevant issues because people were queuing up to purchase just about everything.

This of course all changed in the late sixties, seventies and eighties when the Japanese took the world by storm through their ability to incorporate quality into mass-produced goods. The paradigm that quality and reliability must carry a high price (as with a Rolls-Royce or Rolex) was completely eradicated by organisations, such as Toyota, Nissan, Seiko, Sony and many others. For the first time in history, products of quality and reliability were accessible to us all.

The initial response from Western manufacturers was to wave the patriotic banner, 'Buy American/British/Australian/etc. Let's keep our own people employed.' But customers stubbornly demonstrated a preference for quality products and even slashed prices failed to dislodge their Japanese preference. The quality of Japanese goods remained unassailable for many years resulting in the decline and eventual fall of many global-name organisations.

Eventually (and it took over two decades), Western manufacturers were forced to acknowledge two alternatives: either embrace quality and reliability into their design and manufacturing processes, or go broke. Some were successful, many were not. Ironically, the Japanese learned their quality management skills from an American, James Edward Deming, whose philosophy was repeatedly derided by USA manufacturers, but that's another story.

The quality gap no longer exists. Having seized and fully exploited a once-in-a-lifetime opportunity, the Japanese are back on a level-playing field. Quality and reliability have taken a back seat to quality at a reduced price (from China, India, etc.). Innovation and creative design also offer a major differentiating advantage. Quality is no longer an exception, rather an expectation. Ask yourself, who in today's world would purchase a car or television set with an unreliable reputation?

Arguably, the altruistic Japanese management culture is more conducive to the incorporation of care and pride into the manufacturing processes. On the other hand, many Western organisations have demonstrated an incredible ability to respond through the implementation of effective quality management systems. It is also worthy of note that the Japanese have themselves turned to quality management systems to reinforce their formidable quality reputation.

This is proof (if proof were needed) of the importance of selecting and incorporating the right systems into an organisation. Prior to the late eighties, quality management systems were virtually unheard of. In today's environment it would be very difficult for any organisation to compete without some form of quality management system.

Without a formal system to manage a specific area of activity things are just left to chance, which leaves the door open for your competitors. The question is, therefore, what systems should organisations be considering now to provide a competitive edge for tomorrow?

Systems that raise the capability of an organisation to identify the need for change and thereafter quickly respond must surely be worthy of close consideration. The following articles relate to one such approach.

> There's a saying in the USA that the customer is king.
> But in Japan the customer is God.
> Tak Kimoto Sumitomo Inc.

Are they worth the effort?

KNOWLEDGE AND CREATIVE TALENT exists in abundance within every organisation. Management is failing in its duty if it is unable to harvest these attributes for the benefit of the business. Mention 'suggestion or ideas management systems' to many senior executives and watch their eyes glaze as they attempt to suppress a yawn and strike up a more stimulating conversation with the nearest potted plant.

On the other hand, ask the same executives if they would like to run an organisation where everyone enthusiastically and constantly seeks to improve all aspects of business activity, and only control freaks and fools would decline the offer.

Suggestion systems have been around for a very long time and it is fair to say they have not established a great reputation. There are a number of reasons for this and I will discuss these later, but for the moment let us consider why it is more important than ever to create an environment that forces management to listen to the voice of its people.

Clearly the demands on management are greater than ever, as is the complexity of business. Long hours, longer faces and much longing for early retirement are common features within many organisations these days. Most managers will readily acknowledge that they should be giving far more time to aspects of people value, encouragement, development and reward, not to mention the allocation of time for continuous business improvement.

Organisations have been forced to consistently downsize and we will never return to the days when time and resources were available for issues of a 'non-essential' nature. The crunch, therefore, is to identify initiatives that will provide the basis for improving employee and customer satisfaction levels, encouraging a culture of continuous change (improvement) and removing some of the burden from an overstretched management team.

For many, suggestion schemes conjure images of little boxes filled with derogative comments about the boss. In fact if the boss really believes and expects that the installation of a few boxes will open up a realistic, creative dialogue with his people, then he's possibly worthy of the comments contained.

As we all know there is no such thing as a quick fix particularly if it's fixing boxes on walls. If an organisation is serious about listening and learning with, and from, its people it must demonstrate respect for their creative input and also offer appropriate recognition and reward for their engagement.

Management must surely recognise that the employees of today are more educated and better informed than ever before. The reserve of untapped talent within most organisations can, if utilised, deliver incredible benefits. Equally, the motivational influence for people receiving formal recognition (possibly for the first time) can be infectious leading to a positive and rapid change in business culture.

A formal ideas management system will enable management to devolve the responsibility for detailed aspects of continuous improvement whilst also ensuring that people are consistently encouraged to participate and receive recognition for creative input.

Talent denied the opportunity of expression is without value. I once read of a child, rescued from the slums of Brazil, who became a famous solo violinist. The musical talent was inherent but without access to a musical instrument it may never have been detected. Similarly, an ideas management system provides an instrument to enable talent to be displayed and formally acknowledged.

> All that is comes from the mind; it is based on the mind,
> it is fashioned by the mind.
> The Pali Canon

What benefits will ensue?

THE FACT THAT A BUSINESS INCORPORATES a formal system for encouraging, recognising and rewarding positive behaviour says a great deal about the maturity of that business. It tells clients and customers that management understands the vital importance of engaging its front-line people in improving the products and services that are designed to fulfil their requirements. It tells employees that they matter a great deal and that management acknowledges the true value of their contribution to the success of the business.

The benefits that can, and should, ensue from the introduction of a well-structured ideas management system will include, but are not limited to, the following:

- foundation for a continuous improvement culture
- substantial cost savings
- reduced waste/scrap
- improved productivity
- improved safety awareness/hazard removal
- improved management attitudes (respect for the ideas of others)
- improved recruitment (selection of positive/creative people)
- improved procurement (seeking alternative materials/suppliers)
- improved (simplified) working methods
- energy savings (judicious usage/alternatives)
- space savings (modified layouts/improved flow)
- improved environmental awareness (examine aspects/impacts)
- improved customer relationships (direct feedback and correction)
- improved teamwork (our business versus their business)
- better housekeeping
- enhanced feelings of value (recognition/reward/value)
- better interdepartmental relationships
- more relaxed working environment
- improved employee relationships
- improved first line supervisor performance
- improved attitude to change
- better place to work
- better ability to attract and retain talent
- better ability to identify and respond to threats and opportunities
- better communication flowing up from the people at the 'coal face' to the people making policy and strategy.

'Will it also make us vastly wealthy and irresistible to the opposite sex?' Well, who knows, it just might.

A formal ideas management system is no different to any other management system (finance, accounts, sales, quality, environmental, safety, etc.). The argument for its existence or level of priority within an organisation will invariably be decided by the attitude of executive management or, more specifically, the woman or man in the top job.

As the old saying goes, 'what interests my boss fascinates me', and if the concept of an ideas management system is not regarded as a priority issue at the top, then it is better left on the shelf, along with the many other useful tools that have produced remarkable results for other organisations.

To be successful, an ideas management system must be sought for the right reasons with the end clearly in mind. My interpretation of that end would be an organisation that relishes and seeks change for the better at all levels, within all disciplines, at all times.

To summarise, the advantages for incorporating a successful ideas management system into the culture of an organisation represent a major business advantage that is difficult for any competitor to emulate. That said, the business world is littered with the remnants of many such systems that failed to deliver what was promised.

In the next article I will discuss the reasons why most ideas management systems fail and also identify the hurdles that must be faced to achieve success.

> It is the responsibility of the leadership and the management
> to give opportunities and put demands on people
> which enable them to grow as human beings
> in their work environment.
> Sir John Harvey Jones (b. 1924), English businessman

What are the pitfalls?

GREAT CONCEPTS ONLY ACHIEVE GREAT RESULTS through great application. And all applications require the overcoming of obstacles and hurdles.

In my experience major change programs are undertaken for four reasons:

1. The business is facing a desperate crisis and is forced to 'do something'.
2. A clear identification of need based on a systematic analysis of strengths, weaknesses, opportunities and threats.
3. A fear of being left behind because company X, Y and Z are doing it.
4. The silken tongue of a polished consultant who promises the earth and usually ends up costing it also.

I will not speculate on which of the reasons is the most common but as you would expect, the chances of achieving success are much better when alternatives one and two are prevalent.

Necessity is truly the mother of invention and the need for survival unites and galvanises people to do extraordinary things. Additionally, when an organisation is clear about its needs and what it must do to satisfy those needs, it stands every chance of making a difficult change program work successfully.

When the need for change is perceived out of a fad or in a half-committed manner it usually does more harm than good. When the need for change is not conceived as a priority from within the business but rather is imposed as an external 'nice to have', such initiatives invariably fail.

It has been reported that ninety-five per cent of total quality management (TQM) initiatives fail to produce the expected results. When such initiatives do fail they leave major stumbling blocks for any later actions that may in fact be essential for business survival. The question that should be asked is, 'What did the five per cent of businesses do to achieve success?'

Areas of predictable resistance

When attempting to install an ideas management system it is important to expect and prepare for a great deal of resistance. This may be overt or covert in nature, but it will exist in some form in every organisation.

The underlying causes for resistance will include:

- Experience with previous (similar) programs that failed.
- Managers and first-line supervisors might interpret that they are being bypassed or that their authority/control is being usurped.
- A view that employees have nothing useful to contribute.
- Trade union representatives may fear a ploy to erode their power/status.
- Some senior and middle managers may interpret it as a 'soft' option and a waste of their time.
- Some managers may perceive that the system will be used to introduce uncontrolled and unapproved changes.

Resistance should not be seen as a reason for dismissing an ideas management system—few things worthwhile are easy. It is vital, however, to anticipate resistance and then identify the ingredients for success. This will be discussed further in 'What are the main ingredients for success?' on the following page.

In summary, just about all well-conceived and well-managed business improvement initiatives are capable of delivering results. Like most things in life, however, the results will be dependent on the degree of energy, tenacity and ability of the initiators.

> It's crazy to blame the piano if the student refuses to dedicate the necessary time and effort to master the instrument.
> Glyn Ashley, contributing author, *You Lead, They'll Follow* Volume 3

What are the main ingredients for success?

FROM LONG EXPERIENCE, we have found that there are seven main requirements for the successful implementation of an ideas management system.

Top-level commitment

Unless management is absolutely convinced of the benefits that will ensue as a result of implementing a successful ideas management system, it is possibly better to leave the concept on the shelf. A half-hearted, insincere approach will produce a half-baked system and half-measured reaction from everyone concerned.

A suitable change champion

Possibly the second most vital ingredient is to identify a champion within the organisation with both the ability and the credibility to implement and sustain such a system. This is particularly vital in the early stages when resistance is strongest and before any significant benefits are evident.

A review of the anticipated areas of resistance (as indicated in the previous article) would indicate that the change agent must be well capable of fighting their corner—it is certainly not a job for the immature or the faint hearted. Any astute, career-minded individual will quickly acknowledge that implementing and managing a successful ideas system involves more risk than reversing into the CEO's new Mercedes.

Good system design

The third vital consideration is that of system design. Too complicated and people will fail to understand the system—it will also be costly to administer and slow to respond. Too simple and the system will lose credibility and fail. An internal champion is essential but they may need initial assistance from a suitable consultant. This is particularly important in the design stages because getting it wrong will negate any later opportunity of getting it right.

Clearly defined rules

Unless the program is well thought through and clearly defined it will lurch from one problem to the next. Some of the essential considerations are as follows:

- What inputs are off-limits?
- What denotes an acceptable idea and at what stage will it be recognised—at inception, after acceptance, after implementation?
- What is the target work group?
- How will problems be identified and communicated?
- How will proposals be circulated when they impact on wider areas of business activity?
- How will the change process be controlled/supervised?
- Who will assess ideas and how?
- What criteria will be used for such assessments?
- How will consistency be maintained?
- What measures can be used to positively engage everyone?
- What recognition and reward will be applied and when?
- How will information/data be stored, sorted and utilised?
- What latitude is management prepared to devolve?
- What should be the structure of the suitable award categories?
- How will the flow of ideas be stimulated?
- What are the rules for ideas that have no obvious benefit?

Avoid boxes like the plague

The most common (half-hearted) mistake is to install a number of suggestion boxes and then wait to see what happens. I can tell you what will happen—nothing! What's worse, management are likely to interpret this as an indication that nobody has any ideas worthy of consideration and the program will quickly bite the dust forever.

Apply natural communications

For a program to be successful it must engage people in natural processes of communication. This really works best when solutions are developed through dialogue. This might involve talking with colleagues and others with diverse skills but should always involve the immediate boss. In turn, the boss should be measured and rewarded in accordance with their ability to stimulate active involvement in the process of improving the business. They should also take responsibility for controlling the change process by seeking the necessary approvals from all concerned.

Incorporate into all relevant systems

This may take some time to complete but begin initiating the incorporation of the ideas management system into:

- the corporate or strategic plan
- business unit plans
- performance management systems
- key results area
- key performance indicators
- performance appraisal systems
- position descriptions
- monthly meeting agendas.

Inspect what you expect to happen. What will get measured and reported on, will get done.

By now you will have concluded that there is no simple means of effectively tapping the reserves of knowledge and creative potential that resides within all organisations. The quality guru, James Edwards Deming, referred to this knowledge as 'the gold in the mine'. This comparison is because, like gold, the only way to effectively tap the full intellectual capital that resides within all organisations is to 'work the mine'. The nuggets exist in abundance and await their discovery but only hard work, skill, tenacity and patience will reveal their presence.

How can we retain the momentum of an ideas management system?

W HEN PURCHASING PROPERTY we are advised to focus on 'location, location, location'. With ideas management it's all about 'recognition, recognition, recognition'.

Whilst in the cradle we scream and cry for recognition. With adulthood we usually abandon tantrums (for much of the time) but even the most confident and successful of people have an inherent craving for acknowledgement—a simple pat on the back for a job well done.

Very few organisations successfully harness the enormous motivational power that is unleashed when people are given the opportunity to feel valued and/or receive formal recognition and status for positive, creative input. In my experience, far too many bosses struggle to offer encouragement and praise but never miss an opportunity to criticise.

A formal ideas management system helps identify the kind of positive behaviour that is expected of its leaders. Once the leaders understand that their performances will be measured by their ability to implement and sustain patterns of positive behaviour, the culture of an organisation quickly changes.

The old adage, 'What gets measured gets managed', never fails and when leaders are measured by a yardstick that places a value on the creative, innovative inputs arising from within their area of control, things really begin to happen.

In the early stages of system implementation it certainly helps to inject an element of competition within an organisation to give a clear indication of which divisions, areas, functions (whatever groupings are relevant) are performing best in stimulating the process of continuous improvement.

Simply placing formal measures on aspects of continuous improvement and recognising the best performers automatically elevates and sustains the relative importance of the concept within the organisation.

Maximising success opportunities

The more people receiving recognition the better because winners become converts and converts make the best disciples. The eventual objective must be to implant a culture of continuous improvement through the active involvement of everyone connected with the organisation.

Awards to stimulate group leaders

Gaining the support of leaders is absolutely vital and so awards for the most active contribution from a division, department, function, etc. are highly appropriate. Similarly, awards for the most active supervisor, foreman, manager, etc. will also clearly send home the message that listening to people and acting on their ideas will bring recognition and reward.

Awards to stimulate everyone

Use the following ideas for awards:
- the most active contributor of the year: individual, area, division
- the best idea of the year (all categories)
- the best idea of the month
- the best annual cost-saving idea
- the best annual safety idea
- the best annual environmental idea
- the best annual customer-care idea
- the best annual innovation
- the best annual employee satisfaction, morale, wellbeing idea
- the centurion award for the one hundred most successful ideas (area, individual)
- the annual raffle with all successful participants eligible.

As indicated earlier, the actual categories, though important, are not as vital as the need to create winning opportunities. Just as the system is designed to continuously improve a business, so too must the program continuously improve.

Annual review

It is recommended that the entire system should be extensively scrutinised on an annual basis with the object of defining areas for improvement and with a view to keeping the concept alive and fresh at all times.

Don't expect to plant seedlings today and fell timber tomorrow

IT IS EXTREMELY IMPORTANT FOR AN ORGANISATION to recognise that an ideas management system will only become fully effective when the business culture embraces continuous improvement as the modus operandi. Whether an ideas management system will, in isolation, create such a culture is open to argument but there can be no question that such systems provide an excellent foundation.

It must be acknowledged that people take time to absorb new concepts and come to terms with the new opportunities that suddenly present themselves. Management, in particular, must demonstrate patience whilst also maintaining a reasonably conservative expectation level in the early stages.

Let me assume that you have read the previous articles and are now at base camp wondering, 'Is it all worth the risk and effort?' The answer to this question directly depends on the beliefs of management and the degree of preparation, training and resources that an organisation is prepared to commit. Like climbing a mountain, great preparation, skill and tenacity will generally prevail over a casual 'let's give it a go' approach.

How prepared are you?

- Do you believe that your business would benefit from an ideas management system?
- Do you sincerely believe that the people within your business have a wealth of untapped knowledge and creativity?
- Does the extraction of the untapped knowledge warrant the time/cost of working the mine?
- Can you identify a change agent within the business who has the respect, confidence and ability to implement and administer a formal ideas management system?
- Are you prepared to tend the concept and allow time for it to take root and become established?

The importance of culture

As with a nation, the culture of an organisation is formed over the duration of its life. It is reasonable to say that the older the organisation, the more difficult it will be to change its culture.

Once a culture becomes embedded it can destroy an organisation. This is because the current necessity of constant and rapid change may be incompatible with the traditional 'ways' of a business.

It makes excellent sense, therefore, for a business to take control of its cultural development rather than simply allowing it to happen. When an organisation sets out to create a culture of continuous and rapid improvement, it effectively protects itself from the embodiment of 'sacred' ritual and routines that have no relevance in today's world.

In a culture of continuous improvement, everything is always open for examination and everyone recognises that constant change represents the only basis for survival.

> The only place where success comes before work
> is in the dictionary.
> **Anonymous**

An important tip for evaluating ideas

MANY ORGANISATIONS IMMEDIATELY DESTROY their chances of success with an ideas management system by insisting on assessment rules that are too cumbersome and time consuming. A classic mistake is to assume that every idea must produce a cost saving and therefore have a calculable value.

It is natural that everyone will wish to see an ideas management system generating cost savings if only to pay for its administration, but it is vital to recognise that some ideas have no direct financial connotation. This is true of certain safety and environmental improvements, customer relations issues and the like.

One system that I introduced has stood the test of time—over twenty-two years. Amazingly, the financial rewards have remained consistent throughout, yet the program has delivered results that are a tribute to the creative ability of the people involved. Such are the powers of recognition and personal value.

Suggested evaluation criteria

Keeping an ideas evaluation process simple enables it to be quick and cost effective. The credibility of such systems rapidly declines when the cost of evaluation exceeds the value of the improvement.

A simple evaluation technique works as follows. After having the idea fully explained and clarified, the evaluation team should:

1. Ask, if implemented, will this idea represent an improvement?
2. If the answer is no, ensure that the initiator is quickly informed of the reasons and is awarded a small gift (or allocation of points) to encourage further involvement.
3. If the answer is yes, then ask, 'Is the idea significant enough to warrant a category one award or is it a category two idea?'

If this sounds too simple to be true, please be assured that this process has been successful for twenty-two years over tens of thousands of ideas. The most important issue is not the relative value in cost terms but the incorporation of a workable improvement into the organisation.

Where an idea does have a direct financial implication that is readily calculable then the benefits can, and should, be quantified. If required, ideas that do effectively generate a cost improvement can be linked to a scale of major, moderate and minor. It is not recommended, however, that a direct proportional linkage be incorporated. This is because the extent of creative input rarely corresponds with the ultimate value of an idea and the gold in the mine (when discovered) must pay for working the mine.

In short, it is vital to initiate an evaluation process that is economical to administer, quick to respond, equitable for all and effective over the longer term. Keep it simple.

> And the trouble is, if you don't risk anything
> you risk even more.
> Erica Jong, American author

Step-by-step approach

EACH ORGANISATION WILL HAVE its own specific requirements for an ideas management system—there is no such thing as an 'off the peg' solution. It is highly unlikely that the culture of one organisation will be the same as the culture of another. The uniqueness and differences need to be reflected in the design of the ideas management system.

Factors that will influence the complexity, design and potential success of a system will include:

- the size of the organisation (cost viability)
- the nature of the business (degree of complexity)
- the age of the business (contained by tradition)
- the styles of leadership (open and trusting versus control-based)
- the business status (declining, flat, growing, booming)
- management/employee relationships (degree of mutual trust)
- general morale and degree of positive energy.

Establish management commitment

Before the commencement of any detailed work on an ideas management system it is essential to gain the full commitment of the entire management team. From experience this is never easy because it is often difficult to separate genuine commitment from lip service aimed at pleasing the boss.

A good way to sell the concept is to openly debate the issue after highlighting the potential benefits, identifying the extent of the commitment required and outlining the prospects of doing nothing. It may also be a useful exercise to give everyone a defined period to report back with a better/alternative proposal. In any event, it is essential to gain a consensus for the concept before incurring any costs on system development.

Identify a suitable champion

Even if an organisation has the full support of its management team it is extremely unlikely that an ideas management system will be successful without a passionate champion to drive the system and make it work. Simply dumping the responsibility on a hard-pushed manager (usually the HR manager) is a traditional recipe for failure.

Cascade the concept

Considerable thought must be given to the communication of the concept. Organisations are notorious for a lack of forethought and sensitivity when presenting new concepts. This provides the ammunition for negative/cynical reactions from negative/cynical people.

The aim should be to involve people (including trade union representatives) from the very beginning to convert a concept into a business asset that represents a win–win for everyone. As a successful ideas management system will certainly create such a situation there is absolutely no reason for any lack of transparency.

Policy issues

Initially, it is essential for management to specify and agree to a few general policies for incorporation into the detailed design processes. Specifically these must include:
- Who is eligible to participate?
- What idea inputs are off-limits?
- What recognition and reward structure is acceptable?
- Who will be responsible for setting up and running the system?
- What degree of autonomy will be devolved to the system administrators?
- What controls must be satisfied to effectively manage improvements? (For example, safety, engineering, technical, as-built drawings, customer reaction, etc.)

Technical support

As indicated earlier, however, assigning the right champion for the task is without doubt a major consideration for success or failure. Depending on the experience of the assigned individual (champion), it may be advisable to engage a suitably experienced consultant to assist in the actual system design process.

Team-driven approach

The design process may be improved and expedited using a small multi-disciplined project team. The team, preferably selected by the assigned project leader, should include individuals that carry influence and respect within the organisation.

To be successful an ideas management system must be pragmatic, functional and fair. It must also gain rapid credibility as a workable vehicle for recognising, rewarding and initiating ideas for business improvement.

The importance of system credibility cannot be overemphasised and by involving respected, no-nonsense people in its design the eventual proposal is far more likely to meet needs that may be specific to the organisation. It is also vital to appreciate the value of having the support (rather than possible opposition) of such people when the system is being launched.

Specific design considerations

Whilst the design of an ideas management system must be tailored to suit a specific organisation, there are a number of considerations that must be systematically addressed for the system to function smoothly. These will include:

- Establish a standard format for ideas presentation.
- Develop an effective system for storing/monitoring/collating/analysis.
- Define how ideas will be received/discussed/circulated/developed/initiated.
- Decide the process for impartial, credible ideas review and how, who, where and what frequency.
- Decide the basis for recognition and reward and the frequency, category and value.
- Identify supporting roles for management and others.
- Consider potential areas of conflict, ideas duplication, non-originality and perceived incompatibility of assessment.
- Prepare a small handbook of rules.

Above all, the design objective should be one of functional simplicity. Most ideas management systems fail because of overcomplication and a loss of momentum.

Gaining management approval

Naturally, before launching the scheme, it is essential to gain management approval for the proposals as developed and presented by the project team. Whilst senior management must obviously satisfy itself that the proposals are workable and seek amendment as necessary, it is important that the team is encouraged and empowered as far as possible to run with the system and make it work.

Launching the system

In my experience, it is better to launch an ideas management system as you would a boat, easing it slowly into the water. People are naturally suspicious of pretentious 'big splash' initiatives that are usually here today and gone tomorrow. The most successful system that I have witnessed began very quietly (too quietly in fact), with only one idea being presented in the first two months of implementation.

It is recommended that the project team should make a series of presentations to all employees followed by a question and answer session. These sessions should:

- Clearly instruct everyone on how/why the system has been developed.
- Explain how the system will operate.
- Outline the potential short-term and long-term benefits for all.
- Explain the specific roles and responsibilities of everyone concerned.
- Advise everyone that the scheme represents a learning process for all.
- Ensure that all angles have been covered.

Remember, by including well-respected individuals on the project team the system proposals are far more likely to be positively received.

To kick-start the system it may be advisable to consider a series of special incentives for early participants.

Management role

The best systems are those where management remains totally supportive but does not need to concern itself with the detail. Ultimate success is when employees take complete ownership of the system.

> Innovation: The fuel of corporate longevity.
> **Training advertisement, Decision Process International, December 1986**
>
> Somebody said that it couldn't be done,
> But he with a chuckle replied,
> That 'maybe it couldn't' but he would be one,
> Who wouldn't say no till he tried.
> So he buckled right in with the trace of a grin,
> On his face. If he worried he hid it.
> He started to sing as he tackled the thing,
> That couldn't be done, and he did it.
> **Edgar A Guest (1881–1959), English journalist, from 'It couldn't be done'**

Protecting your business

T HE MINDARIE REGIONAL COUNCIL, a local government enterprise that deals in the business of waste management in metropolitan Perth, was having trouble in 2002. Real trouble—of the physical type. Break-ins, damaged equipment, cut fences, theft of laptops, and the like. Located on the isolated stretch of a main road some twenty-five km north of the central business district, the council's facility was a soft target for unwanted intruders.

Forming the team

The CEO enlisted the support of a local Perth security consultant.

The credentials the CEO sought in selecting a team included:

- membership of the national Security Industry Association,
- licensed security consultants,
- accredited supplier of security and risk management related products and services to international standards,
- experienced and qualified personnel.

The coalition having been formed, the stage was now set for the conduct of a facility risk audit.

Setting the objective

The project team agreed that the objective of the audit was to establish a detailed outline of the current range of security measures in place and the risk profiles they are designed to counter. These measures were then rated for their effectiveness in meeting the likely contingencies that may impact upon the facility, staff, customers and assets.

The process

The project team adopted a fundamental principle and that was to have a theoretical reference point. And this was the relevant standard—in this case, AS/NZS standard for risk management 4360:1999. Other key elements of the process included personal interviews, reviews of existing plans and systems, site visits (including those of the unannounced, discrete and after-hours type). Data was collected, collated and analysed.

A snapshot of the findings

A typical audit of this nature is likely to uncover a raft of findings in the following areas:
- The sources of physical risk.
- The likelihood and level of impact of these risks.
- The standard of existing access systems to premises and buildings, including key controls.
- The standard of the existing communications and alarm systems, including protection from power fluctuations and outages.
- The physical protection afforded to buildings via window types, screens and doors—and not forgetting the roof.
- Mail, package and cash handling systems, including storage.
- On-site monitoring systems, including CCTV.
- Infrastructure security including fuel storage, machinery and service lines.

What about the remedies?

One simple way of laying out suggested remedies (and the project team used this approach at Mindarie) is to categorise events as:
- disaster, e.g. fire, flood
- criminal event, e.g. burglary, vandalism
- personal attack on an employee
- restrictions on operations, e.g. picket lines
- explosion
- extortion/kidnap/ransom
- mail-related event.

The remedies then relate to the protection of people and property against these potential events using one or more of the following:

- physical barriers
- alarm systems
- recording systems, e.g. CCTV
- specialised equipment, e.g. duress buttons, gas masks
- training of staff in emergency procedures, including equipment handling
- development and implementation of systems and processes.

A more secure environment for you and your staff means a more comfortable environment for your customers—and that's good for your business.

Visual management—a superb motivational tool

THERE IS AN OLD SAYING, 'what can't be measured can't be managed'. As true as this statement is, many organisations fail to provide any dynamic feedback to communicate the impact of individual/team action in relation to the bigger picture. I will share an experience that effectively confirms this assertion.

Some time ago I was examining the effectiveness of a team of maintenance engineers in a major process industry. The majority of their work was associated with maintaining a large number of overhead cranes without which the business would simply grind to a halt.

Four shifts were employed to cover the maintenance activities over a twenty-four hour, seven-days-a-week working routine. The overall objective was quite simple—keep the cranes operating at all costs. And guess what? That's what they did.

Costs were escalating but the reliability factor was remaining static. I was commissioned to investigate the problem, reduce costs and improve crane reliability.

Acquiring the facts

My first task was to analyse the costs using the Pareto (80–20) rule to identify where the money was going. As expected, it was quickly determined that 80% of the expenditure related to 20% of failure incidents. The solution was therefore quite simple—tackle the 20% and eat away at the 80% cost factor.

Communicating the problem

Armed with this vital information, I set up a series of training sessions with the four respective teams. It was quickly confirmed that the information obtained from the analysis of worksheets was accurate and the maintenance engineers recognised that the elimination of these faults would have a major impact on the reliability of the cranes.

Root cause analysis

Using an established and proven Japanese technique the maintenance engineers were asked to apply the simple tool of asking 'why' five times in succession.

For example:

The crane has stopped working.

Why? There was a fault on the cross travel motor.
Why? A component was overheating.
Why? Because it was exposed to heat from an adjacent component.
Why? Because of the close proximity of the components.
Why? Because that's the way it was installed.

Question: Can we relocate one of the components?
Answer: Yes.

Result: Root cause of the problem removed.

Similarly, the teams were taught how to prepare cause and effect (Fishbone) charts and also how to analyse computer printout information to identify high cost maintenance activities.

Visual management

To drive the initiative, two large targets were installed in the vicinity of the workshop occupied by the maintenance engineers. The teams were challenged to use their new analytical skills to drive down costs and increase reliability. The targets would be updated monthly, by inserting arrows, to indicate their progress and their prize, when achieved, would be a barbecue for the entire team.

The bullseye on one target represented a 33% drop in the average cost for maintaining the total complement of cranes (approximately forty-five). The outer ring of the target indicated present status.

The other target bullseye represented a 33% increase in reliability as measured by the operations department with the outer ring representing current status.

Results

Within three months both arrows were firmly placed in their respective bullseyes and the targets were revised to aim for even better results—plus another barbecue! As a consequence, the concerned organisation cancelled an order for an additional supplementary crane.

Conclusion

When people fully understand what is required of them and are given the correct information, tools, measures and motivation, they will deliver what is required. For my part I know very little about overhead cranes.

If it ain't broke, fix it anyway

THE EXPRESSION, 'IF IT AIN'T BROKE DON'T FIX IT', may have relevance in certain situations but when used as the basis for initiating business performance improvement it can have disastrous effects. Organisations that react only when things are broke…go broke.

Whilst this may appear to be an obvious observation, in reality very few businesses allocate sufficient time and resources to the process of overall business improvement.

As a simple check ask yourself these few simple questions:

- What percentage of management/staff time (daily, weekly, annually) is actually dedicated to the process of identifying, implementing and monitoring critical improvements into the business?
- Who, if anyone, is responsible for coordinating an overall business improvement program and what level of priority is given to the program in the overall scheme of things?
- What criteria is applied for measuring the success or otherwise of the business improvement program?
- Are all staff actively involved in the process of improving the business?

If your response to these questions is a resounding 'gulp', then don't be too concerned. In reality, most organisations have consistently downsized to a point where simply fulfilling the direct functional requirements of the day represents a major achievement.

Ask any business leader if it is essential to continuously improve business performance and they will inevitably deliver a positive response. But for things to improve they must change and thus overcome inevitable resistance from people who have both motive and reason for protecting the status quo.

Crash programs or quick-fix solutions rarely deliver what consultants promise or what senior management expects. This is not because the concepts are unsuitable (although they may be) but because the programs fall foul of an embedded culture that resists change at all costs. 'We don't do things that way around here, fella.'

All business is nothing more, or less, than a team of individuals combining skills and energy for the purpose of generating wealth or providing a service. Teams that operate in harmony and are most adaptable to change will inevitably prevail over those that foster a reactive, 'can't do' environment.

Changing personalities or the structure of an organisation can obviously introduce quite significant improvements, as can the introduction of better systems, procedures and practices. However, for an organisation to become truly 'fit for life', it must be capable of building a culture that embraces continuous improvement as an inevitable requirement for sustained prosperity. Organisations that actively precipitate and embrace the process of improvement at all levels do not simply happen by chance—they are carefully moulded and nurtured over time.

It is impossible to pursue creativity and participation in a traditional control and command environment. The most critical question for embarking on this course may, in fact, lie in the willingness and ability of management to trust its people, loosen the reins and share responsibility for the future of the business.

The successful implementation of a continuous improvement culture will never be a quick or easy fix. Changing a culture requires commitment, time and tenacity. Once established, however, such a culture will provide the ability to consistently review all aspects of business activity. It will also create an environment where change is expected and desired rather than resisted.

Some of the characteristics that directly influence a positive change culture include:

- Acknowledgement that a culture of continuous improvement represents the only basis for long-term business survival.
- Communicating the futility of internal conflict and politics within the organisation.
- Implementing systems that formally recognise, encourage and reward people for improvement initiatives.
- Encouraging the formation of cross-functional teams to collectively develop and implement complex improvement initiatives.
- Allocating specific responsibility for the coordination of an overall improvement program.
- Giving ample management sunshine to positive actions, cooperative behaviour and people who go out of their way to help clients, customers or colleagues.
- Regular progress updates of the business improvement program. Incorporating the personal characteristics that best fit the desired culture into recruitment criteria.

They have stuffed up again!

> If anything can go wrong it will.
> Murphy's Law
>
> The emphasis in sound discipline must be on what's wrong
> rather than who's to blame.
> George S Odiorne, *How Managers Make Things Happen*,
> Prentice Hall, New Jersey, 1961

'THEY HAVE STUFFED UP AGAIN!' How many times have we all heard that one? Our customer is irate because this is the second time we have not fulfilled their order to their expectations. Or our department has failed to meet the needs of another department.

So often, the blame game now starts:

- 'I did my part, but John let us down again', or
- 'Fred didn't tell me it was so urgent', or
- 'Sales staff should know we can never do that in that time', or something similar.

In the case of a production organisation, the sales department becomes extremely frustrated and blames the production department. Production blames sales for making unrealistic promises or for not making their requirements clear, or for offering something which the company is not equipped to supply within the time and price structure offered.

Similar scenarios can occur within any type of organisation where there is a failure of one or more groups to meet their objective.

Engaging in the blame game is highly unproductive and demoralising for everyone involved. It can become quite destructive. Stress levels can be raised in an undesirable and negative way. Tempers can flare. Relationships can be severely damaged.

What we often lose sight of in such a situation is that our people generally strive to do a good job and probably have tried very hard in this case. A calm and objective analysis will frequently reveal that it is the system that has given rise to the problems.

The role of the manager is to make it possible for staff to do their job, and after that to encourage them to do it. Management has a responsibility to continually listen and to monitor the situation. They need to take action to ensure there are relevant systems and procedures in place, and adequate resources, including staff knowledge and skill sets, to achieve the objectives. Whenever there is a failure, look first to the systems and only after that should you look to particular persons. The manager has primary responsibility to ensure there are appropriate systems in place, and that they are well understood and doable.

A quality assurance system will go a long way to addressing these matters. It will document shortcomings, and identify just how often errors of a particular type occur, and the source of those errors, as well as identifying what actions are required to correct those errors in the future. It takes a lot of the emotion out of trying to get things right.

However, there are many successful organisations without a formal quality system, and sometimes in these groups in particular, there can be a tendency to blame the person or persons and overlook what may be shortcomings in the system.

In any case, when there has been an annoying and frustrating error, it can pay to review the following checklist with your staff:

- ☐ What systems do we have to cover situations like this?
- ☐ Were they relevant and adequate in this instance?
- ☐ Are the procedures well understood by all relevant staff?
- ☐ Are the set-down procedures doable?
- ☐ Do our staff understand the importance of compliance with these procedures?
- ☐ Do the procedures take adequate account of the ability of other parts of the organisation to comply?
- ☐ Are there more or different resources required in order to adequately comply with the system?
- ☐ Are the skill sets of the relevant staff adequate to meet the requirements of the system?
- ☐ Is there a need to revise the procedures?
- ☐ Is there a need for more training?
- ☐ Is there a need for mentoring?
- ☐ Is there something that management can or should do to avoid a recurrence?

Be careful what you wish for …

OKAY, SO YOU ARE TO BE INVOLVED IN CREATING a new information system in the office. You are one of the users of the existing system, and considered the subject matter expert on the processes that the new system will do. The IT guys want to know what you want in the system. Where do you begin?

Technically known as the 'requirements definition phase', or more traditionally the 'analysis phase', this is one of the first steps in the process of developing a system. It is also one of the most fundamental parts. The system is designed and/or configured based on these requirements and they are really the foundations on which the system is built. If the foundations are wrong, it may be difficult to change the system later on. In fact, it is not that uncommon for the requirements to be defined incorrectly, often resulting in a system being built that does not serve the purpose at all.

So how do you specify what you need in a system?

☐ Use clear and concise language to explain each requirement. Back it up with as much evidence as you can lay your hands on. Items such as reports, existing input screens and documentation, such as user procedures, are excellent at showing the designers how the system works.

☐ List everything you can possibly think of, no matter how minor it may seem. It is better to be detailed than sketchy and find something that you assumed would be included is actually not. Something minor, but mandatory, that may have been overlooked could be a real headache to include after the system has gone live.

☐ Be aware that the existing method of doing a set of tasks may be that way because of constraints that the existing system promotes. This may be an opportunity to review how technology may be used to improve the process for which the new system is being designed. If the system is already developed, and the requirements are being put together for configuration/gap analysis purposes, check out the features that the new system may already have. Most advances of late have focused on the online and electronic information transfer components.

☐ Think of all the people who will interact with the new system, both within your organisation and the various departments, as well as external people, such as customers and suppliers. Are their needs being met? What do they want the system to do for them?

☐ There will be a priority put on each of your requirements. Each item is rated in some sort of scale which is normally: mandatory, very important, nice to have, and not really important at all. Each requirement is costed as to the effort it takes to produce. Then the negotiations start to look at maybe what is going to be left out, what is left in, and when each item will be developed. Start this priority setting early, putting your own realistic priority on each requirement.

☐ Review all the requirements several times and ensure that the wording and supporting information make it quite clear about what is needed. These final checks are good for clearing up ambiguity.

☐ Often there will be constraints put on a system because it is a system already developed. Requirements are still important, as it identifies the gaps between what this developed system already does and does not do. In extreme cases, a set of formal requirements shows that the system being put in is actually not going to work at all.

☐ Finally, changing a system is expensive. None more so than when the change is needed because the original design was wrong. Getting it right in the first place reduces effort and the long-term costs. Take the care and the time needed to make sure you have defined all the requirements as you see them.

> ‘
> Too many companies have beautiful, elegant computer systems
> that create more problems than they solve.
> **Susan E Steele, The Wharton School, CFO, December 1987**
>
> Most of the computer technicians … are complicators, not simplifiers …
> They're building a mystique, a priesthood, their own mumbo-jumbo
> ritual to keep you from knowing what they, and you, are doing.
> **Robert Townsend, former CEO, Avis, *Further Up the Organisation*, Knopf, 1984**
>
> The relationship between input and output is sometimes—when input is
> incorrect—tersely noted by the expression 'garbage in, garbage out'.
> **Glossary of Automated Typesetting and Related Computer Terms, Composition
> Information Services, 1975** ’

Making the right technology decision

YOU'D BE HARD PRESSED to find a business these days that isn't dependent on technology in one way or another. From the simplest use of MS Word for correspondence, through to accounting packages and in-house developed systems—not forgetting the ubiquitous email and internet access—we're all out there mouse pointing, fingers tapping and screen saving. But as your business grows or circumstances change, and you require greater functionality, greater operating efficiencies or perhaps integrated solutions for e-commerce, how do you work out what is the most appropriate software to run your business?

The evaluation

A structured evaluation process is critical to making an investment that you are happy with. This is the case, regardless of the size of your business. Many organisations in the top end of town have rued their software decisions, as have many small- and medium-sized enterprises.

We suggest that you structure your evaluation to include the following steps:

1. **Articulate why you are making the investment.** What are your objectives? (If you don't know where you're going, any path will get you there.) This will help others in the organisation understand the project and the benefits, so when you need their help, they are more likely to provide it. This also helps when there are conflicting priorities with other projects and activities. You can then objectively assess which will deliver the greatest benefit to the organisation.
2. **Get hands-on experience of your business processes.** Understand what business processes you need (e.g. order processing) and identify any specific pieces of functionality (e.g. a special price calculation). Get hands-on experience of how the software deals with those requirements. Don't just concentrate on specific function points. It is critical to consider the business process of how it all hangs together from an end-to-end perspective. Your business may change so that you don't need to apply a certain discount structure any more, but you will still need to accept sales orders.

    This particularly means that you should not just take at face value what the salesperson says. You should ask them to show you how the system will satisfy your specific requirements and this means to demonstrate it working. It also means looking at the entire process from start to finish, so that you get to see how easy the system is to use and how things hang together.

3. **Clarify the vendor's support and services offering.** If you can only get your questions answered by calling the overseas support desk at your cost during their business day, you won't be making many calls and could end up with a white elephant. If you have a 24/7 operation and support is only provided during office hours, is this acceptable or not?

   Understand, however, the difference between a support service and a help desk. The former relates to supporting the system from a technical perspective and will log and resolve software problems. The latter provides a user support service to help with useability and functionality understanding issues. Most vendors don't provide a help desk.

4. **Understand how the software will be implemented.** You are buying software to help you better manage your business processes. The organisation that implements the software for you (it could be the vendor or a consulting firm) should have a methodology—this is after all their key business process. They should apply the same sort of rigour to their business as they are helping you to do to yours! Make sure that the methodology is not just a glossy brochure.

5. **Research where else you can get expert assistance.** An overseas vendor may provide the software, but there may be a thriving services industry locally. Are these service organisations accredited in any way? What are the credentials of their staff?

6. **What about future releases?** Understand what the situation is with respect to ongoing product development and your situation with respect to upgrades. You may have to pay monthly or annual maintenance (don't overlook this in your budgeting) to get access to upgrades. If the government changes the taxation rules, you don't want to be out on a limb with your software. Also, with business and technology moving at 'internet-speed', you probably want to be able to keep up-to-date on developments.

7. **Check their track record.** Talk to other organisations that are using the software and have used the same implementation organisation as you intend. Validate that what you have been told is actually true in practice.

8. Make sure that you know what it will cost.

This is more than a licence fee and hardware cost. You need to understand the cost of the implementation (don't forget about your own resources and whether you will need to back-fill for them), and what ongoing costs are relevant. Think about the total cost of ownership (TCO).

Software implementation

ONCE A DECISION HAS BEEN MADE to implement new software in your business, the implementation needs to be carefully managed. Bear in mind that most software packages provide good functionality and are of acceptable quality. Sometimes a major new release will have teething problems, but if you avoid being the guinea pig, generally the software is stable. Most vendors have great success stories and also have some horror stories. Generally, what it comes down to is how effectively you implement the chosen solution.

The following are critical contributors to success of the implementation project:

☐ **Make sure you have a sponsor.** Implementing a new system across your organisation will involve significant change. This will impact on how people do their jobs, even what their jobs might be. Some tough decisions will need to be made. The sponsor needs to have enough clout in the organisation to carry things through, to make decisions and to commit the resources that are required.

☐ **Don't go it alone.** Make use of the expertise of the software vendor or specialist consulting firms who have practical experience in the software. They should know the pitfalls to avoid. They have been there before.

☐ **Go vanilla!** In software parlance, this means don't make programming changes to the system. Most packages provide a wide variety of options (set by parameters like you do with MS Word under Tools/Options) with which you can configure the software to meet your requirements. This should give you the flexibility that you need for most of your requirements. This includes how you take orders, your pricing models, your sales commission structures, etc.

You could go further than what is provided in the software and get the vendor to make programming changes, or worse still, use your own staff to make the changes. This is fraught with danger. Generally, the vendor will only provide you with limited support because they don't know whether the programming change has impacted how the software functions. If you don't go vanilla you risk not being able to upgrade, having a complex implementation and serious cost overrun. This is one of those tough decisions that the sponsor will need to enforce.

☐ **Make sure that the people who will use the new system are involved in the implementation.** You need their input and want to minimise resistance. Business support is one of the critical success factors to an implementation. Common sense tells you that the people who are doing the job best know how it can be improved. Use the vendor's consultants to help you understand what is possible and your own staff to debate the alternatives and help you come up with the best solution.

☐ **Use project management techniques to manage the implementation.** This means that you must understand what activities are required, what deadlines exist (e.g. production of a Business Activity Statement, alignment to financial year end), who is doing what, what defines success, how to manage issues and the resourcing commitment to the project.

☐ **Tell people what is happening.** You are about to make significant change in the organisation. People don't like change. It's important that they start to see what is happening as something familiar and non-threatening. The best way to gain that familiarity is to keep reinforcing your message. Communicate, communicate, communicate. A change management consultant said, 'Communicate until you think you've done too much, and then it still won't be enough'. Sometimes it takes a few times for people to understand what you're saying. Repeat your message. Make it consistent and clear. Provide different types of delivery, so that the different styles of people are accommodated—some people might want to read about what you're doing, for others a meeting or presentation is most appropriate, while others need to touch a new system to absorb it. Find different ways to present the same message.

☐ **What other projects must be initiated?** Look beyond just implementing a piece of software—are there any other things that need to change to make use of the system? You'll definitely need training for your staff, but will you need to change your business procedures? Will you need to inform your customers about anything or will the change be transparent to them? Many organisations overlook the impact the software has on the day-to-day running of their business.

Your business system has the potential to increase your efficiency and business effectiveness. It can also cause you untold headaches! Making the right decision and ensuring a successful implementation is critical.

Waste not, want not

GOT MY FIRST INKLING OF THE MASSIVE POTENTIAL for the waste of time, effort and money in large, bureaucratic organisations when I worked for one. Unfortunately for my employer (the telecommunications and postal services), I was unfocused, unmotivated and bored. This was my first full-time job after a spectacularly mediocre three-year stint as a mathematics student grappling with really useful concepts, such as the development of the real number system based on Piano's Axioms.

But I digress. Back to the subject of waste. In my job, I spent most of my time sitting at a desk which featured an IN tray on the left-hand side, an OUT tray on the right-hand side and me in the middle. About every hour or so a person called a clerical assistant would come round pushing a trolley full of cardboard files and drop some of these in my IN tray and collect any that I had placed in my OUT tray. One particularly bad day for both of us (my employer and me), I decided to check out what would happen if I placed all the files as they were deposited into my IN tray straight into my OUT tray without performing whatever action was required from me. So each time the clerical assistant had disappeared, and checking that my boss was occupied pretending to be occupied, I moved the files straight from IN to OUT.

Guess what happened? You're right—nothing! I thought at least I would get a few phone calls from other distressed employees who were waiting on my actions. About a week later, all the files came back to me. The consequence for me of this prank was nothing. If the mail wasn't delivered that week, then the newspapers certainly kept it quiet. As far as I know there were no riots or other examples of public disquiet with the postal service.

Which, in a round about way, brings me to my theme—efficiency or the consequences of inefficiency. If the figure bandied around by me (and other bandiers of figures) of a waste factor of 30% (Deming) holds to be true, then there is one hell of a lot of taxpayers' money or sales revenue being wasted out there. That is, that 30% of the activities performed by the entire work force of an organisation result in waste of time, effort and money. If the annual wages bill for a hospital is $50 million, that's $15 million wasted each year. If the annual wages bill for a public sector agency of 4000 employees is $160 million, that's $48 million wasted each year. Scary, isn't it? But it gets even scarier!

What causes this waste? The individual characteristics and idiosyncrasies of the human race. Human and system error. Failure to follow proper systems and procedures. Unnecessary activities. Unnecessary duplication of effort. Re-checking, re-working and correcting of errors. Poorly motivated work force. Incompetent management and staff. Stupid decisions. Communication breakdown. Inaccurate perceptions, etc. etc.

Organisations (specifically in this case, groups of managers) are constantly pushing the work force to take on new fads and initiatives— constantly looking for the new Messiah. Wouldn't it be nice if we focused on getting it right in the first place. Doing what we are doing now with less waste. Let's get the basics right before we embrace the latest fad coming out of guruland or academia. (Don't read this line if you don't like plugs. This is the focus we take with our M•A•P•P™ System. I told you not to read it.)

As another example, in the state of Victoria, Australia, the public sector wages, superannuation and leave entitlements in 2003 was $11.02 billion for 245,900 workers. Apply the 30% waste factor and you get $3306 million dollars going down the drain—every year!

The annual selling and administrative expenses for Nike for their financial year ending May 2003 was US$3.14 billion. That's a 30% waste factor of US$942 million! That's a lot of money that is just not doing it. No wonder there is never enough money and the cost of everything keeps going up.

Phew! Okay, so I am getting a little carried away here and these extrapolations just couldn't be true, could they? Notwithstanding that some people tell me that the waste factor of 30% is too low. Whatever. The message still is that we waste one hell of a lot of time, money and effort—much of which could be avoided.

And if you think that this doesn't apply to you because you don't work in a large, bureaucratic organisation, well, think again because the 30% waste factor applies to any organisation with a work force of around twenty or more.

By the way, I chose Nike because they are known worldwide, but I could have used any organisation as an example. By most measures, Nike is one of the most successful companies in the world and I am sure that they would be a leader in initiatives to minimise waste.

Improving relationships

Beating the competition, not each other

CAN YOU IMAGINE A TEAM SPORT where the players focused their energy on out-shining each other and where accentuating and exploiting weaknesses in the game of your team-mates became more important than beating the opposing team? Well, neither can I but in many organisations it is considered to be quite acceptable and even healthy to perform in this manner.

It has always amazed me how much time and energy is consumed within organisations because departments and functions refuse to cooperate or seem totally incapable of working in harmony. I have personally witnessed many situations where business interests have been ignored, and indeed seriously damaged, because of interdepartmental rivalry and political game play.

The difference between sport and business is that the results of poor teamwork are rapidly identified in the former example, whereas if customers decide to withdraw their business or an organisation becomes generally uncompetitive, numerous explanations will emerge which never consider the impact of inadequate business teamwork.

This is hardly surprising because such a conclusion would infer an inadequacy in management ability. After all, is it not the responsibility of senior management to build a cohesive business team that focuses its collective energy on beating the competition and meeting the expectations of the customer?

In truth many organisations never appreciate or acknowledge the real damage and costs that are incurred because of a disharmonious business environment. In a command and control situation it is common for CEOs to promote conflict among functions as a basis of motivation. This 'smile and frown' leadership style certainly keeps people on their toes, if only to deter their colleagues from stomping on them.

Senior management is notorious for skirting round the 'softer issues' (such as functional disharmony) possibly because the 'softer issues' ultimately demand harder solutions. But the sure way to raise the actual importance of a problem is to tag it with a price. How much is it actually costing your organisation to beat up on each other instead of the competition?

Ways to improve a disharmonious business environment:

• Formally acknowledge functional disharmony as a problem that must be tackled for the good of the business.

- Introduce measures of departmental performance that will identify and acknowledge positive, helpful attitudes within departments.
- Consider the benefits for reorganising responsibilities and accountabilities in alignment with the processes that collectively deliver a product or service to an external customer. Aligning your internal performance measures with those of your paymasters will ensure that the important things are the important things.
- Conduct a series of training sessions designed to communicate the importance (to the business as a whole) of tackling the disharmony problem.
- Conduct a formal survey across the functions designed to measure the difference between the efficiency and attitude of functions, as perceived by those who utilise the services and the perception of performance by the functions delivering the services. Conduct a gap analysis and discuss the results with all parties.
- Set up and facilitate a series of internal 'customer care' meetings whereby respective functions openly discuss interface problems, cost implications, uncooperative attitudes and other perceived or real problems. Never forget, 'perceived' problems are always real to the person on the receiving end.
- Set up a joint reward program for improvement solutions that arise from 'Internal Customer Care' forums.
- Use cross-functional teams to jointly solve problems.
- Establish a 'Helpful Colleague' award program. Encourage people to send a card of acknowledgment when they receive outstanding service from another department. These cards could be posted at workstations and form the basis of a 'Most Helpful Department' award program.
- Reward and recognise competent, cooperative, helpful people and recommend the autocrats, politicians, egotists and territorialists to your competitors.

A little something to think about

There is a relatively small steel manufacturer in the USA that adopts a black shark for its logo. However, on closer examination, the shark is a shoal of small fish shaped like a shark.

The message in the logo is clear. We may be small but we represent a big threat to our competitors. This is because we have established the capability to respond in total unison to meet the increasing demands of our customers. They do, too!

Look for positive opportunities

'EVERY MAN I MEET IS MY SUPERIOR IN SOME WAY. In that, I learn from him.' Many years ago, I read this quote by American essayist and poet, Ralph Waldo Emerson, and it has stuck with me ever since. It doesn't matter whether we are talking with the cleaner or the departmental manager, there will be skills, knowledge, perspectives and experiences which that person has and which will be far greater than our own in some way. Always recognising this will help you retain a more balanced and humble perspective.

It is a natural human tendency to look down on people less skilled or less fortunate than ourselves. When finding yourself thinking this way, take the time to remind yourself of Emerson's quote and think of ways in which you could learn from this person. Follow up by exploring these avenues when next you meet. There will be a double benefit from this. You will almost certainly learn something new, or a different perspective, and the other person will be buoyed by the genuine interest you have taken.

Possible areas to explore include:

- Specific aspects of their work and problem areas, and what helps make it easy/difficult.
- What are the most rewarding aspects of their work and what are the most frustrating.
- Any 'tricks of the trade'.

- What aspects of policies, systems and procedures do they find frustrating, irrelevant, obstructing or difficult to put into place.
- What policies, systems and procedures help in the performance of their job.
- What they would like to see changed if they were running the show.
- Where they have spent their early years—either in their job or earlier work experience, or even their childhood.
- How did they arrive at their present job, what would they do differently along their career path, what were the really good decisions they made and why.
- Their hobbies or sport—what skills and attributes are required, and why they find it enjoyable and fulfilling.
- What unused skills they may have that they can see opportunities to use in the workplace.
- Travel experiences—what they liked, disliked, any significant things they learned, any way in which their perspective of things in general may have changed as a result.

(Note from Dan Kehoe: This article was written by Harry Bate who is living testimony to his comment above, '… has stuck with me ever since.' Harry is one of the more courteous, respectful and humble people [despite his many achievements] that I have met. He embodies the truth of Emerson's words.)

> Man never exerts himself but when he is rous'd by his desires.
> While they lie dormant, and there is nothing to raise them,
> his excellence and abilities will be for ever undiscover'd, and
> the lumpish machine, without influence of his passions, may be
> justly compared to a huge wind-mill without a breath of air.
> **Bernard Mandeville (1670–1733), English physician and fabulist,**
> *The Fable of the Bees*, 1714
>
> Respect the man and he will do the more.
> **John Warner Barber (1798–1885), American printmaker, publisher and author,**
> *The Book of 1000 Proverbs*, 1876
>
> The best index to a person's character is (a) how he treats people
> who can't do him any good, and (b) how he treats people
> who can't fight back.
> **Abigail Van Buren (b. 1918), advice columnist**

Simple statement: multiple meanings

IMAGINE YOU ARE THE MANAGER of both Frank and Mary. It does not matter so much what they do, only that they report to you. You look up to see Frank enter your office. He appears agitated. You ask, 'What seems to be the problem?'

Frank replies, 'Mary is too aggressive. She thinks she can boss me around.'

What would you say? How would you respond?

These two simple sentences present you with a number of issues to consider and multiple ways in which you can reply—all with different outcomes. The best response will be the one that allows you to get to the source of the problem.

Before you answer, consider:

- Whether you are going to solve the problem.
- Whether you have the time to coach Frank so he can solve it himself.
- How Mary will react when she finds out Frank has complained about her.
- To what extent you might be part of the problem.

Response 1: Ask questions to identify behaviour and find a logical solution

You respond to Frank, 'What do you mean by too aggressive? What does she say or do? Does Mary really think she can boss you around?'

These questions will help you understand the situation and specific behaviours that cause the problem from Frank's perspective. However, you do not have Mary's point of view. Your questions imply that you are going to take over and solve the problem for Frank.

To find a workable solution, some investigation is needed to understand what is actually happening in the workplace. You might want to observe the two interacting to see the behaviour for yourself or find out Mary's side of the story.

Response 2: Manage the relationship issue— demonstrate empathy

'I can see you are upset Frank. Tell me about what has just happened.'

An empathic response can bypass the need for the fact-finding questioning style used in Response 1. The aim of empathic responding is to help Frank take action to resolve his issues with Mary.

An empathic response accurately acknowledges Frank's feelings. It is also phrased as a statement or observation rather than as a question. An empathic response demonstrates your understanding of the person's situation. It does not mean that you agree with them.

If your response is empathic, Frank will respond with a 'yes' and launch into more detail about the situation with Mary. As Frank tells his story, you will learn whether it is Mary that has upset him or whether there are other reasons for Frank wanting to talk to you. His explanation will help you to determine the nature of the problem.

What not to say:

• 'Talk it over with Mary. Let me know how you get on.'
• 'Frank, can't you see I'm flat out here.'

These responses both score zero on empathy. Frank has come to you for support or assistance in his relationship with Mary. Neither response acknowledges his feelings. If Frank were able to sort out the problem himself he would have done so already.

The first two response styles are based on the assumption that the problem lies with Frank or Mary as individuals, or in the relationship between them. If this is the case, training and/or coaching might well solve the problem. However, the cause of their differences may be due to roles issues.

Response 3: Determine whether there are role issues

Instead of thinking that one or other person is the problem, listen to determine whether the way people view their roles is the source of the problem.

Is Frank not doing things that Mary thinks he should? Is Mary assuming responsibility that is not part of her role? If either Mary or Frank is doing or not doing something that is part of their job role, clashes between them are going to occur. Dealing with the problem as one of 'role conflict' rather than a personality clash can provide a quick solution. This is easier than trying to make Mary less aggressive or Frank more assertive.

To find a solution, sit down with both of them and clarify:

• The goals of the team or work group.
• Each person's role and responsibilities.

- Areas of overlap.
- Processes and procedures for getting things done.

The review might take two one-hour sessions, but will soon enable Frank and Mary to work together productively.

Response 4: Consider performance as the problem

You, as the manager, may have so many other things to do that you are not covering all aspects of your job role. You may be allowing performance issues to go unresolved because your attention is elsewhere. It could be that Frank is not doing what he is supposed to be doing, so frustrating and annoying Mary that she is trying to manage his performance.

Spend time observing what is happening in the workplace to determine the extent of performance issues and try to:

- Clarify the behaviour you want and expect from Mary and Frank.
- Check that you have clearly defined performance objectives.
- Develop your delegation skills.
- Spend time coaching and developing Frank and Mary to ease the pressure on yourself.
- Talk to your manager about your workload.

Getting to the source of the problem

To resolve interpersonal or role differences, bring those involved together so that they can discuss their concerns and arrive at a mutually agreed solution. Be ready to facilitate the meeting. You must be impartial and listen openly to both sides of the story. Put a process in place that will enable both parties to hear each other's point of view and understand the impact of their behaviour on each other. Use your empathy skills to respond to feelings expressed as the discussion proceeds.

The following points will assist:

- Have people talk about behaviour—the specifics of what each person does or does not do, says or does not say.
- Avoid judgmental labels, such as lazy or aggressive, as this will only create defensiveness and result in people becoming angry or withdrawn.

- Give each person time to present their case without being interrupted by the other. If they interrupt, introduce the idea of paraphrasing the other person's grievance prior to adding their response.
- Be prepared to let people have time to cool down if the conversation becomes heated.
- Encourage people to express their opinions rather than remaining silent.
- Allow time for people to find a solution rather than providing the solution for them. Have them think about how they will work together now and in the future.
- Ensure that both parties agree to make changes to ensure that they have reached a lasting solution. If only one party makes changes, it is unlikely to work.
- Establish a follow-up session to check that the agreed changes have at least eased, if not fully resolved, the conflict. Allow people to come back to make further adjustments to agreed changes if the first solution does not work. It may take a few sessions to arrive at a workable solution.
- If the problem is still the same or worse after having the meeting, review your options. Leaving conflict to continue unresolved will ultimately create problems for other employees.
- Call in an external mediator if you are not confident in your ability to deal with the problem. It is easier to resolve a problem early in its history rather than waiting until those involved are unable to tolerate being in the same room as each other.

Gone, but not forgotten

I T OFTEN HAPPENS THAT ONE OF YOUR STAFF will suffer a prolonged absence from work (from three weeks to six months, even more). This creates additional issues for you to address, including how to handle the work now not being done, who can take on extra work in the short-term, what 'tricks of the trade' the person used and which you now need to know to get the job done, whether to try to find a temporary substitute staff member, trying to ascertain how long the absence may be for, and so on.

With all the additional resulting issues, we can often forget to pay adequate attention to the needs of the absent staff member. In case of prolonged absence due to illness, the staff member will almost certainly be suffering low spirits, and perhaps loss of a sense of value and belonging. Lack of appropriate action on your part can lead to long-term morale issues and even loss of the person to the wider market once they have recovered. It is important that you maintain some form of communication link to allow information flow both ways.

By taking appropriate action, you will not only raise the sense of wellbeing of the absent staff member, you will also raise the confidence and spirits of the person's workmates because they will see that you care and so they will feel more secure about their own positions. This will have a positive impact on relationships all round.

Some actions you can take with little effort include:

- Phone regularly to enquire how the person is. At the start this should be every few days, but later it can become every few weeks or so.
- It may be more appropriate to be speaking to the person's spouse or next of kin if the person is incapacitated.
- If there is someone on the staff who is particularly close to the person, ask them to keep you informed. (This should never be a substitute for direct contact from yourself.)
- A card signed by workmates can be very uplifting.
- Send flowers or fruit in hospital. They are a very common gift and can be noticed for their absence.
- If the person has become ill while away on a business trip, arrange to fly the spouse or next of kin to their bedside. Arrange accommodation for the person through the hospital. It will be convenient, adequate and economical.
- Keep others informed of the status and progress of the person.
- Copy the person in on their normal newsletters or reports.
- Ensure they are kept informed of any major developments in the organisation. Share good news with them. Make them continue to feel of value and linked to the organisation.
- If a question arises where you would normally have sought their input, then phone/email them and request a view. This can result in the double benefit of a better decision, plus an enhanced sense of inclusion and value of the staff member.
- If they can work a few hours at home each day, and some matters can still be addressed by them via email, then not only can you email them, but more significantly, you can invite their staff to contact them for support, guidance and approval on some issues.
- When ready, try to accommodate them on a part-time basis if that will help them to get back into their previous role.

> The deepest principle in human nature is the craving to be appreciated.
> William James (1842–1910), American philosopher and psychologist

Tricky or treaty

D EALING WITH THE ISSUE OF TRUST within a work group is a very tricky proposition. If someone has demonstrated that they can't be trusted, it is very difficult for people to continue to trust that person. And once someone has been labelled as untrustworthy, it is very difficult for them to shake that label. But if trust has been eroded by past events, then workplace relationships will suffer.

To regain lost trust takes a special message from that person and willingness by others to acknowledge that this person has made a mistake and sincerely wants to make amends. The special message (which is also an acknowledgment) can be as follows:

'I am aware that in the past, I have said and done some things that have caused me to lose your trust. I acknowledge this, I regret this and I apologise for this. My thinking at the time was poor and not in anybody's best interests. I have realised that I let you down and I let myself down. I now much better understand the importance of trust for all of us. I wish to make amends if you'll let me. I hope to slowly convince you that I can be trusted. I ask you to give me a chance to redeem myself. I'm aware that I will only get one shot at this.'

If your group has the maturity, here is an exercise to improve workplace relationships focusing on trust. If the group lacks the maturity, but you want to help them grow and you would still like to do this exercise, suggest during the discussions that you speak generally of the group, not of specific people.

Ask the group to rate the importance of each of these actions and how effectively you currently do them. Discuss the different perceptions people have and then agree five relationship-building actions that you will focus on over the next month or so. Meet again in a month to discuss progress and agree some new relationship-building actions to focus on. It can be useful to hire an experienced and qualified facilitator to facilitate this process if you want to participate equally with your people and not be seen to be unduly influencing the process.

Work through the following with your group (numbered for reference only):

1. Raise the issue of trust within relationships and the impact of trust on effective working relationships.
2. Agree with your people the context, space and boundaries within which they can make decisions.

3. Check whether people believe there will be repercussions or reprisals if they speak honestly.
4. Identify what you need to do more of to develop and maintain trust.
5. Cite general examples of events that resulted in the perception of a lack of trust.
6. Agree things that you could do that would reinforce/demonstrate trust.
7. Implement new actions to reinforce/demonstrate trust.
8. Inform people of the context and rationale for your decisions.
9. Acknowledge the source of ideas/suggestions. Give credit where it is due.
10. Provide people with the space to set and manage their own priorities.
11. Respect the confidentiality of people where sensitive issues are involved.
12. Ask people what they would like to happen in relation to building two-way trust.
13. Always do what you say you are going to do.
14. Show commitment to decisions made and implement actions to support and follow through on decisions.
15. Be seen to treat all people equally and fairly.
16. Avoid ridicule of other people's ideas.
17. Allow people to get the job done without unnecessary intervention.
18. Show an interest in the issues, needs and wants of all people.
19. Speak positively about the organisation, its management and the intention of key initiatives.
20. Acknowledge things that happened in the past that adversely affected trust.
21. Seek understanding by asking for clarification when you are unsure of something.
22. Allow people to learn from mistakes without repeating them.
23. Agree ways to recover lost ground in relation to issues adversely affecting trust.
24. Follow through on promises made.
25. Adopt a 'can do' attitude in the face of adversity or obstacles.

One for all and all for one

THE RELATIONSHIPS PEOPLE HAVE with each other in the workplace exert a powerful influence on the behaviour of the work group. Most people want to be accepted by the others in their work group and feel a sense of belonging. Acceptance from their peers can be as or more important than acceptance from their boss.

The directives and messages coming from management to the work group may have less influence than the interpretations of those communications by colleagues. People in a work group are often moved more by what they think the work group wants of them rather than what management wants of them.

Why is this so? For many people, work defines their life. The social relationships they form at work have a huge impact on their level of enjoyment in the workplace. Working with people who don't like you is a very unpleasant experience. Compliance with group norms or the unwritten ground rules governing the work group's behaviour becomes an important consideration.

Because no two people are exactly alike in terms of temperament, style, approach, attitude, competence, etc., there will sometimes be tension and conflict. Not everybody is going to get along.

Again, if your group has the maturity, here is an exercise to improve workplace relationships. Ask the group to rate the importance of each of these actions and how effectively you currently do them. Discuss the different perceptions people have and then agree five relationship-building actions that you will focus on over the next month or so. Meet again in a month to discuss progress and agree some new relationship-building actions to focus on. It can be useful to hire an experienced and qualified facilitator to facilitate this process if you want to participate equally with your people.

Work through the following with your group:

☐ Discuss how workplace relationships impact on team effectiveness.

☐ Agree the things you do which detract from effective workplace relationships.

☐ Identify areas where cooperation could be better.

☐ Ask/tell your work colleagues how they/you are feeling.

☐ Agree actions you need to take to improve cooperation.

- ☐ Discuss ways to improve workplace relationships.
- ☐ Share your perceptions of another's behaviour if their behaviour is counterproductive.
- ☐ Agree the things/behaviours that influence effective workplace relationships.
- ☐ Acknowledge where relationships have been damaged and agree a strategy to work together.
- ☐ Seek feedback on your own responses to a conflict situation.
- ☐ Tell people what you are honestly thinking and feeling.
- ☐ Ask others about the things you do that detract from effective workplace relationships.
- ☐ Discuss with senior management what they can do to assist in improving workplace relationships.
- ☐ Ask others to honestly tell you what they are thinking and feeling.
- ☐ Ask others to give you feedback about your own performance or style.
- ☐ Clarify and agree where there are differences of perception about situations and issues.
- ☐ Agree to undertake a process to improve the relationship.
- ☐ Agree where relationships could be better.
- ☐ Focus only on the behaviour that may be damaging the relationship and not the person.
- ☐ Tell others how you react to their style.
- ☐ Identify the things each person does that cause the other party concern or grief.
- ☐ Discuss the benefits of better relationships and the 'downside' of a poor working relationship for you all.
- ☐ Avoid saying things that may damage the dignity and self-respect of others when attempting to resolve contentious issues.
- ☐ Acknowledge things that happened in the past that have damaged relationships so that parties can move forward.

PART 9

Improving learning and development

Mindsets

AS WILLIAM SHAKESPEARE WROTE in *Henry V*, 'all things are ready if our minds be so'. Ever wonder about the range of mindsets held by participants in a management-training course? No? Ever wonder why people attend management training programs, return to work and display little or no change to their management behaviour? Still no? Well, get off this page and go read something else.

If you are organising management training, delivering management training or sending your people off to participate in management training and you expect that 'people problems' will now be solved, read on. Fortunately, some people who attend management training hold mindsets that make them ready to be trained and ready to apply the learnings in the workplace. Sadly, in my experience, they make up only thirty to forty per cent of the participants.

Here are some of the mindsets held by participants that mean that they are unlikely to be ready for learning and even less likely to be ready for application in the workplace. The problem is that once people establish these mindsets, they have trouble letting them go unless the mindsets have been replaced with other ways to think about the management training:

• This will be some bullshit that will bear no relevance to me and my job.

- I'm really busy at work trying to get my job done (read that as the technical aspects of their job, not the 'people management' aspects of their job). Now I have to get further behind by being here.
- This sounds fine in theory, but it wouldn't work in my workplace with my people with my problems.
- I do all of this anyway. This is just reinforcing what I already know.
- I hope Shelley is taking all this in. She really needs this. (Thinks Ralph.)
- I hope Ralph is taking all this in. He really needs this. (Thinks Shelley.)
- I wonder if … (the management trainer) has ever worked in my job. You don't ever get any time to do this sort of stuff.
- My guys would laugh themselves silly if I tried this stuff with them.
- This person (the management trainer) has no idea of the ramifications for me or the ramifications on the relationships with my people if I were to try this stuff with them.
- It's okay for (the management trainer) to suggest this approach; they don't have to deal with the consequences if it backfires. No thanks.
- I'd say this model was developed by some academic who has never worked in the real world.
- I'll be buggered if I know why I am even here. I have no idea just what I am expected to do with this.
- I wish senior management were here. They don't do any of this themselves.

> You can change behaviour in an entire organisation, provided you treat training as a process, not an event.
> Edward W Jones, Training Director, General Cinema Beverages Inc., *Training*, Dec 1986
>
> A man has no ears for that which experience has given him no access.
> Friedrich Wilhelm Nietzsche (1844–1900), German philosopher, *Ecce Homo*, 1888
>
> Learning does not occur because behaviour has been primed (stimulated); it occurs because behaviour, primed or not, is reinforced.
> BF Skinner, Harvard University, *Beyond Freedom and Dignity*, Knopf, 1971

Hit and myth

OVER A PERIOD OF EIGHTEEN YEARS, I designed and delivered over 250 training and development programs for managers and supervisors. These ranged from half-day workshops to one-week full-time residential programs. For most of these years, I laboured under the awareness that what I was engaged in was largely ineffectual. People would come along to these programs, be intellectually stimulated, have some fun, go back to work and pretty much carry on as before. The training didn't really transfer into new and better behaviours in the workplace. With, hopefully, some exceptions, it didn't really make people better managers.

My performance as a management trainer or facilitator was usually evaluated by what are referred to as 'happy sheets'. Scoring high on the 'happy sheet' evaluations was relatively easy. Spend the day playing management games and simulations (at one time I might have held the world record for facilitating the most number of the 'lost in the desert, on the moon, in space, at sea, in the wilderness, etc.' type of simulations) and various structured learning experiences. Keep everybody intellectually stimulated, throw in lots of icebreakers and energisers, make sure people have some fun and, hey presto, high scores on the happy sheet evaluations. And this is not a criticism of those learning methodologies—the causes of the transfer of learning problem lay mostly with, guess who? The people being trained and their managers. Some say it is caused by the culture of the organisation, but managers (and workers) are the culture of the organisation.

What did we create? A lot of happy people as they finished up the training or a lot of better managers in the workplace? How much of the stuff from the training programs was transferred into improved management behaviours in the real world of work with real people dealing with the real problems and the ramifications of people working together? Well, no-one knows—or else the few that do have kept it pretty quiet—because it was not usually measured in any meaningful way. Okay, perhaps I am being a bit harsh and certainly some organisations do it better than others. But you wouldn't want to bet your life on the view that management training was producing positive changes to management behaviour in the workplace. Would you?

Many organisations still conduct management training in this way. Billions of dollars every year largely wasted. The dissatisfaction with this approach was one of the catalysts for asking the question—is there a better way? (Watch out—here comes another plug. Thus the M•A•P•P™ System was born. It was designed to incorporate the criteria below. I told you to watch out.)

What is usually missing from the traditional approach to management training and development?

- Relevance between theory and reality.
- Clarification of the specific management behaviours expected.
- Identification of participants' perceptions of the importance of required/desired management behaviours.
- Identification of participants' perceptions of how effectively they currently perform the required/desired management behaviours.
- Context for learning—the background, the rationale, the why.
- Acceptance of a need to improve by the individual participants.
- Focus on specific and relevant, collective and individual needs.
- Peer awareness of, and support for, better management behaviours.
- Accountability for application in the workplace.
- Monitoring, follow-up and reporting on application in the workplace.
- Measurement of results/improvements to behaviour in the workplace.
- Identification of the support required from higher management.

And just while I am getting these things off my chest, I also have a problem with the inferred message from management trainers/facilitators to real, practising managers—I don't know who you are, your temperament, your psychological make-up, your assets and liabilities as a manager, your people, their temperaments, your unique circumstances, the relationship issues, the history, etc., but I am going to suggest to you how to be a better manager.

Mumbo-jumbo—the A to L of techspeak

WHEN THE COMPUTER BOFFINS start talking about computers, the novice is soon left with little understanding about what is being discussed. This 'techspeak' is really just a form of computer language slang that can be interpreted by a dictionary of techspeak terms.

This article will list some of the more commonly used items/acronyms and terms related mostly to hardware and give a brief explanation. This will help you learn and understand the terminology so that you can impress the 'propeller heads'. There are of course too many to list them all. If you need a more detailed definition of a term, or need to know the meaning of a term not listed, there are plenty of 'jargon decoders' on the Internet.

AUP   'Acceptable use policy' or 'computer use policy'—outlines the way that you are allowed to access a system. This is common in the workplace and for ISPs.

Backup   This is a copy of the data or programs taken so that if something goes wrong later, the copy can be used. It is usually stored onto disks or tapes and removed from the computer.

Bandwidth   There is a pipe that connects the computer to others. This can be a telephone line, or a network link such as Ethernet, or wireless links. The size of the pipe relates to the bandwidth. The bigger the pipe, the more bandwidth, and the faster the computer can transfer information.

BIOS   'Basic Input/Output System'—a program that provides the basic information about the system, such as what hard drives it has, the date and power management. It holds this information in the CMOS when the computer is turned off, and is loaded when the machine starts up.

Blue tooth   A type of high-speed wireless system.

Booting up   This comes from the term 'being pulled up by the boot straps'. It is the powering up, or starting, of the computer.

Burner   A drive that can store information onto a CD or DVD. The laser inside the drive literally burns the information onto the disk.

Byte   A byte is 8 bits (a bit is a single piece of computer information being either 0 or 1), and is the unit of data for one character. Example 10100101 is a byte.

Cache   A piece of hardware that is used as a temporary storage area. Programs will cache information to memory or to temporary disk storage if the information is to be reused again soon. It is often termed as volatile memory because it cannot keep the information in memory when the machine is turned off.

CD-ROM   'Compact disk-read only memory'—a CD that you cannot write information to. It can only be used to read from.

CD-R   'Compact disk-rewrite'—a CD that can be 'burned' or written to only once.

CD-RW   'Compact disk-rewrite'—a CD that can be 'burned' or written to multiple times.

CMOS   'Complimentary metal oxide semiconductor'—a storage area that holds the information about your machine when the machine is switched off. It is used by the BIOS on start-up of the machine.

Cold boot   Starting the computer from when it has been turned off.

CRT   'Cathode ray tube'—a type of computer screen. It describes the heavier, more cube shaped screen using the same technology as earlier televisions.

DIMM   'Dual in-line memory module'—a type of memory module used on a computer. See Memory (RAM).

Disk   Comes in the form of a HDD (hard disk drive), floppy disk, or CD (compact disk) and is used to store data such as files and programs.

DOS   'Disk operating system'—refers to the early forms of operating system used on PC computers.

DPI   'Dots per inch'—an image is made up of many pixels. The number of pixels used to make up the image is referred to as the DPI. The higher the DPI, the more detailed and higher quality the image.

Driver   A piece of code that allows the computer to control a device such as a printer or mouse.

DVD   'Digital video disk'—like a CD in shape, but the technology used to create the disk means that it has a lot more storage capability than a CD and can store entire movies on just one disk.

Ethernet   A type of network used to connect PCs, servers and printers together.

Firewire   A piece of hardware that allows a method of data transfer to be used at high speeds.

GHz 'Gigahertz' or billions of cycles per second. Used in computers as a measurement of the performance of a computer chip or the speed of information transported across a network connection.

Gigabyte A billion bytes of data, or a thousand megabytes.

GUI 'Graphical user interface'—a display screen that shows more than just text, but is also a mix of pictures and symbols. Most modern software packages use a GUI to allow the operator easier ways to navigate and input information.

Hard disk (HDD) This is the disk drive which sits inside the computer (the C-drive on a PC) on which most of your data is stored.

Hub A hub is an Ethernet network hardware item used to connect computers together on the network. It broadcasts packets of information sent from one computer to all the other computers connected on the hub for the correct computer to read.

Kilobyte A thousand bytes of data.

LAN 'Local area network'—a set of network devices (switches/hubs) and cables coupled together for the connection of a set of computers. This network is defined 'local' because all of the computers are typically connected together on Ethernet cable, which has a restriction of 100 metres between links.

LCD 'Liquid crystal display'—a type of computer screen.

Linux An open source operating system derived from another operating system, UNIX. Because it is open source the cost is extremely low (if not free), and is rivalling more established commercial operating systems, such as UNIX and Windows.

Mumbo-jumbo—the M to Z of techspeak

CONTINUING ON FROM 'the A to L of techspeak', this is a list of some of the more commonly used items/acronyms and terms related mostly to hardware.

But don't just stop here! There are plenty of free resources available on the Internet that have seemingly endless lists of terms and detailed explanations. If you have access to the Internet, enter search words such as 'computer jargon', or the term you need to know about, and you should easily find an answer to your query. The most important thing to remember is, when you are presented with a term or acronym that you do not understand, ask for an explanation or research it. Nothing is worse than assuming the answer and misunderstanding the real meaning.

Megabyte   A million bytes of information.

Memory (RAM)   This is the volatile memory that can only store information when the machine is switched on. It is a lot faster to store and retrieve information than on a hard disk, so memory is used to speed up processes performed by the computer and its programs. Generally, the more memory, the quicker the machine will perform.

MHz   'Megahertz'—a measurement used to indicate the number of cycles that a processor is capable of, or a network connection can transfer information. It equates to one million cycles per second.

Modem   'Modulator/demodulator'—converts a transmission from digital to analogue to send down the telephone line. It also converts the incoming transmissions from analogue back to digital.

NIC   'Network interface card'—the device on a machine that allows the Ethernet cable to attach to the PC and it handles all the communications between the computer and the network.

OS   'Operating system'—this is a program that controls the machine, all its devices and its programs, e.g. Windows.

Parallel port   A plug in the back of the machine that normally is used for the printer. Termed 'parallel' because it can send and receive information at the same time.

PCMCIA   'Personal computer memory card international association'—used to connect devices to portable machines such as laptops. It consists of a card similar in size to a credit card and a slot in the laptop that fits the card. Used for devices such as network cards.

PDA 'Personal digital assistant'—small hand-held computing device, e.g. a palmtop.

Peripheral Anything that is external to the computer that plugs into it, e.g. a printer or scanner.

Pixel A small, square dot that is part of a computer screen or printed image. If you look very closely at an image on the screen, you will see it is made up of many dots, or pixels.

Processor (CPU) 'Central processing unit'—the computer chip that does all of the calculations and program selections on the computer.

RAID 'Redundant array of inexpensive disks'—a set of hard drives coupled together to provide what seems to be a single disk. Several configurations are possible (RAID 0, 1 and 5) which provide different levels of backup (called mirrors).

Router A network hardware item that handles Internet or wide area network traffic. Basically, it works by sending a packet of information out over the Internet or wide area network and when a reply is received back, the router knows which machine to send it back to. These sends and receives can number thousands per second.

SCSI 'Small computer systems interface'—a fast systems controller used for devices such as hard drives.

Serial port A plug in the back of a computer into which devices, such as the mouse, are plugged.

Server A computer used to provide a service to a group of other computers on a network. There are many types of servers, such as file, print and web servers.

SIMM 'Single in-line memory module'—an older style of memory module for computers.

Storage Term used for the information that is held on disks when the machine is not powered on. Storage (disks) and memory (RAM) are often confused as being the same thing.

TCP/IP 'Transmission control protocol/Internet protocol'—a method for communication of information between two computers. Packets of data are sent and received in a particular format that is understood by the two computers and is the basis for most LANs/WANs and Internet traffic.

Terabyte One trillion bytes, one million megabytes, or one thousand gigabytes.

TFT 'Thin film transistor'—the technology used in flat screens and laptops. The screen is made up of many tiny transistors and therefore is more expensive to manufacture than a CRT monitor.

USB   'Universal serial bus'—a connection point on a computer that also sends power as well as the signal to the external device.

WAN   'Wide area network'—an extension to a local area network (LAN), where computers are connected to the network over a greater distance, i.e. more than 500 metres. It is also described as a collection of LANs.

WAP   'Wireless application protocol'—a method used to access the Internet and its information through devices other than PCs, e.g. a mobile phone.

Warm boot   Restarting the computer without actually turning off the power, but simply resetting the machine.

Speaking in tongues—the software maze

THE INFORMATION TECHNOLOGY FIELD is full of jargon and acronyms. Even the most seasoned information technology (IT) professional would admit to not knowing all of them. Unfortunately, this leaves the novice computer user baffled as to what it all means. This section tackles the terms most common for software on computers. Remember, there are plenty of Internet sites that list some of the more obscure terms, so hit the Net and do a search for the term you are looking for and you will have a good chance of finding it.

Applet A small program often used over the web to perform a particular task, e.g. when surfing the Net, an applet would be sent to your browser to display a graph.

ASCII 'American standard code for information interchange'—an early standard of formatting text files where each character has a code allocated to it, e.g. the letter X is ASCII 088.

Backward compatible A file is backward compatible when it is used by a certain version of a program, but can be used by earlier revisions or versions of the program, e.g. Microsoft Office XP can also read files from Office 2000 and Office 97.

Bitmap (BMP) A bitmap file is one of the largest graphic files commonly found on a PC. Often used for the background picture on the screen.

Bug A problem with the computer program which causes it to misbehave. Derived from the first computers used where a problem had occurred and a moth found inside the machine was thought to have been the problem.

CAD 'Computer aided design'—a computer program used by draftsman, engineers and designers to more rapidly design.

Codec 'Compressor/decompressor'—a small program or code that is used to handle video files. It effectively decodes (or decompresses) the format of the file to display as video.

Crash This 'accident' happens when a computer program has a fatal error and stops operating. It generally means the computer must be switched off and restarted again to restore the system.

Database A single storage area of data. Think of a database as an electronic filing cabinet controlled by a program. A good database will provide searching and index capabilities, and control the flow of information in and out of itself.

Desktop   A term used by Microsoft Windows—the desktop is quite simply what you see on the screen as icons and toolbars.

Directory   See 'Folder'.

DOS   Disk operating system—refers to the early form of operating system used on PCs.

Exe   'Executable'—a program file that can be run.

File   Files are kept in folders on the disk drive. Each document is a file.

Folder   Think of your computer as a filing cabinet. You need to know where the cabinet is, and where things are stored. A neat and practical system will provide you with a means of easily accessing your data.

GIF   'Graphical interchange format'—a file format for storing and exchanging pictures.

Hung   A program or machine that has stopped midway through doing a process. Often the computer needs to be restarted after it is hung (similar to a crash).

Icon   A small graphic. Often used to launch a program.

Java   A programming language, predominantly used on the Internet.

JPEG or JPG   'Joint photographic experts group'—a format for storing graphics enabling them to be compressed.

Linux   An open source operating system that is a derivative of UNIX. Because it is an open source the cost is extremely low (if not free), and is rivalling more established operating systems, such as UNIX and Windows.

MP3   'Motion picture experts group compression layer 3'—a standard for compressing audio and music files into a reasonable size.

MPEG   'Motion picture experts group'—a standard for compressing video and audio files, used when sending email or attachments.

OCR   'Optical character recognition'—a process of scanning a hard copy document and having a program interpret the characters on the page into computer characters. Often good for clear typed text, but not so good on poor reproductions or handwriting.

OS   'Operating system'—the basic software that controls the computer, all its devices and its programs, e.g. Windows.

Soft copy   The digital form of a physical document.

Virus   A malicious program that is designed to cause abnormal behaviour on a machine. This can range from a simple message being displayed, through to destroying data in storage.

WYSIWYG   'What you see is what you get'—a term used to indicate that what is displayed on the screen is how it will appear when printed out.

Zip files   A compressed format. Files can be zipped or unzipped.

> Computer technology has, quite simply, not delivered
> its long awaited payback.
> **Stephen S Roach, senior economist, Morgan Stanley,**
> *PC Week*, 8 December 1987
>
> Cyberphobia: Fear of computers. Characterised by panic, terror,
> heart palpitations, breathing difficulties, dizziness, trembling,
> going crazy and losing control.
> **Jonathon Siegel, Information Communication Associates,**
> *Inner Guide to Office Automation*, 1988
>
> The machine rules. Human life is rigorously controlled by it,
> dominated by the terribly precise will of mechanisms.
> These creatures of man are exacting. They are now reacting
> on their creators, making them like themselves. They want
> well-trained humans. They are gradually wiping out the differences
> between men, fitting them into their own orderly functioning,
> into the uniformity of their own regimes. They are thus
> shaping humanity for their own use, almost in their own image.
> **Paul Ambroise Valéry (1871–1945), French poet and philosopher,**
> *Fairy Tales for Computers*, Eakins, 1969

Surf's up—Internet and email

WITH THE EXPLOSION OF INTERNET (the Net) usage, and the likely continued dramatic effect it will have on business in years to come, we already have a load of different terms used with the Internet. Listed below are a few of the most common terms that you may hear when venturing near the topic of anything related to either the Internet or email.

ADSL (Internet) 'Asymmetric Digital Subscriber Line'—a form of digital subscriber line that provides a greater bandwidth for downstream traffic (from the provider to the consumer) than for upstream traffic (from the consumer to the provider).

Attachment (email) Used in an email, it is a file that is sent with the email. Even though the pictures or document may appear as part of the email, they are still 'attached' to the email during editing, and then sent as separate components.

B2B (Internet) 'Business to business'—a type of e-commerce that provides a mechanism for one business system to communicate with another business system, e.g. company A's invoice system linking electronically to company B's creditor system.

B2C (Internet) 'Business to customer'—a type of e-commerce that provides a mechanism for a business to communicate with a customer, e.g. a customer ordering an item from a company's online store.

Bandwidth (measurement) For a computer to be a part of the Net, a 'virtual pipe' connects the computer to other computers. This can be a telephone line, a satellite, or network links, such as Ethernet or wireless. The size of the pipe relates to the bandwidth. The bigger the pipe, the more bandwidth, and the faster the computer can transfer information.

Bps (measurement) 'Bits per second'—the number of bits of information transmitted per second from the computer, e.g. a dial-up modem would operate at 56 Kbps, meaning 56,000 bits per second.

Broadband (network) A type of connection to the Internet that is quicker than the traditional dial-up connection. This includes cable, Ethernet, satellite and ADSL connections.

Browser (application)   The program used to collect the information accessed on the Word Wide Web and display it on the screen, e.g. Internet Explorer or NetScape Explorer.

Cookie (term)   A small piece of information held on the PC while you are using the Internet. It may store some details about who you are, or what you have accessed before.

Domain (Internet)   A domain is the 'virtual address' for a web site. Every domain has an associated IP (Internet protocol) address that is a 'network address' and both these addresses are stored on a set of name servers around the world. This allows a domain to be requested and viewed without knowing the physical address where the web site is located, e.g. www.Bsnappy.com.

DoS (Internet)   'Denial of service'—when a web user floods an Internet service provider with many requests for information that then stops others from accessing the service.

E-commerce (Internet)   Trading using online information. Can be as simple as ordering goods online through the Internet, or more sophisticated methods using business-to-business systems.

Encryption (Internet)   The method used to secure data by applying a set of secret keys that scramble the information. A particular set of keys are required to unscramble the code.

FAQ (Internet)   'Frequently asked question'—often used on web sites to display common queries.

Firewall (hardware)   Often a piece of hardware (sometimes software) that monitors the Internet and email traffic coming in from the Internet and either allows or denies the information to proceed further. Used to prevent unauthorised access.

Flame (email)   An email that is insulting. Often sent in the heat of the moment later to be regretted!

FTP (Internet)   'File transfer protocol'—a method for transferring files between one computer and another.

HTML (Internet)   'Hypertext mark-up language'—the language used to write web pages. It uses ordinary language coupled with tags for formatting.

HTTP (Internet)   'Hypertext transfer protocol'—a way web pages are sent over the Internet.

Hyperlink (Internet)   A link on a web page that, when selected, jumps the operator to the linked page.

Intranet (Internet)   A private company-based web site. Only accessible from within the organisation.

ISDN (network) 'Integrated services digital network'—a telecommunication line that is dedicated to a purpose, such as data or voice only.

ISP (Internet) 'Internet service provider'—relates to those organisations providing online services, such as web access, email management and web hosting.

Java applets (language) Java applets are little programs written in Java that are automatically downloaded into the browser to enhance web sites.

MIME (email) 'Multipurpose Internet mail extension'—an encoding system used in transmitting emails. Because email was originally designed to send only text, a format was required to be able to send attachments, such as graphics.

Modem (hardware) 'Modulator/demodulator'—converts a transmission from digital to analogue to send down the telephone line. And converts the incoming transmissions from analogue back to digital.

Portal (Internet) A portal is a World Wide Web site that is intended as a starting site for users when they first connect to the web, i.e. their home page. Many service providers offer portals to the web for their own users. Can be personalised for individual interests. Portals can offer a range of services such as showing news, weather, stock prices and the current temperature.

Proxy server (hardware) Used on a business network to store commonly accessed information downloaded from the Internet. This allows faster access for subsequent visitors of websites by reducing the download traffic.

SPAM (email) Unsolicited email—comes from a Monty Python movie where every conversation is interrupted by people yelling out 'Spam! Spam! Spam!'.

URL (Internet) 'Universal resource locator'—the text-based description for a web page address. Made up of the page name, directory and domain. URLs usually start with http://.

Better planning, better training

BEFORE YOU START any on-the-job training, as always it will pay you well to plan the training. Well, you know that anyway, right? But in reality, we probably rush the most important part of on-the-job training because of a desire to get into it. Curb that desire and do it right the first time.

Use the following as a template for your own planning. Reproduce this but add more lines under each section:

Task

_____

_____

_____

Task performance objective (or learning objective)
To be able to:

_____

_____

_____

Performance standards
Time standards (per unit/cycle, task completion):

_____

Quantity standards (unit per hour/day):

_____

Quality standards (performance indicators):

_____

_____

Performance skills
To be able to perform this task, the trainee needs to perform these actions:

_____

_____

Performance knowledge
To be able to perform this task, the trainee needs to know and understand:

Performance attitudes
To be able to perform this task, the trainee needs to believe that, accept that and think that:

Support actions/conditions necessary to enable task to be done
To be able to perform this task, other people need to perform these actions, or these conditions need to exist:

Aids
Tools, software programs, materials, fixtures, etc:

Safety requirements, gear, clothing, etc:

Blueprints, drawings, diagrams:

Job descriptions, etc:

Learning rules, okay?

> The conventional definition of management is getting work done through people, but real management is developing people through work.
> Agha Hasan Abedi (1922–1995), President, Bank of Credit and Commerce International (Luxembourg), *Leaders*, July 1984
>
> Each mind has its own method.
> Ralph Waldo Emerson (1803–1882), American essayist and poet, *Essays*, 1841
>
> You are only as good as the people you train.
> Lonear Heard, President, James T Heard Management Corp., *Black Enterprise*, September 1987
>
> The more intelligible a thing is, the more easily it is retained in the memory, and contrariwise, the less intelligible it is, the more easily we forget it.
> Benedict Spinoza (1632–1677), Dutch philosopher and oculist, *Ethics*, 1677

COACHING OR ON-THE-JOB TRAINING can be the cheapest, most effective way of improving job performance. Remember, always check whether poor performance is caused by will or skill.

Training techniques

To train effectively, there are a number of steps to follow. The first step is preparation. The second step is preparation. The third step is preparation. Got it? Preparation is tantamount to success.

Preparation

1. What you are training—the skills and knowledge, the equipment and materials you need.
2. Who you are training—find out their level of understanding and knowledge, particularly of technical terms.

How people learn

1. By being given a context.
2. In small, digestible chunks.
3. By practice.
4. By feedback.

Why people learn

1. Give an incentive to start a motive for learning.
2. Acknowledge and encourage during the lesson.
3. Congratulate at the end.

Simple rules of learning

1. **Get your material in the right order:** Points presented at the beginning and end of a training session are remembered better than those in the middle. The two most important points should be given first and last.
2. **Know your trainee:** Adjust your approach to meet the needs and ability of your trainee.
3. **Link your training to the trainee's existing knowledge:** Draw on the previous experience of the trainee and link this to the job to be learnt.
4. **Concentrate on positive instruction:** Avoid negative instruction—just talk about and demonstrate the right ways to approach a job.
5. **Allow them to arrive at their own learning:** Avoid telling them yourself. If a trainee does something incorrectly, rather than point it out to them, ask them what or how they could do that part better. Then let them try again.
6. **Give the trainee feedback on progress:** Tell the trainee how they are doing and give praise and encouragement.
7. **Allow the trainee time to practise:** Practice reinforces understanding and learning.
8. **Top up the training:** Give follow-up training sessions to reinforce learning.

What makes a successful coach?

A SWIMMING COACH, when training their budding Olympians, tells them what to do, shows them how to do it, works on their technique and their attitude, and gets them to practise their skills. They set performance goals and then they encourage, reinforce, cajole, induce and support their swimmers as they attempt to improve their performance.

They monitor progress, evaluate performance, provide feedback, follow-up on things requiring more practice and follow through to ensure that everything is covered.

Coaches work on improving technical competence and mental attitude. They set the context for the program, they give the swimmers information and knowledge, they work on the swimmers' perspectives about themselves, their strategy and their performance. And they help them interpret all this information and knowledge so that it enhances their performance.

This is what coaching and training is all about. And guess what—it works! We produce champion swimmers. No-one disputes that these training methods produce results. This training methodology is accepted practice in all sports all over the world.

While the conditions and motivations are different, a manager can apply all the above in training and coaching in the workplace. Yeah, yeah, so you know all this, but do you do it? Or does it cost precious time to train and coach—time that you don't have because you are too busy dealing with the consequences of ineffectual training in the first place?

It is no surprise that the industry leaders, the organisations really doing best practice, the companies that people want to join and stay, have made the hard decision to suffer short-term pain for long-term gain. They have bitten the bullet and have supported managers who spend more of their time in a training/coaching role.

Organisations spend billions of dollars each year ensuring that their staff are capable of meeting today's demands and the challenge offered by the future. Training can represent a cost effective means of ensuring that the team is properly equipped to achieve the goals of the organisation. It also represents an investment by the organisation in the individual to ensure a lack of competence does not contribute to frustration in the job. And it is way better to err on the side of overtraining rather than undertraining.

Advantages of training your team

1. You gain a better awareness of your people. By working closely with them in a training environment, you can better understand their needs and wants, their perspectives, their context.

2. Training is a public relations exercise. It demonstrates a cultural value through action. Through training, people develop confidence and security, which produces cooperation and respect.

3. Your own career is progressed. As people respond to the training it not only improves output but also makes people aware of your capacity to lead and 'make things happen'. All good leaders surround themselves with highly competent (read well-trained) people.

4. Effective training produces a time saving and therefore allows you to devote your own time to other things as the competency of your team grows. Sure, it costs time in the short-term, but it will pay off in the longer-term. All desired outcomes cost time and effort.

5. Training promotes health and wellbeing among the work group not only by providing a discussion forum but also by developing closer team bonds. People can see that there are other dimensions to their colleagues that they may have missed before.

> Order and simplification are the first steps towards the mastery of a subject—the actual enemy is the unknown.
> **Thomas Mann (1875–1955), German novelist and essayist,**
> *The Magic Mountain*
>
> Definition of a good executive: a man who has successfully trained others to discharge his responsibilities.
> **Anonymous**
>
> Thomas Watson (Founder of IBM) trained, and trained and trained.
> **Peter Drucker, management consultant and writer,**
> *People and Performance*, Harper & Row, 1977

Heads up

CHECK YOUR JOB DESCRIPTION. Is there a statement describing your role as a coach/trainer? No? Well, put one in. As number one priority. Gasp. Okay, then write it in invisible ink. Just as long as it is at the forefront of your mind. Or ask yourself how much of your time each week do you spend on coaching, training, and we'll include mentoring as well? (They all have the same ultimate objective—improved performance.) One hour? Two hours? For many of you the honest answer will be zip.

Hang on. I lead a high-performance team. Totally competent. Totally able. Totally motivated. We have no problems. Great. Congratulations. Give me a call. We can use you and your team as role models in our next book. For the rest of you, read on.

Pretraining check list

1. **Learn what your people already know:** It is dangerous to make assumptions about what people do or do not know. By finding out what they already know, you will make the training more interesting and avoid misunderstandings. Ask them to tell you or show you what they know about the process or task. Then focus your training on the gaps in their performance.

2. **Illustrate or demonstrate:** The talking head approach to training went out with the ark, or should have. Training to be effective is interactive and participative. By illustrating, demonstrating and

involving through skills practice and immediate feedback, you bring training alive. Use show and tell—with most emphasis on show.

3. **Encourage and ask questions:** Two-way communication ensures that your message is received and understood. By actively encouraging your people to ask questions you gain that all important feedback necessary to assess their level of understanding. Prepare your own questions in advance. Give them two to three minutes towards the end of the training session to reflect on questions. Asking, 'any questions?' is next to useless.

4. **Provide the big picture:** By allowing people to see things in context, you ensure they have the key links necessary to stitch separate pieces of information into a meaningful pattern. The time you invest in providing this 'big picture' will be repaid when they understand what the outcome needs to be. Morale is also positively affected in that they take a greater interest and therefore increase their job satisfaction.

5. **Follow-up to all training is vital:** All too often we allow people to see training as an event and not as a journey. Coaching will form a key strategy in assessing individual competence, but it should not be the only follow-up. There is benefit in reviewing the training once people have had an opportunity of applying the skills back on the job, so that the individual as well as you obtain feedback as to their progress. Clarify what is expected of people and set up a series of short meetings to review application and progress.

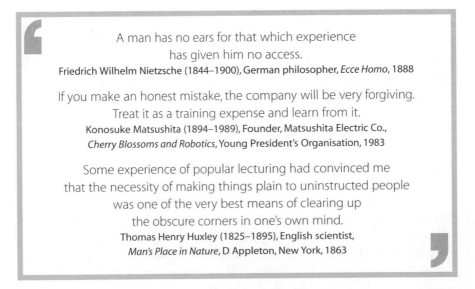

> A man has no ears for that which experience
> has given him no access.
> Friedrich Wilhelm Nietzsche (1844–1900), German philosopher, *Ecce Homo*, 1888
>
> If you make an honest mistake, the company will be very forgiving.
> Treat it as a training expense and learn from it.
> Konosuke Matsushita (1894–1989), Founder, Matsushita Electric Co.,
> *Cherry Blossoms and Robotics*, Young President's Organisation, 1983
>
> Some experience of popular lecturing had convinced me
> that the necessity of making things plain to uninstructed people
> was one of the very best means of clearing up
> the obscure corners in one's own mind.
> Thomas Henry Huxley (1825–1895), English scientist,
> *Man's Place in Nature*, D Appleton, New York, 1863

Too busy?

AVOID COVERING TOO MUCH AT ONCE...

'M TOO BUSY TO SPEND TIME COACHING PEOPLE. Anyway, it's best to learn by experience. Is it? Yes, provided what people learn is what we want them to learn. Unfortunately, there are a hell of a lot of people who learn nothing through experience. That's where a good coach comes in. Yes, it will cost you time, but as you are sick of us saying—no pain, no gain. It's short-term pain, for long-term gain.

Guidelines for successful on-the-job training

- Be completely and thoroughly prepared. Believe that there is a direct correlation between the amount of time that you put into preparation and the quality of your training. As a bare minimum, allocate a ratio of 1:1 preparation time to training time.
- Be enthusiastic—it's catching. Check your own level of enthusiasm for the task/process.
- Be as relaxed as possible. This will help your people to relax as well. Be aware of any inner tension you may be experiencing which will show through your tone or facial expression.
- Express confidence in them.
- Avoid telling and showing too quickly. Check their level of comprehension after each key step. Get them to show/tell you what they have learnt. Move at their pace.
- Avoid stretching them too far beyond their current level of competence.
- Avoid covering too much at once. Too much input interferes with learning.
- Remember that any feelings of incompetence that you help to generate will lead to lowered self-esteem. This will interfere with

learning and performance on the job. Give them permission to make mistakes.
- Remember that all learners are different. What you say and what they interpret may be very different.
- Encouragement and praise reinforce learning, so look for opportunities to use them.
- Encourage questions and answer them enthusiastically. Accept that any questions (no matter how dumb to you) are good questions.
- Use active listening techniques (see *You Lead, They'll Follow* Volume 1).
- Ensure that your body language is sending the message that you want them to 'hear'. Think—how am I looking and sounding to them?
- Don't be afraid to admit ignorance, but make sure that you get an answer as soon as possible.
- Don't be sidetracked from your main purpose. Digressions may be interesting for you, but they will be confusing for them.
- Work at making your training as pleasant as possible for all concerned.

Follow-up actions

No matter how well you present a training session, your efforts will have been wasted if they do not result in improved job performance and results.

You have to be a transfer agent as well as a trainer. The role of a transfer agent is to help individuals apply what they have learned in the 'real world'. Every step in the training process should be developed with an eye to what they have to do on the job.

Following training, implement specific activities aimed at helping them to put it together. Discuss appropriate follow-up activities with them. Agree what you will both do and when. These should include:
- giving opportunities for immediate use of the skills,
- extension activities,
- provision of job aids to support performance,
- showing interest in the staff member's on-the-job performance.

Some of these activities may involve a temporary rearrangement of routine for you and other members of your team. Some of these activities may require the active support of other members of your team. Negotiate with others and motivate them to assist.

Apply some creative thinking when developing the appropriate follow-up activities to enhance the transfer of learning.

Checklist

V ERY FEW MANAGERS ARE GIVEN training and coaching in training and coaching. You got that?

Use this checklist before, during and after conducting a training/coaching session to help you prepare, execute and evaluate:

1. **Motivate and orientate the person**
    - Explain the context and purpose of the job/task/process.
    - Explain what you will be doing in this training session and how it relates to the job. Define your learning objectives and present them visually. Allow the person time to absorb them.
    - Encourage them to ask questions throughout.
2. **Present necessary information clearly, orderly and completely**
    - Break the task/process down into key steps and key activities for each step. Highlight critical activities or safety aspects.
    - Always use show and tell with more emphasis on show.
    - Provide information in manageable chunks—in a logical, connected sequence.
    - Use visual/physical aids.
    - Use practical situations to illustrate information.
    - Avoid or explain jargon that may be unfamiliar.
    - Look for signs of comprehension/lack of comprehension or that they are distracted or switched off.
    - Check for understanding—ask them to demonstrate or summarise the key points once or twice during the session.
3. **Demonstrate where necessary**
    - Go slowly—at their pace.
    - Demonstrate one skill at a time.
    - Make sure they can understand.
    - Explain what you are doing as you do it.
    - Repeat the demonstration if necessary.
4. **Provide the opportunity for step-by-step practice**
    - Move at the staff member's pace.
    - Give them time to work things out for themselves.
    - Let mistakes happen only if the consequences are minimal.
    - When you see a significant mistake about to happen, ask the staff member to think again.

5. **Give feedback**
   - Specify what has been done well and what needs to be improved.
   - Focus on the performance, not the person.
   - Always give the good news first—here's what you did well, here's what you can improve on.
   - Be encouraging and supportive—express confidence.
   - Involve them in looking for solutions.
6. **Set follow-up activities**
   - Ensure that the tasks are relevant and worthwhile.
   - Avoid giving too much help as this may encourage dependence. It is better to help them find solutions than to give solutions.
7. **Show interest in on-the-job performance**
   - Check initially to ensure that the skills are being used correctly. Incorrect use of skills may become a habit, which is hard to break.
   - Your interest demonstrates how important you believe the job and the staff member to be. Explain that you are there to support, not condemn.
8. **Provide encouragement and support throughout**
   - Show your interest and willingness to help.
   - Provide as much as the individual needs.
   - Always express confidence.
9. **Evaluate the effectiveness of your training**
   - Compare what is with what should be.
   - Determine how you will bridge any gaps.
   - The training task is not complete until your learning objectives have been achieved—use them as a final checklist.
   - Identify the ways you could improve your training performance.

PART 10

Improving sales and service

Planning to fail?

'VERY FEW PEOPLE PLAN TO FAIL though many fail to plan' is an adage that should be borne in mind when discussing key account management. It is widely accepted that twenty per cent of a company's accounts generate eighty per cent of its business. Therefore, managing the business of these accounts to ensure optimum benefit to your business is vital. One element that can make a difference and help to ensure success is the development of an Account Business Plan.

A proper Account Business Plan should satisfy the criteria of being simple to understand, realistically address the key issues and something that can actually be used to manage the business.

The Account Business Plan must be written through consultation between both companies as input from both is vital, otherwise there is little motivation for either party to adopt and adhere to the plan. It is used as a guide for the business and establishes benchmarks that are used to assess performance. The Account Business Plan is used to drive the business through all levels for both parties and should be used as the basis for business review meetings.

Examination of the effectiveness of numerous Account Business Plans suggests that the most effective contain the six sections detailed below and do not consist of more than ten pages. In fact, there are very few businesses that would require more than one page per section—a total of six pages.

The six sections are:

1. **Account details:** lists all the relevant details of key personnel, their positions, areas of responsibility, and contact numbers and addresses for both the company and the customer. A simple table format is ample for this section.

2. **Objectives:** list three to five major objectives that will be focused on during the course of the year. The first should always be the attainment of the total dollar sales forecast that has been agreed to by both parties. Other objectives can concern specific products, markets or initiatives that will impact market shares or attainment of the other objectives. They should be **SMART** (Simple, Measurable, Attainable, Realistic, Time-constrained) objectives.

3. **Factors affecting business:** this is a critical section of the plan and therefore many people find it the most difficult to compile. It should contain details of aspects that contribute to the success of the business as well as details of the major factors that are retarding the business between the two companies. The essence of this section is to identify the factors that something can be done about by either party. In other words, it should identify what new, better or different things can be done to grow the business and what existing things should continue to be done. Market conditions, such as reliance on favourable seasonality, that affect all companies including competitors should not be included. It is likely that you will be able to identify four to six major factors affecting business.

4. **Business forecast:** this should be a single page that details the agreed sales forecast for the plan year between the two companies. It should be expressed in terms of product volume and prices. To provide a perspective, it should also contain sales data showing actual results for the last two years so that trends can be identified. It is important that both companies analyse the trends and understand the reasons for them. A copy of this page should be updated monthly and used as a basis for business review meetings with the account that should focus on the factors that cause variations to achieving the forecast sales.

5. **Forecast assumptions:** this section identifies the assumptions that underpin the forecast for major products in the Account Business Plan. The assumptions are things that will be done, usually to counter factors affecting business. If everything remained constant,

then the forecast for next year would be identical to the actual result of the previous year. A forecast assumption then is something that will occur or be done that will change the result from the previous year's result. It may take into account competitor activity, market conditions and actions that either of the two companies will undertake.

6. **Promotional activity program:** provides details of the major elements of the promotional activities that will be carried out to help achieve the forecast sales. These are most likely to have been identified in the forecast assumptions section. The cost (and source of funding), timings and who is responsible for what should be determined. Staff training is an important element of this section. A calendar should be drawn up and unless circumstances in the marketplace change, it should be adhered to. Implementation of the promotional program and changes due to circumstances should be discussed at the business review meetings.

Stick with the truth, please

YOU HAVE TOLD YOUR SALES STAFF not to try to sell by 'knocking' your competitors or their product. You know such negative talk will not necessarily sell your product and can lead to damaging perceptions about your organisation and, by association, its products or services. If you learn of this taking place you can, and should, counsel your staff.

However, what should you do if you learn that another company is unfairly criticising your products or services in the marketplace? The following are some useful tips:

- Check the accuracy of the information you have received very carefully. Ascertain what was said and, if possible, who said it. You may need to phone the customer first hand to do this properly.
- Consider who ought to be phoned in the competitor's organisation and told of the reported criticisms. The person to be phoned should be sufficiently above the level of the reported criticiser so that they will feel free to take corrective action.
- Now identify who in your organisation could be considered at approximately equal status with the person it is proposed to phone.
- Have this person (it will very likely be yourself) phone the manager in the other company. Say something along the line of, 'John, thanks for taking my call. We are competitors in the marketplace and in our

company we respect your right to compete. We are very comfortable with healthy competition and I believe you have similar views. On that basis, I feel the need to alert you to a report I have received that one of your employees is behaving in a way that I believe you would not condone. I would be grateful if you could please check it out and take any desirable corrective action if you find the claim to be true. I am told that last Thursday at XYZ company one of your sales people stated that our ABC product is made from inferior materials. This is quite untrue and misleading. I am sure your policy is to compete on an honest and fair basis. Could you please look into it? Once again, thank you for taking my call.'

- Usually, the person you have called will accept that you have phoned in good faith and will act accordingly.
- If you hear of the criticism being repeated in the marketplace, then you should again call the person in the other company and say you have heard that the problem has continued. Have they had an opportunity to follow up on the previous conversation? What was the outcome? Could they please now pursue the issue again, as a matter of priority?
- In my experience, the action described above will cause the offensive behaviour to stop. If, on the other hand, it does not, then, depending on the seriousness of the matter, you may feel the need to refer the matter to your general manager who can phone the corresponding manager in the other firm. Or you may like to write a letter outlining your concerns. If you decide to write a letter, be especially careful not to make any statement or claim you cannot substantiate.
- It is very important that at all times during these communications you are respectful of the other organisation and its people. Any apparent lack of respect will motivate the other firm not to act in support of you.

> A lie can be halfway around the world before
> the truth has got its boots on.
> **Proverb**
>
> Trouthe is the hyeste thing that man may kepe.
> **Geoffrey Chaucer (1340–1400),** *Canterbury Tales*

What do your customers really think?

WHY DOES IT MATTER what your customers really think? Patricia B Seybold in *The Customer Revolution* (Soundview Executive Book Summaries vol. 23 no. 6, June 2001) cites three key characteristics that highlight the importance of the customer.

These are as follows:

1. Customers are in control.
2. Customer relationships count.
3. Customer experience matters.

Now, have you been too afraid to ask for fear of the answer? Not sure where to start?

Perth consultant, John Lowe, in conjunction with the Mindarie Regional Council—a regional local government in the waste management industry in metropolitan Perth—developed a model in late 2003 to do just this. It is a simple, workable model to help you measure your customer's views of your business:

1. **Establish your project objectives:** Are they about benchmarking, profiling of customer groups, measuring awareness of public relations campaigns about acceptance of change, identifying areas for improvement, general feedback, etc.? An example of an objective for a customer service measurement project is, 'ABC company to determine the position of all customers on the current suite of fees and charges'.
2. **Define your methodology:** Who do you want to collect information from, how, where and at what time? Is face-to-face better than mail-out or telephone?
3. **Identify your sample sizes:** What is significant? What is affordable? What is manageable?
4. **Frame your questions:** Some examples are as follows:
   - Thinking about your visit today, how would you rate your overall experience?
   - Have you had any trouble today in relation to the following ...?
   - What do you consider to be the best aspects of ...?
   - How could the facilities and customer service at ... be improved?
5. **Assemble the data:** Use tables, charts, summaries and graphs to do this. The following is an example of a tabular layout for data relating to the acceptability of existing fees and charges.

	Customer group			
Rating	A	B	C	Total
Acceptable	10	25	38	73
Unacceptable	5	15	12	32
Total	15	40	50	105

6. **Analyse the data:** What does the data tell us about our business? What are the strengths and weaknesses? What are our skills like? Do we have the right type of people and are there enough of them?
7. **Improving the business:** The McKinsey 7–S Framework (Thomas J Peters and Robert H Waterman Jr, *In Search of Excellence*, Harper & Row, 1982) is a useful guide to a structured approach to this. Zero in independently on staff, structure, skills, systems, style, shared values and strategies to catalogue the areas for improvement. Some examples of improvement strategies are:
   – provide additional staff in particular areas;
   – provide existing staff with particular training;
   – improve existing communication means with customers;
   – establish a customer-focus group.
   And lastly, check. Monitor the changes to determine their effectiveness and on-going contribution to better customer service. Remember, no customers—no business.

And pigs can fly

THE CUSTOMER IS ALWAYS RIGHT AND PIGS CAN FLY. Let me stick my neck out here a little. I'll bet that in most disputes between the customer and the supplier, the customer is more often in the wrong than in the right. I've done extensive research on this consisting of a sample of one—me. Now this requires absolute honesty, but I reflected on times that I have had some sort of dispute with the supplier of goods or service and counted the number of times I was actually in the wrong. They outweighed the number of times that I was in the right by a ratio of about 2:1. Not that I admitted that I was in the wrong at the time and a couple of times I did not genuinely know that I was wrong.

So where does that leave you if you are a provider of customer service? Well, if you close your eyes together very tightly and squint at that little puff of cloud up there, you know it does look like a pig flying!

In reality, the customer is not always right and there will always be some dishonest customers who are trying to pull a scam. But, ignoring the liars and cheats, at that moment in time they are right. Dead right. According to what they know, to what they understand, to what they think they need or want, to what they perceive and expect, they are right. And until you alter or inform their understanding, their knowledge, their needs, their wants, their perceptions and expectations, they will stay right.

If the prosperity of your organisation is dependent on attracting and maintaining customers, here is an exercise you can do with your group every six months or so. Ask the group to rate the importance of each of these actions and how effectively you currently do them. Discuss the different perceptions people have and then agree on five key customer service actions that you will focus on over the next month or so. Meet again in a month to discuss progress and agree some new customer service actions to focus on. It can be useful to hire an experienced and qualified facilitator to facilitate this process if you don't want to be seen to unduly influence the process.

As a group rate the importance of each of the following actions:

☐ Discuss the reasons for, and benefits of, improving customer service.

☐ Discuss ways to improve customer service.

- [ ] Discuss the impact your area has on the ability of your internal customers to deliver services to external customers.
- [ ] Ask customers how they would like to see you improve services or introduce new services and then use their suggestions in your plans to improve things.
- [ ] Identify what your customers need to do to help you help them.
- [ ] Identify how and why customer service breaks down.
- [ ] Check with customers that you have understood what they have told you.
- [ ] Demonstrate an interest and enthusiasm for what you are doing.
- [ ] Discuss with senior management the actions you require from them to help improve customer service.
- [ ] Check regularly that the service provided meets customer expectations.
- [ ] Check regularly that all key systems and procedures are capable of meeting customer expectations.
- [ ] Establish how soon the customer needs the service provided and then inform them of when you will be able to comply.
- [ ] Provide customers with feedback in relation to progress.
- [ ] Establish customer expectations by confirming with them what it is they want done and the standard to which they want it done.
- [ ] Provide accurate, timely and consistent information at all times.
- [ ] Seek answers to unknown questions from those who know.
- [ ] Identify the training needs of staff in the area of customer service and then provide the appropriate training.
- [ ] Identify ways to cooperate more effectively, internally, during the provision of customer service.
- [ ] Implement agreed actions to improve customer service.
- [ ] Check to see that the customer's needs have been met.
- [ ] Define your roles in relation to customer service, then document the key things that you are responsible for in this area.
- [ ] Discuss and agree who your customers are.
- [ ] Identify customer expectations and perceptions of your service.
- [ ] Agree with other areas that influence customer service ways in which you can improve customer service.

Blunders

OW MANY TIMES have you (or some other person in your company) walked away from a negotiation feeling that you lost, because the other party got a better deal than you did? Have you ever wondered why it is that some people are consistently able to negotiate better outcomes than others?

There has been much written about the merits of achieving a win–win outcome through negotiation. The truth of the matter is that more often than not, the negotiated outcome favours one party more than the other and the reason for that is quite simple—the 'winning' negotiator, in all probability, made fewer mistakes during the negotiation process.

I have not yet met a person (and that includes looking in the mirror) who has not made mistakes during a negotiation. The sad thing is that some of us make the same mistakes over and over again and never learn from our past experiences.

One way I have found to be helpful is to critically review each negotiation that I have been involved in, or witnessed, to determine what mistakes are made. For years now I have been compiling a list of such mistakes and the total now exceeds thirty-five and keeps growing.

Here are some of the more common (or the most damaging) mistakes that occur in negotiations. Avoid them if you can and you will increase your chance of gaining a more favourable outcome:

- **Inadequate preparation.** Preparation for a negotiation is an involved process and may take a lot of time, but is well worth the effort. Resist the temptation to take short cuts and, if possible, rehearse the negotiation with your colleagues.
- **Tight parameters.** If the range that you have set for your negotiation parameters is too tight, you will stifle the flow of the negotiation through being seen as inflexible.
- **Loose parameters.** If the range that you have set for your negotiation parameters is too wide, you will lose credibility due to the amount of 'ground' that you will have to give to reach a conclusion.
- **Giving concessions.** Never give anything—the other party accords no value to something received free. Make sure that you trade concessions to get the proper value for your concession.
- **Making assumptions.** Use questions to uncover relevant information, don't assume knowledge of what is important to the other party. Probing is also an important source of power in a negotiation as it enables the questioner to lead the process.
- **Being impatient.** The quickest way to end a war is to lose it, but the quickest way to conclude a negotiation is to give in to the other party's demands. Be prepared to take time to reach the desired conclusion—the result will be worth it almost every time.
- **Acting instinctively.** In many cases the first or instinctive response is not the best. Take the time to consider alternatives before responding to a proposition—the best responses are often counterinstinctive.
- **Acting predictably.** Every negotiation situation is unique and requires a tailor-made approach. Bringing unpredictability into the equation makes it more difficult for the other party to second guess your responses or intentions.
- **Eagerness to please.** This is one of the deadliest mistakes, although wanting to please and be liked is quite normal. Unfortunately, in a negotiation, you may have to displease the other party by saying 'no'. Similarly, a good negotiator must, from time to time, appear to be unreasonable—it goes with the territory.
- **Not listening.** Listening is essential to achieving a positive outcome of any negotiation. Active listening means listening with understanding, not just to the words but also to their meaning in the context of the negotiation.

- **Dubious tactics.** There is no place in an ongoing business relationship for tactics that are questionable or better suited to a one-off negotiation situation, such as selling or buying your own house. An unfair tactic will almost certainly 'come back to bite you'.

> The mark of a good negotiator lies in not only making good agreements, it also lies in avoiding making bad agreements.
> Peter Baartz, contributing author,
> *You Lead, They'll Follow* Volume 3, 2004
>
> All governments, indeed every human benefit and enjoyment, every virtue and every prudent act, is founded on compromise and barter.
> Edmund Burke (1729–1797), English statesman, orator and writer, during conciliation with the American colonies
>
> Nothing gives one person so much advantage over another as to remain cool and unruffled under all circumstances.
> Thomas Jefferson (1743–1846), third President of the United States
>
> Many things are lost for want of asking.
> George Herbert (1593–1633), English clergyman and poet

Tactics and dirty tricks

I N MOST COMPETITIVE SITUATIONS, the outcome is often determined by the tactics that are employed. Notwithstanding all that has been written about the value of striving for a win–win result, a negotiation can, and should, be viewed as a competitive situation. I am sure that if you read this article you will recognise many of the tactics as they are described.

Tactics are the actions that are taken during a negotiation, in support of the overall strategy, and are very much a part of the whole process. They are more likely to be successful if they are used in a subtle manner and should be varied according to the situation.

Dirty tricks are simply tactics that are employed by the other party. One of the best defences against any dirty trick is to recognise it for what it is—this renders the dirty trick harmless and minimises its impact on the final outcome. This is why the tactics you use must be subtle as, once they are exposed, their impact is severely limited.

There are a large number of dirty tricks that can be employed in any negotiation situation. Indeed, many successful negotiators are able to switch from one to another without drawing breath. Twelve of the more commonly used ones (including a couple of personal favourites) are described below. It could well be to your advantage to familiarise yourself with them.

Dirty trick	How it works
The decoy	Asking for something the other party cannot possibly give and then using that as the basis for a trade-off. In other words, the other party feels obliged to concede a point to 'balance the books'.
The precedent	Quoting a like situation or past example when a third party has been granted the concession you seek. The implication is that your prospect (compared to others) is being unreasonable in their demands.
The nibble	Where the major issue is agreed upon first and then little added extras are asked for, and easily agreed to, as they appear insignificant in relation to what has already been agreed.
The budget bluff	When the other party states that they have reached the limit that has been imposed on them. This allows them to 'draw a line in the sand' without appearing to be unwilling to negotiate.
The competitor	Where a comparison is made with an offer from your competitor to force you to lower your price or to grant more concessions. The old 'I can get it cheaper elsewhere'.
The flinch	A visible reaction to a proposition designed to lower the other party's expectations of agreement. The opposite can be to show no reaction whatsoever which is equally disconcerting.
The future	Negotiating a better deal on a small order on the implied promise of future larger orders. Similar in concept to using a 'loss leader' in a retail store.
The drag	Protracting the process so that the time and effort invested increases in importance and concessions will be given so that 'all that effort is not wasted'. The subtlety here is to give the appearance of moving forward while actually spinning your wheels.
Good guy– bad guy	The classic tactic as demonstrated in TV cop shows. Used in a team negotiation where one person adopts dominant behaviour and the other is friendly or conciliatory. Unless you are a schizophrenic, do not try this one by yourself.
The walk away	Only to be used if you mean it. When all else fails, by walking away from the negotiation table, surprising results often occur. Be warned, however, that once you reach the door, there is no turning back.
Funny money	Technique where the real cost is reduced to a very small amount on a per unit basis when a lot of units are involved. Alternatively, the amount can be summed when giving a concession.
The stall	This involves the use of small talk, distractions, side issues and the like to try to build time pressure by slowing down the negotiation process. Works very well if the other party has a plane to catch.

The free goods fallacy

THE PROVISION OF FREE (BONUS) GOODS is often used as an inducement to gain an order. This is done based on the belief that the provision of free goods is a better financial proposition for the company than granting a discount off the selling price (SP), but all is not what it seems. Indeed, there is a fallacy inherent in this practice. In reality, the provision of free goods has exactly the same impact on a company's financial position as granting discounts of an equivalent percentage. Because of the tendency to give a higher percentage of free goods, this practice can actually cost more than granting discounts.

Hypothetical

A customer wants to order a pallet of 320 × 2 litre bottles of Xtron that has a 'normal' selling price of $3.60 per bottle and a cost of goods sold (COGS) of $1.20 per bottle. The sales representative has been told to offer the choice of either 5% discount or 20 free bottles in every pallet of 320 bottles. This is equivalent to a 6.25% discount from the customer's perspective.

At the sales promotion launch meeting, the sales representative was told that free goods (especially with high margin products like Xtron) cost the company much less than giving discounts. On a sales call, the sales representative offered a customer the choice of deals—discount or free goods. The customer, being astute, chose the free goods option.

The reality

The customer chose the better deal (equal to 6.25% discount) and therefore is very happy. The sales representative has followed directions to get the order and is therefore very happy. The company accountant is very unhappy as the deal has cost an additional 1.25% compared to giving a 5% discount because of the fallacy of free goods.

The maths

There is absolutely no difference to the financial result for the supplier if he offers 20 free bottles in each pallet (buy 300, receive 320) as opposed to offering an additional discount of 6.25% on the 'normal' selling price for the whole 320 bottles.

Free goods:	320 bottles @ COGS $1.20	= $384.00
	300 bottles @ SP $3.60	= $1080.00
	0 bottles as free goods	= $0
	Gross profit	= $696.00 or 64.4%
6.25% discount:	320 bottles @ COGS $1.20	= $384.00
	320 bottles @ SP $3.375	= $1080.00 (6.25% discount)
	Gross profit	= $696.00 or 64.4%
5.0% discount:	320 bottles @ COGS $1.20	= $384.00
	320 bottles @ SP $3.42	= $1094.40 (5.0% discount)
	Gross profit	= $710.40 or 64.9%

The explanation

Under either scenario, the company must manufacture 320 bottles and the customer receives 320 bottles. There is quite clearly no inventory impact difference to either party.

Unless the customer has the market demand capacity for the free goods, they would be foolish in the extreme to accept them. This simple fact negates the argument that the customer may be unwilling to buy 320 at the discounted price but would be willing to buy 300 at the higher price and receive 20 free bottles.

If they are willing to accept bonus free goods, they must have a perceived market demand and therefore must be able to sell the whole quantity at the discounted price. It depends on the negotiation skills of the people involved.

The danger

Because of the widely held belief that the provision of free goods 'costs the company less' there is a tendency to give them out in greater volume than a comparable discount across the total volume. This will actually result in costing the company more. Depending on the internal accounting methods, giving free goods may hide the true average selling price and may, albeit slightly, reduce the sales figures to that particular customer.

The question of who pays the freight for free goods sometimes causes difficulty but in most situations, because they are part of a shipment, whoever pays for the shipment pays the freight on the free goods. Freight can be a small, hidden cost associated with the provision of hidden goods.

The recommendation

Use discounts rather than free goods—percentages are easier to round up or down than physical stock items. You can't give a fraction of a bottle, it's all or nothing. When using free goods treat the percentage as an equivalent discount.

Ensure that all relevant people in the company understand the true cost of free goods—every item given free is one less item you could have sold at a discount.

Kerbside counselling

SOME TIME AGO, I SAW A SALES TRAINING FILM in which a sales manager accompanied a sales representative on a sales call. After one failed sales call that resulted in a lost order, the sales representative turned to his manager and asked, 'Why didn't you save the order?' The sales manager answered, 'I don't want one order won by me. I want hundreds of orders won by you.'

The role of a sales manager includes responsibility for developing the selling skills of the sales representatives in the team. No amount of classroom training or role-playing will accurately reflect how a person will perform in a 'real life' situation. On the job observation is the answer. To achieve this, it is essential that the sales manager accompany the sales representative on live sales calls with customers or prospects.

One of the critical issues that need to be understood is that the role of the sales manager, in such circumstances, is limited to that of an observer. During the actual sales presentation, if things start to go wrong, the sales manager must resist the temptation to jump in and save the sale. Such action is counterproductive as it may damage the ego of the sales representative and may not reveal where the problem lies. The job of the sales manager is to carefully note what is happening during the sales call and then to use that information in a 'kerbside counselling' session.

Effective kerbside counselling takes place immediately after the sales call and is enhanced through proper preparation. Some simple steps to follow are listed below.

Before the sales call

- Gain an understanding of the call objectives from the sales representative.
- Review the customer (or prospect) account status. This will help cement the valuable habit of keeping customer records up-to-date—a notorious weakness of many sales people.
- Preview the sales call plan for likely objections, problem areas and recommendations.
- Clarify your role is that of observer—you simply intend to 'shut up and listen'.

During the sales call

- Observe, listen and refrain from interrupting. This is difficult to do but most customers will understand the situation, as it is not an unusual occurrence.
- After the introductions and greetings, comment only when invited by the customer or the sales person. Remember that some customers may try to take advantage of your presence and ask for a better deal.
- Discretely take notes of the strengths and weaknesses of the sales representative. This is sometimes hard to do if you are paying attention to what is going on during the sales call.
- Note particular aspects of the call that go very well or very poorly.
- Avoid jumping in and saving the sale when you sense things are not going well. You may be surprised at the number of times the sales person salvages the situation when given the opportunity to do so.

After the sales call

- The golden rule is to use reflection (see *You Lead, They'll Follow* Volume 2) as the major technique during this session.
- Spend some time determining the key learning points that you wish to make and relate these to what happened during the sales call.
- Identify some positive aspects of the sales call so that you can indulge in a little ego stroking.
- Commence the counselling session by asking, 'How did you feel the call went?' or 'What did you achieve compared to your call objectives?'

- Add supporting statements to the explanations given by the sales representative. This is when you should use specific examples of what happened during the call. Try to avoid generalities—they are often of little value as they (generally) lack definition.
- Analyse the strengths of the sales representative that were exhibited during the call and seek their input in so doing. 'What did you feel you did well?' or 'What aspect of the call were you really comfortable with?'
- Make comment on the positive aspects but do not go overboard in your praise. The more 'gushy' the praise the more ineffective it is. Ensure that you use specific examples to illustrate the strength being discussed.
- Analyse the weaknesses but try not to call them that. Avoid asking, 'Well, what did you do wrong?' It is much gentler and more productive to ask, 'How could the sales call have been improved?' or 'What would you do differently next time?'
- Suggest ways that the sales representative could improve during the next sales call—this might be using more benefit statements, asking more questions, being more positive during closing or any one of a number of other professional selling skills.

Finally, a kerbside counselling session should not last more than fifteen to twenty minutes and, particularly if the call did not go well, should not be conducted while driving to the next call—an emotional driver is not a safe driver.

AFTERWORD—
THE NEW WAY TO MANAGE

T HE ROLE OF THE MANAGER has changed dramatically from what it
was ten or twenty years ago. Back then, a manager primarily had to
be technically good at their job. If they had some people skills too,
well, that was a bonus. Nowadays, a manager's focus is more on
managing the human and conceptual issues that impact on the delivery
of high-quality products and services. Today's managers still need to be
technically competent, but they require a broader and different set of
management skills than their counterparts of yesterday.

On a bigger scale, another emerging and absolutely critical focus for
today's manager is the contribution they can make to developing
organisations—small, medium and large—that are sustainable
economically, socially and environmentally.

From *Organisational Change for Corporate Sustainability* (Dunphy,
Griffiths and Benn, Routledge, 2003): 'Wherever we are in society and
the world of work, we can engage in the debate about the social role of
the corporation. All of us can contribute to a redefinition of
corporations to ensure they become major contributors to
sustainability rather than social and environmental predators
undermining a world fit to live in ... to ensure that all corporations are

instruments of a broader social purpose than the generation of short-term wealth for shareholders ... it is vital that corporations make profits—but not at the cost of destroying the future viability of society and the planet'.

Fortunately the fundamental principles of managing people haven't changed too much. The adage, 'Treat people reasonably and fairly and most of them respond reasonably and fairly' still prevails. However, because of the changes in society and the marketplace—a better educated workforce, different expectations and attitudes of the workforce, new safety and environmental laws, increased technology, new industrial relations practices, increased competition, increased costcutting, increased job mobility, greater consumer awareness and expectations, globalisation and, hopefully, greater awareness and enlightenment about the management of our workforce—the focus of today's manager is more likely to be on the following:

- How to constantly get more out of less—less money, less staff.
- How to get staff to embrace, adapt to and willingly implement constant requirements for change.
- How to manage consultation.
- How to establish a process to get staff willingly and actively involved in continuous improvement.
- If people behave according to how they perceive everything, how to incorporate their perceptions in the day-to-day management of the organisation.
- How to remove fear from the workplace.
- How to manage staff so that they act of their own volition to improve profitability and productivity.
- How to manage and improve team performance through the active participation of team members.
- How to create an environment where team members learn from each other.
- How to get ownership and commitment to focus on the critical areas most requiring action.
- How to harness the power of the team to use peer group pressure as a constructive agent for positive change.
- How to change behaviour in the workplace.
- How to carry out a role with a greater emphasis on facilitation and support.
- How to set up and manage 'self-managing' teams.

We have been learning how to answer these questions for over twenty-four years, and we have attempted to describe our learnings in this series. However, I was not satisfied to just put these ideas into books—I wanted to try something else. I wanted to design and develop a new management tool—a process that both managers and staff would gladly use and that would address each of the above questions. Hence, the M•A•P•P™ System was born.

I had long been critical of the traditional ways organisations had tried to change behaviour. As a management consultant, I had first-hand experience. Myself and my ways of thinking and doing were often part of the problem. This had been frustrating me for years because I knew that there had to be a better way. So, just like in the cartoons, one day I was sitting at my desk when I had a sudden flash. At last—a breakthrough!

This simple idea (how often are the best ideas the simple ones?) became the embryo for the current M•A•P•P™ System, but not without a long and frustrating gestation. As usual, I had to overcome the knockers—people with whom I worked who couldn't grasp the concept. But this was the least of my worries. From the moment we began marketing the early version of our new management tool, we attracted huge interest within Australia and overseas. With great expectations, we waited for the flood of orders. Alas—no flood, just a trickle.

The downside of this was that we very nearly went broke. The upside was that, thinking there must be something wrong with the M•A•P•P™ System, we kept on developing it, refining it and improving it. Eventually, the true reasons for the lack of sales dawned. One: I was a lousy salesman. Two: our process was new, innovative and different to what the managers with whom we were negotiating were used to. At the time, it was also unproven. So for managers to agree to buy our product, they had to step outside their comfort zone and take a risk. We then discovered an interesting and revealing situation. Senior managers would rather spend their money on strategies that were demonstrably ineffective and too often a waste of time, effort and money, but with which everybody was familiar and used to, because they were 'safe'. Hmm.

There is a happy ending. Gradually, persistence and determination paid off and we can now add 'tried, tested and proven' to our statements of facts about the M•A•P•P™ System.

The great and inspiring Dr Ken Blanchard, who was lecturing me and other students on the topic of leadership at the time, said, 'If you don't blow your own bugle, somebody will come and use it for a spittoon'. However, far be it from me to blow the bugle for the M•A•P•P™ System. So, if you are interested, here's what managers and staff have to say about it:

- 'Fantastic. This is simply fantastic.'
- 'Where was this process twenty years ago?'
- 'After six months of using this process, we are more than ever convinced that this is the way to go.'
- 'The M•A•P•P™ System has become a valued part of our self evaluation and improvement of our performance.'
- 'I found the exchange of perceptions mildly threatening, but in the end I found it to be an extremely satisfying experience.'
- 'We are very pleased with both the process and the results of our Team Improvement Program using the M•A•P•P™ System ... Congratulations on developing a process that actually delivers.'
- 'On the basis of our evaluation, we have decided to extend the application of the system to fifty additional staff incorporating six new work teams.'
- 'Having now been using the M•A•P•P™ System for three months, I am happy to describe both the process and the results as brilliant. There has been a significant improvement in both communication and motivation since we started using this process. I recommend the M•A•P•P™ System without reservation.'
- 'This is a process which we will definitely use as a standard way to improve our business. I recommend the M•A•P•P™ System to any organisation. Thank you!'
- 'This system has exciting potential in application to a wide range of industry for improving the performance of individuals and teams.'
- 'The general response from the many managers who examined the M•A•P•P™ System is that it provides a simple yet comprehensive approach that effectively facilitates the drive for a quality culture. This is achieved through a well conceived, action-based, continuous improvement process which utilises peer group pressure to monitor and achieve positive results.'
- The employee involvement that has been fostered through the use of the M•A•P•P™ System, coupled with the structured approach ... has contributed to a fifteen per cent improvement in plant reliability. The process has been accepted by all users and we plan to continue to use it as standard practice for future improvements within our business.'

How do you …

- Get staff to embrace, adapt to and willingly implement constant requirements for change and innovation?
- Change old habits, old ways of doing things?
- Change negative, counterproductive attitudes to more open, more flexible, more productive attitudes?
- Transform the culture of your organisation or work group?
- Focus the energy of a group to resolve a critical problem?
- Establish a process that motivates staff to willingly and actively engage in continuous improvement?
- Incorporate employee perceptions into the day-to-day management of the organisation?
- Eliminate the crippling impact of psychological fear in the workplace?
- Use peer group pressure as a constructive force for improvement?
- Create an environment where people in a work group learn from each other?
- Increase ownership and commitment of employees?
- Set up self-managing work groups?
- Improve individual performance in the workplace?
- Create a supportive context for training?
- Apply a process that motivates employees to willingly implement better ways of doing things in their workplace?
- Get people to willingly act to remove the blockages that are limiting improvement and progress?
- Provide a tool to managers and workgroups to use in their workplace to do all of the above?

☑ The M•A•P•P™ SYSTEM

Visit our website: www.mappsystem.com

☑ The M·A·P·P™ SYSTEM

Managing Actions for People and Performance

Different   Innovative   Powerful   Practical

This is not a training event—it is an ongoing implementation process applied in the workplace.

Tried   Tested   Proven
over ten years of applications

with over 400 work groups from many different industry sectors in Australia and overseas

Created, designed and developed by Dan Kehoe

The M·A·P·P™ System is an implementation tool—a framework and a structured process—used by managers and work groups in the workplace to motivate and engage staff to implement actions which will improve areas critical to their business or service.

It is a tool used to improve organisation and individual performance. It is primarily used to improve productivity and/or leadership and management. The system can be applied as a self-managing tool with or without external process facilitators.

We have licensed, trained and accredited M·A·P·P™ System consultants in many countries.

To find out more, contact us at dk@mappsystem.com or visit our web site at www.mappsystem.com

WHAT IS THE *SPACE* CONTINUUM®?

A range of tools which can be continuously applied to achieve sustainable improvement in what matters most to your organisation or work group.

It recognises that:
- Every organisation or work group is in its own space.
- Every organisation or work group is evolving with unique circumstances and needs.
- Every organisation has initiatives already underway.
- People tend not to resist their own ideas.
- Every organisation or work group has the collective learning and wisdom to resolve every problem and benefit from every opportunity, given the right tools.

The *SPACE* Continuum® operates in three distinct spaces in the organisation.
- *SPACE* 1—**Analysis and assessment**
  Identifies focus areas for change, improvement and development.
- *SPACE* 2—**Attitude shift/formation/re-alignment**
  Changes counterproductive attitudes, resolves past issues and baggage, and develops better attitudes to prepare for, adapt to and participate in, sustaining improvement.
- *SPACE* 3—**Behaviour change and implementation**
  Provides a structured, action-implementation process to enable the implementation of actions required for sustainable change, improvement and development.

- We have adapted Open Space Technology (*SPACE* 1.1) for application in the corporate/business world and added a structured, action-implementation process to deliver sustainable improvement.
- Our Team Values tool (*SPACE* 1.2) enables the governing values agreed to by the work group to be implemented in the workplace and demonstrated in the way we work.
- Our Team Effectiveness Assessment tool (*SPACE* 1.3) enables groups to measure current team performance and incorporates a structured action-implementation process to deliver sustainable improvement in team and individual performance.

- Our Organisation Performance Diagnostic tool (*SPACE* 1.4) not only identifies areas for improvement that will lead to greater efficiency, productivity, customer and employee satisfaction, and profitability but provides a structured, action-implementation process that delivers sustainable improvement.
- Our Customer Perceptions Survey tool (*SPACE* 1.5) measures customers' perceptions of service delivery against staff perceptions of service delivery and incorporates a structured, action-implementation process to close the gaps and exceed customer expectations.
- We have developed Attitudinal Competence Att-C® (*SPACE* 2) which addresses the problem of self-defeating or counterproductive attitudes.
- Our M•A•P•P™ System (*SPACE* 3.1) can be used to improve any aspect of organisation, work group or individual performance through a structured action-implementation and behaviour-change process.
- We have resolved the problem of transfer of learning from the training room into the workplace with our M•A•P•P™ System (*SPACE* 3.1).
- Our Ideas Management System (*SPACE* 3.2) has won international awards from Europe, the USA and the Middle East.
- We have developed a Self-managing Performance Management tool (*SPACE* 3.3) using self and peer assessment which enables work groups to address under-performing people themselves.
- Our Visual Management tool (*SPACE* 3.4) is a simple and powerful way to motivate a group of people to reduce costs, increase sales or improve a key function.

We can:
- Facilitate the implementation of all or any of our tools depending on your needs.
- Operate in a partnering relationship with your own internal consultants/facilitators.
- Train your internal consultants/facilitators in the implementation of all or any of our tools.
- Train your managers in the implementation of all or any of our tools.

The *SPACE* Continuum®
Creating the space for sustainable improvement
For small, medium and large organisations
Created and developed by Daniel Kehoe with David Deane-Spread
For more information and a no-obligation demonstration visit
www.space123.com

INDEX